Black Dollar$ Matter!

Teach Your Dollars
How to Make More Sense

Another dose of reality
By James Clingman
Author of __Blackonomics__

Professional Publishing House   Los Angeles, CA

Cover designed by:
Khalid Z. Briggs
[IAM] | Producer | Director | Creator | K.Briggs
Specializing in Creative Direction, Production Management, Brand Management, and Graphic Design.
Contact me for your next project!
IAMKBRIGGS@GMAIL.COM

Book Formatting by:
Jessica Tilles of TWA Solutions
www.twasolutions.com

"*The nation's most prolific writer on economic empowerment, Professor James Clingman is considered by many to be the most thought-provoking, solutions-oriented, and perceptive commentator on the too-often ignored critical subject of Black economics. His syndicated column, Blackonomics, is an absolute must read for anyone serious about Black empowerment, and so is this book, Black Money Matters. Professor Clingman most definitely matters as well.*"

— **A. Peter Bailey,**
Journalist, Author, Lecturer, Educator

Dedication

For my wife, Sylvia; Love you forever!
"Thank you for being here…"
And
For my daughter, Kiah;
I love you unconditionally.
I wish we could
"Do it all again."

My time has come; I'm at the end of my road
Sometimes were hard, but I carried the load
Most of my time on this earth was great
But our time was the best, even though you came late

In my autumn years you were exactly what I needed
You set me straight and the warnings I finally heeded
I was adrift at sea without even a rudder
Where I'd be without you still makes me shudder

So don't be too sad, and don't cry too long
Just know that to me you will always belong
I know it's tough; I know it's hard
But smile through your tears and trust in the Lord

He gave you to me and He gave me to you
You'll always have us whatever you do
Your recollection of fun times will help you get through
Sit back and remember whenever you get blue

Walk tall little princess; stand straight and stand proud
Look up and imagine I'm there in a cloud
Be happy and thankful for what we have shared
Stay strong, be brave, and never be scared

Though it's hard to let go, now that you're grown
I know you're prepared to make it on your own
The hard work, the stress, and the tears that you shed
May God's grace repay you with great joy instead

May the man you select be strong, loving, and kind
Treat each other well and you both will be fine
He'll never love you the way that I do
But that's not his role; he is not supposed to

No one and nothing can take what we've built
Our love will live on like grandma's quilt
And although I knew one day it would end
Like you, I wish we could do it all again
Your "Daddy Jim"

What's in this book, and
Where can I find it?

2010

2011

2012

2015
Practical Solutions

Introduction

My Last Go-Round
"The Urgency of Now"
MLK

For 22 years, since March of 1993, the Blackonomics newspaper articles have circulated throughout the U.S. and various foreign nations as well. In addition to the syndicated column, a website, a book, a radio show, and a TV show by the same name, Blackonomics, have been in the public venue. It struck me, as I began to wind down my activities in the economic empowerment arena, that after writing four books on the topic, containing more than 315,000 words, more than 1000 newspaper columns and magazine articles averaging 800 words each, speaking at many national and local events, and teaching Black Entrepreneurship at the University of Cincinnati for 12 years, that what I have said should have been more than sufficient. But then I thought about Dr. Amos Wilson and his writings. I also thought about the five "M's," Marcus, Medgar, Malcolm, Martin, and Maynard. They did not quit.

In March of 2013, I tried my best to decrease my writing from once each week to twice a month, but for various reasons I could not. The main reason was that there was still so much to share, so much to teach, and so much still to do to help bring Black people into a state of true economic freedom and power. So I kept on writing.

Now that I have been weakened by ALS, I decided to do something I said some years back that I would not do: write another book on economic empowerment. My thoughts back then were that I had said everything that needed to be said on the topic, and I did not want to be redundant by writing another book just for the sake of doing so. I have overruled myself. Redundancy notwithstanding, we need reinforcement and repetition especially on issues related to economic empowerment, because we are so slow to act on the basic economic principles that will carry us forward. It seems we like to talk about what we need to do rather than do it. So I guess this can be called an economic empowerment marketing and advertising campaign. Some have called it preaching the "Economic Gospel."

Herein is my strongest effort yet to elucidate the nuances and the obvious connections between politics and economics. Moreover, as others before me have done, my task is to do everything I can to convince Black folks in particular that our emphasis must be returned to economics over politics, as it was when we owned economic enclaves across this nation. I know that's hard for some of us, because we have been seeking political power since 1965. Irrespective of our feelings about our favorite politicians, the status quo will remain the same until we demonstrate our willingness to use our dollars to affect public policy. Everything else is just rhetoric.

I am not advocating an "either or" scenario between the two disciplines; certainly our actions in response to them must be "both and." We must understand the priority, however; which one comes first, which one depends on the other, and which of the two can achieve real power faster. We have struggled with politics for 50 years now, since we abandoned our economic base of business ownership and mutual support. Five decades should be enough to convince us that if and until we have a strong economic base, a position of strength from which to negotiate our grievances with politicians, we will never have real political power. I hope this book convinces you of that hard cold fact and will lead you to work on obtaining real economic power, collective and individual, as quickly as you can.

Since my last book, <u>Black Empowerment with an Attitude</u>, written in 2007, many economic issues have affected this country and, in particular, Black people. Since that time also, Barack Obama was elected to the highest office in the land, an achievement that has not escaped my sometimes unpopular query in several of my newspaper articles and TV shows. In addition, since 2007 Blacks have come to realize that we are no better off, economically speaking, and I would add politically as well, than we were when Martin Luther King, Jr. spoke at the March on Washington in 1963. While many Black people thought our problems would be solved, or at least dealt with on a political level, when Obama was elected, they are highly disappointed. Our relative unemployment rate is the same as it was in 1963, our incarceration rate far exceeds our percentage of population, our overall health and access to healthcare has declined since then, and our median family net worth pales in comparison to that of Asian/Indian Americans and White Americans.

We are now third in population, behind folks who call themselves Hispanic. Our votes are ignored by one party and taken for granted by the other. (As I write this, 40,000 people are converging on Selma for the 50th anniversary of "Bloody Sunday" to march, once again, for voting rights.) Our aggregate annual income of $1.2 trillion is mainly used to create wealth for everyone except Black people, because we spend the vast majority of it at their businesses. Politics has not and will not solve these issues. We must solve them ourselves, by "the work of our own hands," as Martin Delany told us.

This book deals with the political and economic issues that affected us between 2008 and March of 2015; it directs the reader's attention not only to the problems we face as individuals and as a collective, but also to practical, achievable, and appropriate solutions. It points us to a way out of the economic ditch in which we have remained for decades since the 1960's, when we owned more assets, relatively speaking, and controlled economic enclaves across this country.

As my friend George Fraser told me over 20 years ago, "There is a book inside each of us, Jim. You should write yours." I took him up on that challenge and wrote four. Now I feel there is one more book inside of me, and this is my final effort (I "really" mean it this time.) to capture the art and science of Blackonomics in book form.

This is my final attempt to enlighten, to inspire, to challenge, and to change our thinking in such a way that it has a positive impact on those who come behind us. It encourages the elders among us to pass the baton to the young warriors among us, but our passing it must be with patience, direction, advice, and counseling.

Considering the issues we have faced in the past few years, it is incumbent upon Black people to take the reins and drive us to economic empowerment. There are too many pressing situations that are having a negative impact on our lives; the trials we face also do not bode well for our progeny, and for us to continue to rely on symbolic gestures and vicarious living for our relief will lead to our ultimate demise.

This is why we must rethink the words of MLK, when he talked about the "urgency of now," which he spoke not in a political campaign speech, but out of his deep concern for our future welfare in this country. Thus, I use his words once again, within the context of economic empowerment, and I pray we will gain a better understanding of something else MLK said, "Why we can't wait."

The term, "Black Dollars Matter!" is in response to our efforts to tell the world that "Black Lives Matter!" To most, that's a very obvious reality, and there should be no need to impress that reality on any human being, except of course, those who would take Black lives unjustifiably. Thus, our protests against police killing Black men continue. In order to implement a Black dollars strategy in response to the killings, we must understand the relationship between public policy development and economic empowerment. Once we get a handle on that, I contend we will be well on our way to winning this battle.

Each day we can see how much "Black Dollars Matter!" to everyone else's wealth and well-being. Question is: How much do they matter to Black people? Are we willing to leverage our dollars and use them as we return fire against those who hold us in disregard? Are we willing to make small sacrifices to impress upon those who, in the words of Bob Law, have a "depraved indifference" to our abuse by the justice system? Those questions, and more, deserve our answers as we delve into the realities of our existence and survival in this country and throughout the world.

Just as Black dollars matter, Black votes matter as well. Sadly, our votes only matter when it's time for us to cast them. Thereafter, we are left alone, no support, no advocacy, and no reciprocity for our "precious" and "powerful" votes, as some like to call them. Thus, in order to fully grasp and execute an appropriate response to the issues we face, Black people must see the connection between economics and politics in the same manner as other groups do. More importantly, we must utilize that connection to our best advantage, just as other groups have done.

Understanding that economics runs politics, it is incumbent on us to work together, to organize ourselves, and then to do the work that must be done to gain true economic and political power—not mere influence, but real power.

This book contains one section for each year from 2008 to 2015; each section deals with political and economic issues during that period of time. The last section, 2015, speaks to "what now?" It gives us solutions to the challenges we face going forward.

I trust you will do three things: Read this book; enjoy the book; learn from it; and execute initiatives that will bring economic empowerment to fruition for Black people. It's not difficult, in light of all the resources with which we have been blessed. We have the knowledge, but we must also have understanding, and then have the wisdom to apply it to our lives, both individually and collectively. Remember: Once you know better, it is incumbent upon you to do better—or, no better for you. Take a seat, please; class is about to begin.

James Clingman, March 7, 2015

Preface

"My son, pay attention to my wisdom; lend your ear to my understanding…do not depart from the words of my mouth…lest aliens be filled with your wealth, and your labors go to the house of a foreigner." Proverbs 5:1-10

"Whoever loves money never has enough." Ecclesiastes 5:10

"Money answers all things." Ecclesiastes 10:19

"And when Simon saw that through the laying on of the apostles' hands the Holy Spirit was given, he offered them money, saying, 'Give me this power also, that anyone on whom I lay hands may receive the Holy Spirit.' But Peter said to him, 'Your money [will] perish with you, because you thought the gift of God could be purchased with money! Acts 8:18-20

"The love of money is the root of all evil." 1st Timothy 6:10

Command those who are rich in this present world not to be arrogant nor to put their hope in wealth, which is so uncertain, but to put their hope in God, who richly provides us with everything for our enjoyment. Command them to do good, to be rich in good deeds, and to be generous and willing to share. In this way they will lay up treasure for themselves as a firm foundation for the coming age, so that they may take hold of the life that is truly life.
1 Timothy 6:17-19

The Bible and other holy books speak a great deal about money. There is certainly no shortage of books written by hundreds, maybe thousands, of authors on the subject of money. They tell us how to obtain money, how to spend money, how to save money, how to invest money, how to lose money, and even how to steal money. Money is ubiquitous in our society, nationally and globally, and as such we must learn about it, how to use it to our advantage, how to leverage it, how to circulate it and make it work for us, and how to multiply it.

Money in and of itself is merely a means to an end, as "The Preacher" wrote in Ecclesiastes 10:19. The powerful rulers of his time, if they ran out of money, after spending it on debauchery and excess, could simply raise taxes or even extort more money from the citizens. Sounds like present day politics, doesn't it?

But the warning, "Whoever loves money never has enough," is quite true, and similar to a contemporary economic precept, "The more money you have the more you will spend."

So what does this say about Black people in America, who have an aggregate annual income of $1,000,000,000,000? What does it say about us when it comes to our spending habits? What does it connote regarding our failure to invest and multiply our dollars? What does it say about our conspicuous consumption of everything everyone else makes or does, while we ignore or even boycott our own businesses? What words come to mind? Slothful? Shameful? Sad? Stupid? Sinful?

Good stewardship is a very important aspect of economic empowerment, and it gets high marks in the spiritual realm as well. With that in mind, how can Black people have so much money flowing through our coffers each year and yet remain at the bottom of every good category and at the bottom of every bad one? Looks to me like we have been cast into "outer darkness."

The good news is that the bad news is not so bad, or as one brother put it, "The bad news is a lie." It is not too late for us to turn this thing around and get back on the road to economic security and self-determination. A small percentage of our voting capacity and our financial resources, strengthened by a spirit that "cannot be crushed" as Ken Bridges used to say to the MATAH, will allow Black people to take control of our destiny. It will create in us an even stronger consciousness, awareness, esteem, love, and respect for one another. It will engender us to our children and grandchildren by creating a legacy from which they can benefit.

So don't buy in to what Spiro Agnew called the "nattering nabobs of negativism." All we need is a cadre of dedicated, committed folks who are willing to make relatively small sacrifices, the positive impact of which will accrue to Black people as a whole. Everybody will not and does not have to participate; just a small percentage, some 2% according to the One Million Conscious Black Voters and Contributors movement, and we are on our way. By the way, if you have not already joined that movement and believe you are among the two out of every 100 Black people in this country who are conscious enough to act in addition to talk, just go to www.iamoneofthemillion.com_and sign up.

Now let's start teaching our dollars how to make more sense.

2008

How we got here.

The year 2008 ushered in some very hard times, especially for Black folks. Paradoxically, we were ecstatic and in a constant state of euphoria about the real possibility of a Black man finally becoming President of the United States; at the same time we were losing our homes and, collectively losing as much as half of our wealth in the process because our asset base resided in real estate. Sadly, after the celebration in November of that year, our cloud-nine disbanded and we came crashing back to earth where it did not take long for reality to set in.

News flash! A recession is on the way; oops, make that a depression for Black people.

Thanks, U.S. Treasurer, Henry Paulson and Fed Chairman, Ben Bernanke, for letting us know. Whew! If it weren't for you we probably never would have found out about this. Thanks, guys! We almost missed this one; we never even saw it coming. It sure is a good thing to have the two of you in Washington watching our backs. With your combined Wall Street experience, your financial acumen, your Ph.D.'s from MIT, and all of your knowledge of economics, you have guided us along this treacherous economic path, protecting us and calling out the pitfalls every day, and we certainly thank you for your assistance. What would we do without leaders like you?

How are things going for you and your families? We trust everything is fine. We know you have tucked a little something away for the dark days ahead. We are sure your mortgages will be paid, you will have plenty of food to eat, and your children and grandchildren will be all right as they "struggle" through this economic crisis. Don't worry. Things will be tough, but keep your heads up; you'll get by.

What about your friends and associates? How are they faring? We know they may miss out on their bonuses this year and will not be able to purchase all those cars, yachts, jewelry, condos, and summer homes they were planning to obtain. But, not to worry; with the two of you still at the helm, even though the ship is going down, they can be confident that you have a couple more tricks up your sleeves. How did Ben put it? "We have a few more cards to play," or "we have not used all the tools in our toolbox yet." Man, are we happy to hear that good news.

While we don't understand all those nouveau finance terms like "collateralized debt obligations," and "credit default swaps," we are confident that with all of your knowledge of banking, credit, and the stock market, you will continue to protect us from the horrors of a Wall Street collapse. After all, aren't a lot of your friends working there?

Even though we are struggling to pay our bills, rents, and mortgages, trying to avoid the increased credit card fees levied by the banks, and trying to give our children a gift or two for Christmas; even though we are working hard to put food on our tables and hold on to our jobs; and even though many of us have already been laid off; we are comforted just knowing that you have our best interests at heart.

You know, we were well aware of this recession months ago, at least in our households and in our communities, so pardon our sarcasm at the beginning of this note. But we understand that until it hits the upper echelon of our society it's really not a true recession. After all, the economic condition of Black and poor people is not nearly as important as that of the Wall Street gang, the CEO's, the bankers, the politicians, and all the rest who keep this country running so smoothly.

Not trying to take anything away from your expertise or knowledge of financial matters, but sometimes the grassroots folks just know certain things. Some call it intuition; we call it "mother wit." As we began to see gas exceed $4.00 per gallon and our food costs rise to a point where we had to return to the good old days of pinto beans and cornbread for an entire week, we knew we were in for a rough ride.

But now, just when we thought we had reached the bottom, the worst has happened; there can now be no doubt about our terrible situation. With all due respect to your prognostications and recent announcement on the recession, Mickey D's has raised the price of a double cheeseburger from $1.00 to $1.19! They even took one slice of cheese, which cost them 6 cents, off our favorite sandwich, and now they call it the McDouble. That's it; ball game over. Time to start looking for a window to jump out of; now we really know how bad things are.

Sorry for boring you with our problems; you have more important things to consider. We just wanted to say how much we appreciate you, Ben and "Hank," for all you have done to us – uh, I meant to say, "for us;" and let us not forget about your predecessors, John Snow and Alan Greenspan. We owe a debt of gratitude to all you guys for the work you have done

As we look across this country and see millions of people sinking further into debt they cannot handle, we can thank the politicians who passed the bankruptcy bill that makes it even more difficult for individuals to file, despite being forced to because of medical catastrophes and the like. We can thank the greedy CEO's with their cavalier attitudes toward our plight, as they continue to take home their millions in salaries and bonuses. We can thank the bankers and financiers who have already received billions of dollars, some of which went to parties, vacations, and to purchase other banks.

We thank you, Ben, for your ability to create money "out of thin air" as they say. And we thank you, "Hank," for getting Congress to give you sole control of $700 billion to dole out to whomever you choose. You guys are so smart!

Reflecting on all that has happened in the past few months, we know that with all your credentials and all of your compassion for us, just as you gave the corporations their welfare checks, we know you will get around to us soon. Keep up the good work guys.

The arrogance of political power.

Arrogance, ignorance, and incompetence. Not a pretty cocktail of personality traits in the best of situations. Not a pretty cocktail in an office-mate and not a pretty cocktail in a head of state. In fact, in a leader, it's a lethal cocktail. — Graydon Carter

This nation is being destroyed by greedy, conniving, arrogant people. Our political leaders have taken this country to the edge of economic meltdown and political chaos with their lies and deceit. I often wonder if they think they will ever die and have to account for their actions. It is shameful and sad that they are so engrossed in their own personal enrichment and have literally disregarded most of the people in this country. But, it's also sad to think that most of us go along with the program, whether by omission or commission, by allowing these leaders to continue doing their dirt.

Even sadder is the fact that our children will surely pay the price for our apathy and our weakness in the face of impending disaster. When I ask myself, "What are we afraid of? What do we have to lose? Why do we allow ourselves to be played? I cannot for the life of me come up with acceptable answers.

The people in power are so arrogant and aloof in their dealings with the folks for whom they are supposed to be working. The "American people" are so laid back and shy when it comes to our response to the nonsense, because we simply do not want to know what is happening. We want to remain in our ignorance, thereby having no responsibility or obligation to act in any way to change things.

We ratchet-up our enthusiasm for politics, especially this year (2008), and traipse to the polls like lemmings, believing we will find salvation there. Fact is, we will only gain an emotional up-tick from the upcoming elections, both national and local because our investment in the political process is that of amateurs. Despite being involved for decades, and despite having elected Black officials all over this country, we are still politically impotent and ineffective in most cases. In other words, we still get played.

The arrogance of our top political officials is off the chart. They thumb their noses at us and could not care less that we know what they are doing. Our ignorance, in many cases, is off the chart as well. We do not pay attention to what's going on around us; we do not have a real grasp of our history; and we do not critically analyze what is being said to us via the nightly 30-second sound-bites.

The arrogant lord over the ignorant and strut their power over the weak with impunity, as though there is no higher authority or price to pay for their despicable actions. But take a look at current conditions and you will see that there is a price to pay for both arrogance and ignorance.

Financial institutions are in deep trouble, and when they sneeze, we get pneumonia. The housing bubble has burst and we are paying dearly for it; families are losing their homes by the hundreds of thousands across this nation. Unemployment is on the rise, and inflation is taking hold. Mass layoffs, such as those seen in the late 1980's and early 1990's are returning to the forefront – 4000 from Merrill-Lynch alone. Food prices are reaching unprecedented levels; and who knows where the price of gasoline will end up this year. Many of the ignorant are still dying for the arrogant in Iraq, while billions of dollars flow like oil from corrupt hand to corrupt hand, through Halliburton, Blackwater, and KBR.

The Saudis and other oil rich nations refuse to increase production and help lower the price at the pump, while China and India have increased their demand for the precious commodity. We owe more than we have; we import more than we export; we have a deficit that is out of control; and we have a dollar that is probably worth about 35 cents by now. All of this and much more, and the arrogant tell the ignorant to mimic Bobby McFerrin, "Don't worry, be happy."

What's the answer? Experts in economics and business can't agree on what to do at this juncture in America's history, so who am I to pretend that I have the answer. Here is what I do know though. Black folks are at the bottom of every good category and at the top of every bad category in this country; we cannot afford to sit back, mired in ignorance and apathy, waiting for the arrogant to save us. Newsflash! They ain't comin,' y'all.

After 400 years in this country, after suffering under the worst treatment, pushed to the end of the line in every stage of progress, and relegated to second-class citizens, Black Americans remain the most vulnerable of any group.

We must stop volunteering to be ignorant of the things that matter; we must open our minds to the real conditions of this country and the world; we must spend more time critiquing, analyzing, and appropriately responding to the power of the arrogant; and we must design and execute economic initiatives that benefit our people and our children, the way others are doing, without apology.

The arrogance of the powerful leads to the ignorance of the weak, and that leads to the perpetuation of the status quo in this country. They will continue to treat us like mushrooms by keeping us in the dark and feeding us bull dung. We will continue to think we are players while we are really being pimped. We must wake up; there's more to life than sports and entertainment.

Power corrupts, but Amos Wilson taught us that powerlessness also corrupts. Powerlessness is derived from ignorance, and we do not have to be ignorant if we don't want to be. Information is too plentiful and too accessible. Get it! Act upon it!

Consumers are being consumed.

"Conspicuous consumption of valuable goods is a means of reputability to the gentleman of leisure." Thorstein Veblen, Economist, coined the term, "Conspicuous consumption."

In light of the fact that the broad components of this country's Gross Domestic Product (GDP) are consumption, investment, net exports, government purchases, and inventories, and consumption is by far the largest component, totaling roughly two-thirds of GDP, why haven't consumers been bailed out yet? Instead of the most vital segment of the GDP receiving relief, we see the high and mighty getting billions of dollars. What's up with that?

Private consumers, who provide the major portion of GDP, are being consumed by the conspicuous consumption of corporate covetousness. Pardon the alliteration.

How do you feel about the fact that those folks who earn millions of dollars already are at the front of this new millennium soup line? First they allocate and disburse half of the $700,000,000,000 to Wall Street types, investment bankers, and banks that used their windfall to purchase more banks rather than make loans to us, the consumers. Now consumers are faced with depreciating homes, which comprise the vast majority of our wealth, upside-down mortgages, evictions, the inability to get a loan, even for an automobile, and massive layoffs of thousands of "consumers."

To top it all off, we have a guy named Madoff, pronounced "Made-off," bilks his investors out of $50 billion and receives a punishment of house arrest in his multi-million dollar home. To add insult to injury, the SEC was asleep at the wheel (or were they?) and allowed this debacle to occur despite some of its investigators having knowledge of the Ponzi Scheme.

By the way, Charles Ponzi, for whom the scheme is named, received a five year sentence and a ten-year sentence for stealing a few million from his "suckers" in the 1920's. Prior to Ponzi, another guy named William Miller, received ten years in prison for bilking a million dollars from his lemmings back in 1900. Today, for taking $50 billion, Madoff gets house arrest – at least for the time being. He "made-off" with the money and "made-out" with the authorities.

With such little regard for the consumers of this country by those who are steadily grabbing all they can get, at the expense and demise of those upon whom they depend to purchase their goods and services, you would think we would change. You would think the consumers of this country would change our behavior and use our collective leverage to maintain and raise our economic empowerment.

But we are too busy buying everything they make, and everything they are selling, in our "I gotta have it" mode; we are crazed with our obsession to accumulate "stuff" so much so that we would stampede a Wal-Mart and kill a worker who was just trying to earn some extra money on a temporary job. We, the consumers, as critical as we are to the vitality of this country, are acting like children instead of adults, despite being on the verge of total economic collapse.

Consumers are being consumed and subsumed by the higher order of merchants, bankers, and government officials who need us most; and the sad part about it is that we are allowing them; no, we are helping them in their efforts to do so.

Look at some of our more affluent entertainers. Look at their videos, television shows, and the commercials that emphasize the outlandish, the gaudy, the buffoonery, and the conspicuous consumption. BET is literally a potpourri of crime/prison flicks, bump and grind videos of tattooed, blinged-out characters that have all the possessions any ten persons could ask for.

Listen to the lyrics of some of the rap songs and tell me if consumption is not the watchword of these folks. They promote everything from champagne, to cognac, to watches, to clothing, to perfumes and colognes, to cars, and houses that contain everything except libraries.

Look at some of our athletes, rich beyond our wildest imagination. Many of them, having exhausted the limits of ownership of "things," have moved to the point of really believing they have arrived, and are at a point where they cannot and will not be punished by the system if they get caught committing a crime. Thus, they do the most ridiculous things to put themselves in harm's way, losing their careers and, in some cases, the consumer items they held in such high esteem.

What's fashionable about going to jail? What's iconic about being in a commercial that demeans your people? What's commendable about being used by hidden hands to keep your people, especially the young people, always seeking material possessions – at any cost?

These and other examples comprise the folly and the foolishness of consumption at any cost. And for those of us who are not rich athletes and entertainers, we too carry much of the responsibility when it comes to our condition in this country. We see what is happening in our neighborhoods every day, but we fail to do anything about it. We do not act appropriately when it comes to supporting ourselves and our own businesses.

We are indeed being consumed by our own consumption in many cases. We are also being abused by a system of business and government that places more value on those who have than on those who have not and those who need. We saw what happened when the demand and use of gasoline went down; we must do the same thing when it comes to our general consumption. If we fail to do so, soon we will be unable to purchase even the minimal items that we need to survive. We must not continue to be consumed by our own consumption – nor anyone else's.

Barackonomics – Are you cashing in?

Nothing happens in this country without something being sold. "Money isn't everything, but it ranks right up there with oxygen." — Tony Brown

There was Reaganomics in the 1980's, and some of us had the "Reaganomics Blues," a song written and sang by Cincinnati Judge, Leslie Isaiah Gaines, during that time. Old Ronnie ushered in a period of economic empowerment, still recalled by some as the best ever. To this day, the "Conservatives" are making every attempt to reincarnate the Great Communicator, by holding séances otherwise known as political debates, like the one we saw held at the Reagan Library in Simi Valley, California, during the Republican primary (2008). Those folks love themselves some Ronald Reagan – and they loved Reagonomics.

Now we have Barackonomics. No, we have not seen the result of Obama's economic policies yet, but the current environment is rife with excitement, anticipation, and "hope" for the "change" millions voted to see. We will soon find out what the big picture holds; but even prior to the election, Obama-mania ushered in a new language, a new zeal for politics, and a new economic arrangement for Black folks.

Always watching for the economic advantages available to Black people, during the campaign I saw hordes of brothers and sisters making money. Although it was reported that the lion's share of the $650 million or so raised by the campaign flowed into the dominant media outlets, Black owned media receiving very few of those party favors, some of our more enterprising Black entrepreneurs managed to hitch a ride on the Obama gravy train.

I attended one of the Obama rallies held at the University of Cincinnati, during which I saw Black vendors – as matter of fact, I saw only Black vendors selling everything from Obama Action Figures, to Obama Bobble-Head Dolls, to glow-in-the-dark thingamabobs, to placards, buttons, glasses, cups, banners, and T-shirts of all designs and themes. Barack should have copyrighted his name and image.

My old friend and world renowned painter, Gilbert Young, called me to announce his latest creation: a painting of Barack Obama signed and endorsed by "Prez" himself. The painting is titled, "History+Hope=Change." Now you know there will be bushels of money made from that painting. And, as they say, "It's all good!"

I can't recall seeing Black vendors selling Reagan items, or those of the other 42 Presidents for that matter; no, not even Clinton and Kennedy. (I wonder if Gilbert Young did a painting of Reagan; just kidding, Gilbert.) So I was encouraged to see so many Black folks cashing in on Barackonomics, at least as long as the phenomenon lasts. It's about time.

It's good to see Black folks finally getting in on the economic side of politics, especially the folks at the bottom of the heap. Yes, big business got its share, as it always does; the television companies and their affiliates, newspapers, radio stations, and the major marketing and advertising firms received a windfall from the Obama campaign. But, finally, thousands of brothers and sisters got in on the act as well.

My advice is for them to stay with Barackonomics as long as they can. Come up with new ideas, new products, and new services to sell. The ICE Supreme Man, Ashiki Taylor, in Atlanta, created a new flavor "Obama Medley;" Farley's Coffee Executives, Raymond Wilford and Ricky Tillman have developed an Obama "Hero's" Blend. I am sure there are hundreds of other enterprising Black folks across the country making money via Barackonomics, and I see no problem with that.

I do see a problem with Black folks just settling for the moment, however. We had better get a good understanding of the fact that economics runs politics, and this time is no different from all the other presidential elections when it comes to economics. Let's not merely live for the moment and then go back to sleep in the next couple of months. Let's take the small lessons of Barackonomics and do big things with them. Let's support one another with the knowledge that there is enough, more than enough, to go around.

Don't back off now; raise the bar even higher. Be creative and innovative; devise new entrepreneurial ventures and strategies to capitalize on Barackonomics. You cannot pay your bills with hope, history, or hysteria. Emotional investments do not pay dividends. Euphoria is not bankable. Inspiration that is not followed by perspiration - taking some action, doing some work - will be as fleeting as a shooting star. If we do not turn, "Yes we can!" into "Yes we did!" beyond the election, beyond the inauguration, and beyond the parties, then shame on us.

Allow your inspiration to catapult you to collective economic empowerment by establishing equity funds, bartering groups, urban gardens, food cooperatives, rotating credit associations, small business associations, cooperative purchasing programs, youth entrepreneurial training programs, and all of the entities we need to survive and thrive in this dire economic environment. If we do these things, and more, we will have justified our emotional euphoric response to Barack Obama being the 44th President of the United States. If we fail to do these things, we will miss out on the economic benefits that always find their way to the "special interests." Aren't we special? Don't we have our own interests?

You had better believe the "big guys" will capitalize on their investment in Barack Obama. Question is: "Will we?" Let's understand that part of the "change" we voted for is grounded in economics, at least I "hope" it was. And let's commit that the "change" we receive will be much more than mere "chump change."

Who's got our back?

"We have no permanent friends and no permanent enemies, just permanent interests." — U.S. Representative, William "Bill" Clay

Having been concerned for many years about the reluctance among politicians, local and national, to directly cite the economic disparity that still exists between Blacks and Whites in this country, a search of my "keeper" files turned up the following quote: "We could pretend it's not true, but decade after decade of slavery followed by decade after decade of segregation followed by decade after decade of discrimination has an impact. It has an effect. If you're African American in this country today you have about – on average – 10 percent of the net worth of White families. Ten percent – average net worth of [B]lack families is about $8,000; [while that for] White families is about $80,000. And let me tell you, we're not moving in the right direction. African American children who were born into middle class families in the 1960's are now living in poverty."

Former presidential candidate, John Edwards, made that statement in 2008, and to my knowledge he and Jack Kemp are the only candidates that spoke directly and specifically on behalf of Black people in his country. It is intriguing that the 2008 campaign saw the candidates vying to see who supports Israel the most. They were so busy pledging their allegiance to Jewish people by committing their (and our) unwavering support to the extent of going to war and "obliterating" countries that attack Israel.

Hillary suggested she would wipe out Iran if they make a move on Israel; Obama described Israel as our most important ally and said he would respond with force if that country was attacked; and McCain, along with his sidekick, Joe Lieberman, turned and old 1960's hit into a theme song for more war with the catchy title, "Bomb, bomb, bomb, Iran," all in an effort to assure the Israelis that we've got their back. In that backdrop I wondered why there was little or no mention of the candidates' support for Black people in this country. Who's got our back, y'all?

The rationale for Obama not being able to mention Black folks in his speeches, unless it is mitigated by the negative side of Black life in America, is understandable. He cannot get elected by 13% of the population, many of whom don't even bother to cast a vote anyway. Hillary and McCain are a different story. Although the so-called Black vote is so important to a Democrat being elected, it is and has been taken for granted. The Republicans, of course, have all but written off the so-called Black vote; it's obvious judging from the way they shun our institutions. That kinda puts us in a pickle, as they say; it's a real conundrum for Black people in America. Who's got our back?

It is rational and reasonable to suggest that Black people, having been in this country as long as Whites have, and having created much of the wealth of the United States, should be so well positioned that we have some priority when it comes to maintaining our allegiance. It is reasonable to think that any political candidate, especially the ones running for President, would at least acknowledge the contributions made by Black people and speak out boldly about the injustice against Blacks that has continued for centuries, as U.S. Representative Thaddeus Stevens did in 1867 when he called for reparations for formerly enslaved Africans. In the current campaign, we cannot even get an honorable mention. It's all about our support for Israel. I wonder if we would go to war if Ghana is attacked. Why didn't we go to war when the slaughter of 900,000 Tutsis was taking place in Rwanda? Who's got our backs?

The answers are obvious to most of us; those answers reflect the underbelly of this country, still grounded in racial animus and a hierarchy that has been sustained "by any means necessary." The answers point to the fact that our backs are still exposed, politically, socially, and economically, and we are still taking lashes from an overseer who is constantly telling us our name is "Toby" not Kunta Kinte.

The world is a dangerous place to live, and Black people are the most vulnerable; not so much because of evil people, but because of the people who say and do nothing about it. In the words of Sir Edmund Burke, "Evil persists when men of goodwill do nothing." Striking closer to home are the words of MLK, which he probably would say to Barack Obama today, "In the end we will not remember the words of our enemies but the silence of our friends." Will the President have our backs?

The greedy trample the needy

"Those who shut their ears to the cries of the poor will be ignored in their own time of need." Proverbs 21:13

In recent history, there has been no better time than now for us to see the chasm between the so-called have's and the have not's. We are witnesses to the biggest rip-off since the Great Train Robbery. As if Halliburton and all the rest of the Iraq war crooks were not enough, the bar has been raised even higher now with the housing/mortgage/banking crisis. A couple of years ago folks were making so much money, via unethical and illegal means, so much so that they must have thought their gravy train had no caboose. Now they realize that the light at the end of the tunnel was that of an oncoming train.

I have long been amazed at the arrogance of the powerful, and the greed they display in their endless quest for *filthy lucre*. Anything goes. No holds barred. No rules. No ethics. Many of those who benefitted tremendously from their financial shenanigans, making billions of dollars along the way, are now wringing their hands and whining about how we have to fix the problem that they created. Yes we do need to fix the problem, but all indicators point, once again, to the fact that the needy will suffer because of the misdeeds of the greedy.

How long do you think this country will be able to get away with the way it treats and mistreats those most in need? How long will we last under corrupt, money-grubbing, profit-at-any-cost shysters and politicians who couldn't care less about our children's future? How long will America survive, perched high upon its throne of world leadership, if it continues to arrogantly thumb its nose at "the least of these"?

We have seen some of the worst behavior by some of the worst characters, perpetrated upon those who can least afford another financial blow in their lives. Greedy corporate executives, who rape and pillage their companies, get away with their dastardly acts with a bundle of cash in their bank accounts, while the needy watch their 401-K's deflate. Greedy political insiders cut deals and structure contracts that fatten their pockets while the needy try to figure out to pay the rent and stay warm this winter.

If these are not signs of societal decadence in its highest form, I don't know what is. Right now, no one, virtually no one, is running this country. George Bush is an afterthought to most folks in Washington and around the world now; Cheney is living out his "bunker mentality," and only God knows where he is; Cabinet members are shopping their resumes to find that next job; and Congress is too busy with *one-upsmanship*, as they jockey for position in the next administration. In other words, brothers and sisters, we are definitely on our own.

The greedy are certainly sticking it to the needy, and most of us feel like there is nothing we can do about it. Well, there are things we can do about it. We have to muster up the will to act on basic economic principles that will protect us against economic predators and the hazards of being dependent on folks who have no interest whatsoever in our wellbeing.

That old adage, spoken and implemented by our elders, "Do for self," rings even truer now. Black people are at the mercy of those who own the resources of this country and the world; we are too dependent upon the largess of folks who only see us as a group to pacify and dismiss; and while the elitists among our people continue in their reveling and conspicuous consumption, much of which is mimicked by our youth, collectively we are caught in a downward spiral of economic despair. In light of the tremendous amount of resources we have at our command, both financial and intellectual, we can do more for ourselves by working closer together and sharing those resources with one another.

Black people across this country should set up bartering groups through which goods and services can be traded instead of being purchased with U.S. dollars. It makes sense that if the value of the dollar is dropping, we will need more of them to purchase the necessities of life. How do we get more dollars? Barter a portion of our goods and services with one another.

Especially now, in a time of financial uncertainty when banks are on the ropes, Black folks should form Collective Empowerment Group Chapters across this country and leverage reciprocity from the banks and other businesses that we often complain about. Churches must get together across denominational lines and beliefs to take care of their business. It makes no sense to complain about anything that you are not willing to do something about.

Black folks should establish their own investment pools and loan funds in order to create and grow Black businesses. How can we expect to advance in this country if we don't create and maintain jobs for our children? Are they to grow up and continue the cycle of seeking jobs from others rather than creating jobs for themselves and their peers?

It's one thing to rail against the greed and corruption that have overtaken this country; it's another thing to act appropriately to take care of ourselves, despite the actions of the greedy. Collectively we have already demonstrated that we can do whatever we want and need to do. The lessons are there for us to use over and over again. We must follow them.

The greedy will continue to trample the needy; that is, if they are allowed to do so. It's time to rally around the economic principles that led our ancestors to own and control economic enclaves all across this country. Get busy!

Turning our energy into synergy

"And if one can overpower him who is alone, two can resist him. A cord of three strands is not quickly torn apart." Ecclesiastes 4:12

With all of the challenges Black people face in this country, from economics to politics, from crime to unemployment, from health care to education, and the list goes on, it is incumbent upon us to find effective and efficient ways to confront those challenges. You may call them problems, which gives many of us an excuse to become overwhelmed and fall into a state complacency – and then make no attempt to do anything about our situation. But, with every challenge there is an opportunity, and Black people can take advantage of them if we choose to do so. In my opinion, the most efficient way to get relief from our collective doldrums is through synergistic tactics and strategies.

Synergy: "The working together of two or more persons, organizations, or things, especially when the result is greater than the sum of their individual effects or capabilities." The original meaning of the word, synergy, was "cooperation" and was used to describe physiological efficiency. You can also read about synergy in the Bible (1st Corinthians Chapter 12) where the writer uses the human body to describe how we can be diverse yet unified through the synergistic process.

Thus, we have the pattern for collective work, despite our having different approaches to the same challenges. We can and must work together, cooperatively, if we are going to move forward in a country that is hell-bent on maintaining status quo, which for Black people means that we are, as we have been for centuries, relegated to the bottom level of every good category and the top level of every negative category

This is not meant to be a diatribe on the problems of Black folks; it is not a woe-is-me pronouncement. Rather it is a call to arms, a reflection of our opportunities, and an introspective look at the possibilities that lie within and among our people. I believe, as I have written about for 22 years now, that there is nothing we cannot do as a collective, determined, focused group of people in the wealthiest and most powerful country on the face of the earth. Irrespective of the "leadership" of the moment, regardless of who resides in the White House, and despite the clandestine efforts of those who want to keep us solely dependent on the largess of "new slave masters," as the new in vogue saying goes, "Yes we can!"

Synergy is the answer. Our collective economic clout, exercised properly, consistently, and from a position of strength, will take us to heights not seen since we succumbed to the integration trap. Before you get scared, I am not suggesting that Black people should not have fought for public accommodations; I am not positing that we should have stayed separated. I am saying, however, that prior to integration we had greater economic control of our lives because we worked together in support of one another. In other words, we functioned like a whole body rather than a bunch of disjointed body parts all doing their "own thing."

We took integration as if it was a privilege to support the businesses of others, albeit, at the expense of supporting our own. We looked upon integration as an opportunity to assimilate into a majority pool, thereby, causing our Blackness to disappear, which to some of our people was quite all right with them. They didn't want to be Black anyway.

Instead of appreciating the economic enclaves we built during segregation, we abdicated our economic authority over them; we turned our children over to others to educate; and we went about our lives thinking that all we had to do was elect Black folks to public office and everything would be just fine after that. We thought we had finally "made it" to the big house, while most of our people were well on their way to the "poor house."

Now, after forty years or so, we have come to a point where we can truly see the error of our ways and, as I said before, we must look for and get busy on realizing the opportunities that lie beneath the problems. The only way for us to reverse this downward spiral is through synergistic work. We must look for ways to capitalize on the individual resources, both financial and intellectual, that we have accumulated over the years.

We have hundreds and maybe even thousands of Black social and religious organizations; we have many efforts and causes being worked on by thousands of brothers and sisters across the country; we have schools and informal educational programs; and we have skills and talents in every form of endeavor. With all of that going for us there is nothing stopping us from pooling those resources, creating synergy from our individual energy, and bringing to fruition the rich rewards that are certainly due to our people. For every challenge there is an opportunity. Question is: Will we seek and take advantage of the opportunity through synergistic means for the collective benefit of our people?

We like to quote the economic philosophies of Marcus, Malcolm, Martin, and Maria Stewart. We love some of the sayings of Booker T. and DuBois. Our main dilemma is caused by not following through on their instructions to us.

Here are two quotes to consider: "We must cooperate or we are lost!" "We should not allow our grievances to overshadow our opportunities." Let's get busy, brothers and sisters. Put your egos aside, get in touch with other groups and like-minded individuals, and utilize the synergy of our collective and cooperative work.

The politics of fear and loathing

Fear results in paralysis of a people and creates a dependency on politicians for physical protection and provision of essential needs.

Have you noticed the intensity, the urgency, and yes, the expediency in the political arena these days? All of the swagger, chest-bumping, conniving, and hate-filled speech by the talking heads and pundits really let us know what this political game is all about. If you look beneath the sound-bites and the flowery speeches you cannot help but notice the seedy side, the down and dirty side, the ire and animus, the angst, and the ultimate aphrodisiacs: money and power. Of course, we are on the sidelines cheering for our "team" while our purported "teammates" are busy playing the political game to its fullest. One team will win the prize. What will Black people win?

Of course, that last question was rhetorical, that is, unless someone has an answer for it other than the usual symbolic ones. Viewing the politicians from President George Washington on down, along with their cronies and detractors, discloses a great deal about how ruthless some of these folks are. It shows how hypocritical some of them are and how they would stop at nothing to make their team victorious.

A close look will reveal the nature of some of these so-called political leaders as they lie, cheat, and steal better than most of those in jail for having done so. The raw hate and disdain they espouse on television shows is second to none. The way some of them have even run across the field to the other team, and taken the playbook with them, is utterly disgusting. They have no conscience; but that's politics, right?

Some of these characters display despicable behavior by saying terrible things about their opponents; they tell outright lies about one another; they continue the "dirty tricks" made famous by Nixon and his crew; and they exhibit such a high level of hypocrisy with their "do as I say, not as I do" imperative. And these are the folks we elect to public office, the ones we put in charge of life in the U.S. and its locales. Who's crazy in this scenario? Do we really believe they will make things better for us?

In 2002 we were deluged with the notion that America was vulnerable to an attack by Iraq's Sadaam Hussein (Remember that "mushroom cloud" quote?); now we are told to fear a nuclear attack by Iran with a weapon they don't even have. We should also be afraid of terrorists coming to this country and blowing us up; the message is, "be afraid; be very afraid."

Continuation of the fear strategy was John McCain's only hope to win the Presidency; he kept stoking the fire of fear and trepidation by positioning himself as the only one who could protect us from the fearsome Iranians and what they were then calling "Al-Queada in Iraq," the group that was not in Iraq prior to the big lie told by the neo-cons and then convincingly perpetrated by Colin Powell. What chutzpah these guys and gals have. Or, is it plain old deceitfulness, loathing for those on the opposite side, and an unquenchable thirst for power and money?

This idea that all they have to do is frighten the timid U.S. populace and they can have another four or eight years of rule says a great deal about the so-called "American people." Are we really that scared? Is our main political priority centered on being protected from rogue states that we could wipe off the face at the flick of a switch?

In answer to that question I refer you to Abraham Maslow's Hierarchy of Needs Model, which says our first and most basic priorities are physiological needs like air, that we "can't see," as Jill Scott put it in her timely and timeless song, "My Petition." Maslow said we also need water, a constant body temperature and, oh yes, that other essential known as food. We can update Maslow's words by calling these things groceries, rent or mortgage payments, and utilities.

Second to our basic needs are safety needs, which kick in only after our physiological needs are satisfied. In other words, fear is cast aside when it comes to feeding ourselves and our families. One writer says, "Adults have little awareness of their security needs except in times of emergency or periods of disorganization in the social structure (such as widespread rioting [or explosions in buildings]). Children often display the signs of insecurity and the need to be safe." What a telling statement.

Are we really just a bunch of children, afraid of the big bad boogey man called terrorism? Are we depending upon politicians to "protect" us, to pat us on our heads and make it all better? What a sad state of affairs for supposedly intelligent adults who are willing to suppress their physiological needs for their safety needs.

Maslow was right in his needs assessment; he was also right when he said, "If the only tool you have is a hammer, you tend to see every problem as a nail." That's the neo-con model. According to them, every problem we have is grounded in fear of those they call our enemies, thus, all they have to offer as a solution to the problem is war and more war, maybe for the next 50-100 years, as John McCain intimated we would be in Iraq. I guess he was right, especially since we spent $785 million to build a new embassy compound in Iraq, the largest and most expensive U.S. Embassy in the world!

We will never reach our collective "purpose-fulfilling" stage, called self-actualization, if we stay on our present political road of fear and loathing.

Is it too late for Black people?

Only if you have given up, thrown in the towel, called it quits; but as long as you're breathing, you can always change your mind—and change your behavior.

For a precious few individual Black folks, it's definitely not too late; they are doing just fine. No matter what the economy brings, I am sure most of them will continue to be financially secure. Of course we have some who, despite their tremendous wealth and fame, will continue to purchase all the "bling" they can possibly possess and end up broke in a few years. But, as many of my readers know, I have always been about collective economic empowerment, which is the reason for my question: "Is it too late?"

Although I truly hope and pray it is not too late for Black people to make a serious move toward collective economic empowerment, the closer I look at our situation in this country the more doubtful I become of a positive outcome.

I am not a pessimist; I continue to work for our collective advancement, but always with one eye on reality. And the reality is that in spite of all the messages, all the lessons, all the instructions, all the examples, all the admonishment, and all the sacrifices made by our forebears, we are still in an untenable state of affairs.

What's our problem? Have we grown so complacent in our own dysfunction that we are willing to continue the status quo? Do we really believe that someday someone will ride down our streets on a white elephant or a white donkey and rescue us? Have we finally succumbed to the ultimate okey-doke by subscribing to the fallacy that Black folks just cannot – or will not – work together when it comes to economic empowerment? Have we "fallen and can't get up"?

As I look at our situation in America, having modeled my life after those who have urgently called for Black economic empowerment, I don't like what I see. In 2008 Black folks were mired in the worst conditions since we got our "civil rights." Despite the possible election of a Black President, Black people in general were still at the bottom, steeped in poverty, poor health, short life spans, crime and disparate punishment, unemployment, and poor education.

In all of our grandeur, all of our pomposity, all of our red-carpet flash, all of our champagne-sipping-braggadocios-arrogance, we have sunk to new levels of selfishness, self-hate, and insecurity. Our collective prosperity is virtually nonexistent because we have fallen for the ploy that directs us toward "I" rather than "we."

As for the so-called "committed" brothers and sisters, they spend so much time being philosophers and information junkies that they seldom if ever get anything else done. Our dear brother, the late Joe Seyoum Lewis of Atlanta, Georgia, called these folks "Rapolutionaries." Some of our folks have so many ideas, strategies, responses to and complaints about the current plight of Black people, but yet they seldom if ever participate in economic initiatives that will move our people forward. What is wrong with us, y'all?

Is it indeed too late for Black people to secure a solid economic foothold in this country? Is it too late for us to collectively rally around sound economic principles and strategies such as those implemented by other "Tribes" in this country? Is it too late for us to lock-down a prosperous economic future for our children? Is it too late for Black people to use the power of numbers to build and sustain a true economic movement?

If Katrina was not enough for us to see that we are on our own, I doubt that the latest economic debacle will do anything to shake us. In many cases we have grown comfortable in our complacency and psychologically immune to the "emergency we now face" as MLK warned us before he was killed.

We have had recent warnings by Dr. Claud Anderson, in his books and speeches on Powernomics; we have heard from Amefika Geuka, in his brilliant "Black Papers," especially the one titled, From Rhetoric to Action;" and the latest watchman on the wall to warn us is Bob Law, noted radio personality, who issued his "Appeal for Appropriate Behavior" among Black people.

All three of these brothers agree on the simple principle of economic support for one another. They all agree that we should use more of our tremendous annual income to support one another, thereby, creating "conscious Black millionaires." If only those who consider themselves "conscious" would purchase CD's, books, and other items from conscious brothers and sisters, if only we would patronize the businesses of conscious Black people, if only those of us who are supported would, in turn, recycle that patronage to other conscious Blacks, we would create "instant" conscious Black millionaires who would surely, I repeat, "surely" use their financial resources to build an economic foundation for our people.

I have written about Ashiki Taylor and his product, Ice Supreme; I have shared information about Compro Tax, 200+ offices across this country that we can and should support; I have told you about Farley's Coffee and other Black owned businesses that we can support; I even listed, free of charge, Black owned businesses in my latest book, Black Empowerment with an Attitude." So what are we waiting for, a deep depression before we decide to act on our own behalf? I hope not, because then it <u>will</u> be too late.

Empower yourself and empower our people, through mutual support. If the "conscious" among us fail to respond to our appeal for appropriate behavior, can we depend on the chosen few who have "made it" to use their resources to change our untenable economic position? I kinda doubt it. Is it too late? No; not as long as we're breathing. Just start doing more with what you have, and we will succeed.

2009

Hold the apology; give us our 40 acres.

"We demand an apology for enslaving us, talking about us behind our backs, and calling us names right to our faces! And you better not do it again."

"Oh, okay, we're sorry." They went away smiling and back-slapping one another, "Is that all they want? We got off much easier than I thought we would."

Are Black folks special or what? In 2009, the U.S. Senate, and maybe soon to be followed by the U.S. House of Representatives, issued an apology for the enslavement of Black people in this country. Wow! How cool is that? After a couple of centuries of being enslaved, and 145 years after we were so-called "freed," we finally get a formal apology. Despite Congressman Thaddeus Stevens' 1867 resolution for reparations to Africans in America, we have finally reached the pinnacle of respect: An apology.

The timing of this apology is obviously suspect. It comes at a time in our history when we are constantly being made to believe that everything is fair now, that relationships between the races have reached the ideal point of "equality," and Black people have nothing more to complain about when it comes to our progress in this nation. After all, we have Black President.

In my opinion, apologies are highly overrated, especially those given to Black people for slavery. Here's why. Jews got apologies and reparations. Japanese people got apologies and reparations. Native Americans got apologies and reparations. And now, Filipino veterans are scheduled to get "reparations" from the Stimulus Package to the tune of $15,000 for residents of the U.S. and $9,000 for non-residents, along with an apology, of course..

Want a parallel? Check this out. Speaking on behalf of the stimulus for Filipino soldiers, Senator Daniel Inouye said, "It's a matter of honor and the good name of the United States." He noted that in 1941,

President Franklin D. Roosevelt promised the benefits, but Congress reneged on the pledge in 1946."

That sounds similar to General William Sherman's field orders that called for 40 acres of land to be given to formerly enslaved Africans, which was revoked by President Andrew Johnson. That was in 1865.

Want a more recent example? Here ya go. In 1921, after the destruction of Black Wall Street in the Greenwood District of Tulsa, Oklahoma, the president of the local Chamber of Commerce released a statement to the press that contained the following: "The deplorable event is the greatest wound Tulsa's civic pride has ever received...Leading businessmen are in an hourly conference and a movement is now being organized ...to formulate a plan of 'reparation' in order that homes may be rebuild (sic) and families as nearly as possible rehabilitated." Nice words, but it never happened, folks.

The latest case taken to the U.S. Supreme Court for reparations for the survivors of the Tulsa Riot, petitioned by Professor Charles Ogletree and his team of lawyers, was turned down by the Court. Everybody else gets reparations; Black folks get apologies. They get substance; we get symbolism.

Suggestion to the U.S. Senate: Don't stop with an apology; that does absolutely nothing for the economic empowerment of Black people. If you ask me, it is insulting. Did it take you hundreds of years to figure out that slavery was wrong? Did it take that long for your conscience to be pricked? Did it take centuries to bring you to this latest point of contrition? C'mon, "gentle-ladies" and gentlemen.

With all of the precedents for reparations for people who were abused in some form or fashion, not only should an apology have been issued long ago, somebody should have picked up where the U.S. Congress, during Thaddeus Stevens' time, left off. Imagine how things would be for Black people now if someone with a backbone, someone with a conscience, someone with a moral and ethical foundation, would have insisted and acted upon the appropriate response to the aftermath of slavery.

We would not have had the "noneconomic liberalism" from the so-called do-gooders, the White liberals who "helped" Black people by giving us programs, projects, and everything except those 40 acres promised by General Sherman – everything except a way for Black people to become economically empowered. And we would not have the so-called White conservatives (nor the Black ones either, I suppose) wringing their hands and whining about the lack of self-help and personal responsibility among Black people; and conservatives' blame-the-victim tirades would not even be an argument now.

It would have been great if someone would have just paid Black people, given them some land and then followed Frederick Douglass' advice when he responded to the lingering question of his time: What to do with the Negro? Douglass simply said, "Do nothing with us," leave us alone and we will make it for ourselves. He intimated that Black people, without interference, terrorism, racist laws and Black Codes, and equal opportunity, would be all right; we would economically empower ourselves by supporting one another and advancing in our individual fields of endeavor. We demonstrated that acumen in Tulsa on Black Wall Street, but angry White folks burned it down.

Douglass was really on to something, but even after 250 years of enslavement, Black folks still suffered under the latest racist act du jour, whether it was in the form of negative public policy, private sector exclusion, Klan nightriders, voter intimidation, criminal injustice, prejudice, and/or discrimination. After all of the trauma, the torture, the maiming, the lynching, the racism, and exclusion, don't you think a mere apology to Black people is way too little and much too late, that is, unless that apology is followed by some form of reparations? Get a clue, U.S. Senate, and you too, House of Representatives. You can keep your apology. Where do we sign up for our 40 acres?

The Morning After

"It was the most memorable time in my life; it was a touching moment, because I never thought this day would ever happen. I won't have to worry about putting gas in my car; I won't have to worry about paying my mortgage. You know, if I help him (Barack Obama) he'll help me." — Peggy Joseph, Black voter from Florida

On January 21, 2009, after the Inauguration, the festivities, the parties, the formals, the "pomp and circumstance," the tears of joy, the line-dances, and the speeches, I wondered what our next action items would be. I wondered if we would even have one action item. I wondered if Black folks would immediately get back to work on the things that negatively affect us, and continue to move forward on the positive issues. On that morning after, I wondered if we would muster up the same kind of energy we displayed during the run-up to Barack Obama's election. I wondered if we would remain excited and enthusiastic about working to "change" our economic condition, improve the education of our children, reduce crime in our neighborhoods, and strengthen our overall social condition. I wondered.

After the party, would we remain focused on those and other important issues, or would we awaken on the morning after with a terrible hangover? A hangover so bad that we say, "I am glad that's over; at least I don't have to worry about it for another four years." Would we then sit back and relax in our easy chairs, thinking we had it made, and retire to a life of complacency?

When it comes to economic empowerment, we cannot afford to stop fighting because we have a "Black" President. The education of our children will not improve through some hocus-pocus sleight of hand. The crime in our local communities will not subside as a result of someone doing something in Washington, D.C. The discrimination against and mistreatment of Black people in social, economic, and political circles, on a local level, will not magically go away because Obama is in the White House. But you already knew that, right?

So, what now? That question has been asked thousands of times in the past few months. What are we to do now that we have the "First Black President"? The first thing we had better do, and continue to do, is pray for the brother and his family; they surely need it. Then we must realize that with his election, the work has only just begun. Whether you supported his candidacy or not, you should make every effort to bring to fruition the victories for which we have been fighting long before Obama even thought about running for President.

Locally, of course, we must continue to fight for inclusion and equity in development projects, i.e., contracting, construction management, and ownership. We must continue to fight for justice in our courtrooms from our judges and prosecutors. We must fight for real representation from our politicians in return for our votes. We must show up at school board meetings and fight for our children's education – and be participants in their education rather than mere observers.

Wouldn't you like to see Black people expend the same energy on the essential tasks necessary for our full liberation as we saw during the 2008 presidential campaign? Imagine the possibilities, as the saying goes. Picture Black people putting our money together for a common cause, the same way we did for Barack Obama's campaign. We had enough money to send to the campaign; let's do something similar with our money when it comes to contributing to an equity or investment fund for our own businesses. Let's use some of our money to support our organizations, our institutions, and our own businesses. Let's start a "safety net" fund in our neighborhoods to help our less fortunate brothers and sisters in their time of need.

As I reflect on all of the money that was raised during Obama's campaign, some $650 million or so, and yes I know the vast majority of it did not come from Black folks, it is amazing that we never even blinked at such a sum. But when it comes to our putting a little money together to help one another, you can't find some Black people with a search warrant. That's sad.

So let's consider what took place on Tuesday, January 20, 2009, and then let's think about the morning after. Let's think about the year after, the decade after. Let's understand that there is much work to do, work that started before Obama, and work that did not end with his ascension to the highest political throne in the land. After the party, think about all the money we spent to throw the parties and celebrate the occasion. Then, figure out what your particular niche is and get back to work; that is, if you took a respite from the essential work of liberation and building a future for our children.

Some of us did not take a few months off; some of us continued to work right through the euphoria and excitement of Obama's election. We didn't have a hangover on the morning after. We got up and got right back to the work at hand. The work of economic empowerment, political representation, the proper education of our youth, criminal justice rather than injustice, and social equity for Black people, is absolutely essential for our survival and growth in this country.

Not only on the morning after, but on subsequent mornings, make a commitment with yourself and your own consciousness to make a difference. We have to do this work ourselves.

Obama ain't yo mama!

"Hush little baby don't say a word; papa's gonna buy you a mockingbird. If that mockingbird don't sing, papa's gonna buy you a diamond ring."

Now that many believe we are living in nirvana, having reached the absolute pinnacle of our society's glory; now that some think we have entered a post-racial era, replete with the all the trappings of idealism, sweetness, and light; now that we have achieved the collective dream of millions of people who thought they would "never live to see the election of a Black President;" and now that we have been politically inebriated for about 100 days; it's time to sober up.

Having drunk the intoxicating elixir of "change," "equality," "yes we can," and "togetherness," it's time for Black people to go on a serious coffee binge. As the song once said, "Back to life, back to reality." We still have much work to do among ourselves; we still have to fight for what we want and need; we still have to agitate, as Frederick Douglass taught us; and we still have to demand our equitable piece of this rock they call the United States of America.

As one of my Whirlwind members wrote, "Now is the time to fight harder than ever; folks singing 'we are one' is no guarantee of equality and equity in U.S. society. A horse and jockey are 'as one,' unified in the goal to succeed and achieve, but certainly are not equals!" Brother K, in Wichita, Kansas, had it absolutely correct. Now is the time to fight even harder. Why? Because opportunities are available to us now that did not exist prior to Obama's ascension to the throne. That is, if we read the tea leaves correctly.

My good friend, Bob Law, restaurateur in Brooklyn, New York and former national talk radio personality, expressed his exasperation at what seems to be the only reason Black folks wanted Obama to be President: "Black people just wanted to have a Black President. That's all. We had no other agenda than that."

So I ask, "What is our collective agenda now that we have a Black man in the highest office in the land?" Why aren't we beating down the door of the White House demanding some reciprocity for our enthusiastic support of Obama's candidacy and ultimate victory? Everyone else is.

Seems to me we are so enthralled with the symbolism of it all that we have forgotten what politics is really all about: Self-interest, in case you need to be reminded. The parties and celebrations were nice, but now it's time for serious work. If we allow these four years to pass without achieving a higher level of collective economic advancement for Black people, we are simply foolish, and we will deserve what we get.

So don't sit back and think that things will change simply because Obama is in office. Don't think he is going to personally take care of your needs. Obama ain't yo mama; he is the president of a country that is still run, by and large, by White men who have, by their past resistance to change, proven time and again that Black folks will have to fight for everything we get in this country. I think it was Douglass who also said, "We may not get everything we fight for, but we will certainly have to fight for everything we get."

As individuals, we must understand and act upon the fact that things are still about the same for most of us; each of us still has to work for what we want and need. Collectively, we must form a broad-based coalition and submit a national Black agenda that addresses our needs and desires for this government of ours.

Do you think we can do that without some of us caving in, breaking ranks, and selling out? Do you think we can do that without worrying about who will be the HNIC? I think we can, at least those of us who are conscious and dedicated to the uplift of our people and a secure future for our children.

Please don't fall for the okey-doke again, brothers and sisters. Be more than just happy to have a Black man in the White House. The results of our happiness and euphoria should be something tangible to which we can point and share with our children. Brother Obama's children are fairly secure right now; their father and mother are millionaires twice over. They should be just fine. They are "in the house," as we like to say. The question is: "Where are Black people in general?

Finally, let's go back to the post-racial society charade that some are promoting as a result of Obama's election. An excellent example of how some of us are thinking now is the national "I Pledge" [to Obama] campaign that was featured on TV after the election. If you have seen the commercial, replete with celebrities, movie stars, athletes, and entertainers, you may have noticed that each of them pledged to do things like feed hungry people, spend time tutoring, recycling, and other celebrity feel-good stuff. You can see it on You Tube.

Of all the pledges, the one that struck me as strange and out of sync with all the others was that of Michael Strahan, former New York Giant football player. He said, "I pledge to consider myself an American, not an African American." No other person of any of the various ethnic groups featured in that video said they would give up his or her identity; the Black man was the only one who volunteered to do that. Go figure.

As I said, Obama ain't yo mama. Don't sit back and think you will be clothed, fed, employed, educated, sheltered, and included, simply because a Black man sits at the top of the political food chain. Get real and get to work, before we miss another opportunity to build something for ourselves – something that will last far beyond the next four or eight years.

Building Bigger Barns

Pro Basketball all-star, Allen Iverson, built a home in Atlanta for $4.5 million in 2009. It was foreclosed and put on the market for $2.8 million. Iverson bought a mansion in Villanova, PA, for $5 million, and ended up selling it for $2.6 million. Iverson also lost his posh $3.875 million Cherry Hills, Colo., mansion to foreclosure after defaulting on the mortgage, according to the Denver Post.

Anyone familiar with the Book of Luke (Chapter 12) will recall the passage about the young man who had accumulated so much "stuff" and decided to tear down his old barns and build bigger ones in which to store his "stuff." In other words, he had great excess and was not the least bit interested in sharing it or using it to glorify God. The young man was so proud of what he thought was his own accomplishment – accumulating so much material wealth – that he never considered the temporary nature of earthly treasure, nor how he could use his treasure to help others

Are Black folks in that same collective mindset today, accumulating more and more "stuff" and in danger of facing the reality of losing that "stuff" to someone else, as the parable says? Are we so engrossed with getting more and hording it to the point of forgetting where it came from in the first place? Have we overlooked the fact that we are supposed to be good stewards over what we have? And finally, do we think we will live forever, surrounded by our "stuff"?

Those verses show how the young man, after saying he would simply build more barns, was called a "fool" by God; he was told he would die that night, and his great wealth and all of his "stuff" would go to someone else. It goes on to say that this is how it will be with anyone who stores up things for himself but is not rich toward God.

No, this is not a sermon. I just want to point out the wherewithal among Black people, both financial and intellectual, and to suggest for the umpteenth time that we should use our resources in ways that will enhance our collective empowerment, especially among those less fortunate.

A feature in the National Black News Journal cited an article by Forbes Magazine that listed the wealthiest Black folks in America. The top ten individuals had a total wealth of more than $6.5 billion. Wow! I bet they have some huge barns.

Individual wealth among Black people, coupled with our collective annual income of around $900 billion, has already built thousands of big barns across this country. But, what has that tremendous amount of money built that will last well beyond our time? Has it and is it building a solid collective economic foundation? Is it building a strong infrastructure, which is necessary to sustain our children's future well into the next century? Are we using our collective resources, big and small, abundant and meager, to uplift the "masses of our people," as Jackie Robinson lamented?

During this economic crisis, especially among Black Americans, isn't it ironic that we are suffering the most from this latest recession, but we are still in second place when it comes to group income. We are still the most educated Black people on the face of the earth, but we have yet to figure out how to carve out a piece of the U.S. economy for ourselves. We are the majority in several large cities but we are still calling ourselves "minorities" in those cities and settling for small percentages of the business and jobs therein.

We have a competitive advantage in several industries, because we purchase the majority of various goods and services, yet we do not control their production and distribution. I guess we are too busy building bigger barns for all the "stuff" we buy from others.

Our children are suffering in an education system that has no interest in teaching them how to learn; and new prisons are being built every day. We pray, sing, shout, and dance in church more than any other group; and we have ornate edifices within which to do those things, but most of our church buildings are built by non-Black construction companies.

We are the most accommodating, forgiving, supportive, patriotic group of people in this country, and yet we do not love, trust, and respect ourselves enough to stand up and be counted, to use our billions of dollars to leverage better treatment from those who mistreat us every day. What irony there is in our predicament.

I trust we will get ourselves together, start to pool our resources, no matter how great or how small, get busy doing the work of economic empowerment, and taking more control over our children's educational needs. I pray we will see that the solution to our paradoxical situation is not in building bigger barns for all of our "stuff," but rather in building an economic foundation – a collective economic legacy that we can leave for our progeny.

Black by Default

"Like Jews throughout history, the Japanese see an essential need to preserve their unique ethnic and racial culture, even as the tribe expands to virtually every corner of the world. 'We must adjust to this new culture, but our children must remain Japanese,' explains [Yukio] Ohtsubo."
Quoted from the book, *Tribes*, by Joel Kotkin, (pages 124-125)

A conversation with Baba Sanyika Anwisye, from St. Louis, inspired the title of this piece. We were discussing Black people and the fact that many of us keep our Blackness, our African heritage and culture, in a "fallback" position. Baba Sanyika shared with me that only when a system, strategy, institution, business, or initiative, owned and operated by White people does not work for Black folks, will we begin talking about starting our own. When things return to what is called the "norm," Black people immediately move away from self-reliance back into our assimilationist mode.

As I thought about that and reviewed recent history, it began to be quite clear that we do rely heavily on White people to take care of our every need. And, as Sanyika declared, I agree that many of our people are simply "Black by default." Instead of continuously working toward self-reliance, we only fall back to that position when our chances of assimilation are threatened. Does O.J. come to mind?

Take education, for instance. We have made every attempt to assimilate into school systems that care very little about our children. As a fall back tactic we started creating our own schools. Shortly thereafter, when we thought White controlled schools were "getting religion" and "coming around," we stopped supporting our own schools and went right back into theirs.

Look at Back owned businesses. As soon as we were allowed to patronize White businesses, we abandoned our own and assumed we had assimilated to the point that we were welcome and acceptable in their stores, hotels, and restaurants. We found out later that we were still mistreated and exploited in many cases, so we defaulted to the rhetorical effort of creating "our own" businesses again.

Politics anyone? We knew we had it made when we were finally given the right to vote, for the third time, in 1965. Assimilation was a sure bet then. We elected Black folks in droves during the past 45 years, but in political circles, both locally and nationally, we have failed to break the "glass dome" of real political power that has accrued to Whites in this country. What are we doing about that? Even with a Black President we are still trying to fit in.

"Black by default." What an interesting term Baba Sanyika came up with. His point was that we are overlooking a most important aspect of our existence in this world. While we are busy falling back and being Black by default, we fail to realize that our legacy is grounded in having already done the things we now rely on others to do for us. We were born self-reliant; our very nature is to take care of ourselves; our history, in this country and long before we were brought here, demonstrated self-reliance. We had no fallback position, no default position; we were simply and proudly Black people, doing what we had to do to survive and thrive.

Why do some of us "go back" to being Black only when something that is White-oriented is not working for us? This is not an indictment of White people and the systems they have developed; rather it is a stark indication of our dependency and our notion that someone else's "ice is colder" than our own. It points out the dangers of our constant attempts to assimilate into a 400 year-old system that has shown us in no uncertain terms, time after time, that we are "less than."

Giving up one's culture and heritage, abdicating one's own responsibility of self-reliance, and literally walking away from one's economic base, as Black people did in the mid-1960's, have led us to our present condition. Now many of us find it necessary to move to our default position of being Black because the systems we believed in are not working for us and White folks, in general, are too busy trying to take care of themselves to be concerned about fixing our problems.

W.E.B. DuBois described Booker T. Washington's program of self-reliance as having "come along at the correct psychological moment," at a time when the nation was "ashamed of giving so much sentiment to Afro-Americans and was turning to the task of making money." This scenario has occurred many times over in our history; we must learn, once and for all, that we must be vigilant in our quest for self-reliance.

Richard Allen's Free African Society, back in late 1700's, adopted the slogan, "To seek for ourselves." We must be the Black people we once were in this country, and we must put an end to simply being Black by default, and start being Black on purpose.

Can't we all get along?

"The President, he's got his war
Folks don't know just what it's for
Nobody gives us rhyme or reason
Have one doubt, they call it treason
Tryin' to make it real, compared to what?"
Les McCann

Looks like Rodney King is living in the White House these days, y'all. Before you start writing your letters and e-mails to me for having the nerve to say something negative about our President, consider our current situation. We need to open our eyes and our minds to the reality of politics, once and for all, by understanding the nature of the beast.

You've heard the story about the frog that allowed the scorpion to get on his back for a ride across the pond. The frog said he would do it if the scorpion would not sting him. The scorpion assured the frog he would not harm him in return for the ride across the water. When they reached the other side, the scorpion stung the frog; and as the frog lay dying he said, "You promised you wouldn't sting me," to which the scorpion replied, "I was just being true to my nature; you knew I was a scorpion when you agreed to give me a ride."

Lying, backstabbing, grandstanding, accepting bribes, assassinating one's character, cheating, stealing, cursing, and fighting are among the characteristics on display among many of our politicians. In other words they are a mirror of society in general. Too often we hold them up as paragons of integrity, ethics, and morality, only to be let down when they fall from grace.

We send them to Washington with more financial security than most of us could ever dream of having, and they pass laws that adversely affect us but have no effect on their lives. They debate Social Security and healthcare but are not required to participate in the same programs they legislate for us. They determine how we will live, without having to be subjected to those same rules, and without having to pay a price for being wrong. What a life, huh?

Now we have a President who seems to think he can change the political landscape; he seems to believe that hundreds of years of political gamesmanship can be swept aside, and common sense will prevail. He subscribes to the notion that all he has to do is make a speech, do a town hall meeting, or an interview explaining his agenda, and all will be well in Washington and in this country. He seems to be asking the Rodney King question over and over again. And coming from the President of the United States, someone who knows how politics works, it sounds even more ridiculous.

Barack Obama was swept into office by a riptide of emotion, hope, and exasperation at the previous eight years. He was ballyhooed and ushered in on the fragile wings of instant stardom and fame, so much so that he even believed the hype. But, now that he is in office, and the crazies have come out of the woodwork, he finds himself having to respond to the ire of many of the same folks who hailed him as their new chief on January 20, 2009.

Obama is busy plugging holes is the dike and is fast running out of fingers. He was forced to take time to have a beer with two guys who had a spat, and offered it to us as a teachable moment that would demonstrate we can indeed all get along. He is on the road explaining his healthcare plan, trying desperately to get his opponents to get on board and get along with him as well. He is attempting to be all things to all people, albeit disciplinarian when it comes to Black people; but that's another article. All this in his utopian endeavor to help us all get along.

Memo to President Barack Obama: After Rodney King was beaten senseless by those police officers, all he could utter is "Can't we all get along?" All he could muster the nerve to say before the cameras of the world, before a public shocked beyond their imagination at what happened to him, recorded for everyone to see, was "Can't we all get along?" It was his time to shine, his time to teach, his time to enlighten; but he blew it big time and squandered his fifteen minutes of fame with that immature, naïve, rhetorical question.

In this country, Mr. President, as you well know, the political system of which you are now at least the titular leader is a system grounded in rancor and adversity, a system that wreaks of discord, a system comprising childlike adults who always want their way, and a system based on a 250-year struggle for the ultimate aphrodisiac: Power. You are in charge of a system whose participants have fought like cats and dogs over every little thing, and now you pose the question, "Can't we all get along.

After years of being beat up, all while watching it take place before our eyes on the evening news; most of the folks who elected you are not down with the Rodney King inquiry. We expect much more from you. Get some backbone, stand up to the political thugs and do the right thing. Don't go down as simply a "big-baller," be a true "shot-caller." And how about looking out for Black folks every now and then too? After all, you are the President.

Politicians have been battling for centuries, and have demonstrated in no uncertain terms that the answer to the question, Can't we all get along?" is an emphatic, unequivocal, unapologetic, "NO!"

Black Selling Power

"Black purchasing power is now at [$1.2 trillion]…but Black economic influence and its benefits aren't commensurate with this purchasing power."
Marian Wright Edelman

Much has been written, discussed, researched, and analyzed on so-called "Black Spending Power" or "Black Buying Power," as some would call it. For Black consumers especially, but also for other so-called "minority" groups in this country, the respective aggregate amounts of money earned each year, and then spent, are staggering. In addition, and again especially for Black consumers, our aggregate "buying power" can be described as a perpetual cash register, ringing, buzzing, and chiming 24/7/365. Why do we and others always pontificate about Black "buying power" and seldom, if ever, discuss Black "selling power"?

Comparatively speaking, there is very little "power" in spending, especially for those doing the spending. There are a few assets we can buy that can give us a modicum of power; real estate is one, and other items that appreciate rather than depreciate. They give us the power to control, to some extent, our economic future if we manage them properly.

On the other hand, if we concentrated more on selling than on buying, more on producing rather than consuming, and more on saving rather than spending, we could harness our "selling power" and take greater control of our collective economic future. Who do you think has more power, the buyer or the seller?

Black selling power makes the case for us to get more involved in teaching our children entrepreneurship, at least teaching them how to think the way an entrepreneur thinks. It makes a great case for more Black businesses and, just as important, the growth of those businesses. It makes the case for Black people to revert to the ways of our past by producing more of our own products, controlling the distribution of our products, and circulating our dollars among ourselves a few times before they make their exit from our neighborhoods.

Other folks are counting and keeping track of our dollars better than we are, brothers and sisters. Others are monitoring our spending habits and designing advertising and marketing campaigns that give them the power to reach into our pockets and purses, as well as our checking and saving accounts, and withdraw whatever amount they want.

The numbers are available for all to see. "Black spending power" is said to be nearly $1 trillion annually, folks. How much of that money is being spent at Black owned businesses? How much of the money earned by other groups is being spent at Black owned businesses? Apparently not very much is spent with us because Black businesses combined, had annual revenues of just over $88 billion according to the 2002 economic census, and we have the least amount of annual revenues per individual business as well.

Considering the fact that so-called Black spending power is nearly a trillion dollars, and yet aggregate Black business revenue is currently around $135 billion according to the 2007 economic census, we must change our economic game plan. At a minimum this scenario strongly suggests that Black people are not supporting Black businesses to the degree we can and should - and neither are the other groups. By redirecting our so-called "buying power" we can increase our own "selling power," and create wealth for ourselves. At present, our spending power translates to power for the businesses of others, allowing them to create wealth and increase their selling power even more.

Something is drastically wrong with this picture. Maybe that's why statisticians keep blowing smoke at us regarding our "spending power." I guess it makes us feel good to know we have so much money. However, if that money only stays with us for a short while, and if it does very little to create wealth for Black people, it is not doing its job to the maximum degree. Our dollars are not making sense, and we must teach them better, by using our dollars more intelligently.

It's not about how much money we have; it's about what we do with what we have, and how long we hold on to it. The Empowerment Experiment (formerly known as the Ebony Experiment), being conducted by John and Maggie Anderson in Chicago, is even more important when we juxtapose the stark realities of Black "spending power" against the potential of Black "selling power."

I leave you with this thought: You could make a case for the term "Black Spending Power" to be classified as oxymoronic in light of the fact that there is very little power in spending, in and of itself and without a Black consumer consciousness, which is what most of us do every day. So why not move away from that term and build our "Black selling power"?

The power to sell more increases our power to produce more, to distribute more, to establish more businesses, to grow those businesses; and that power can be used to solidify our economic future and pass something more than a few depreciating items on to our children.

We must take greater control of our economic destiny. Yes, it will take sacrifice; just ask the Andersons about that – as well as those of us for whom it is a habit to search for Black businesses to support. But isn't the sacrifice of driving a little further, paying a few cents more, and encouraging our Black businesspersons worth our children's future?

A legacy of "selling power" will be significantly greater and much more important than a legacy that simply states how money we earned and spent each year. Let's consider ways to increase our selling power; we will be much better off for having done so.

Audacity still intact, but my hope is fading fast.

Oh, determination is fading fast;
Inspiration is a thing of the past.
Can't see how my hope's gonna last;
Good things are bad and what's happy is sad.
The Temptations

I don't think anyone who knows me would say I am cowardly or reticent when it comes to speaking the truth, not only on economic issues but also on political issues; my middle name could be "audacious." Well, as I have grown older and wiser, my willingness to take the risk of telling the truth, no matter who is listening (or reading), is even stronger. But, like many of my friends and associates have expressed, my hope for significant change continues to diminish.

I am not condemning the future of our children, however. The hope to which I am referring is now - during my lifetime. There are things I would like to see before I make my transition, but based on what I see these days, both economically and politically, my cynicism increases daily.

Our President, whose book is titled, <u>The Audacity of Hope</u>, taken from a sermon he heard by Dr. Jeremiah Wright, interestingly enough, stirred hope in millions of people when he demonstrated his audacity to confidently run for the highest office in the land. His victory buoyed Black folks to heights we had never experienced; we were bold, no longer timid and willing to take a backseat in politics; we had won! Our hope was sky-high, and it still is among some of us.

That was then, albeit, not too long ago, but this is now. For me, it all started with a debate between Hillary and Barack when someone in the audience asked candidate Obama about the negative effects of illegal immigration on "African Americans." Barack Obama started answering the question in relationship to Whites, Hispanics, Asians, minorities, and then African Americans. He emphasized the other groups and de-emphasized Black people. A slowly pitched softball was lobbed at him and he chose not to swing on behalf of Black people.

Next we had a series of speeches given to Jewish people, Gay and Lesbian people, and Hispanic people, which were uplifting, hopeful, and supportive. In some cases concessions were made. Then, in speeches to Black people, the latest of which was to the NAACP, President Obama continued his assault, as he said he would, against the wrongdoings and irresponsibility of Black men especially. No concessions, just "tough love," as some have deemed it.

Even on his walk through the slave dungeons of Cape Coast, and standing at the Door of No Return with Anderson Cooper, when questioned about the effect of slavery on African Americans, Obama immediately included his assertion that it not only affected Blacks but Whites as well. I am sure Anderson Cooper was comfortable with that answer.

Now, with the Henry Louis Gates situation, we see our President speaking in support of Gates' rights and then doing a Michael Jackson moonwalk in response to the outrage voiced by the FOP, news commentators, et al. Is it just me, or is there a leaning by our President to always accommodate the White psyche while ignoring the Black psyche?

Is this selective outrage on Obama's part? There are many Black men who have experienced similar and worse treatment than Professor Gates. It is happening every day. Is our President mimicking the pig in George Orwell's Animal Farm by placing so much emphasis on the Gates incident and implying that, "We are all equal, but some of us are more equal than others"?

I know, I know, "he has to do what he has to do" because he is the "President of all the people." But, aren't Black people included in "all the people"? Clarence Thomas is Justice for all the people too, right? As I said, my audacity is strong, but my hope is fading.

Obama's "audacity of hope," is not enough for Black people to make the progress necessary to secure a bright future for our children. Our President must have the audacity of reciprocal support for the millions of Black people who so enthusiastically rallied around him. He must have the audacity of courage and strength to speak up for us too, and stand on what he says. Under-girded by the audacity of a Black consciousness, our President could set the stage for beneficial change for Black people in this country.

It's all right to scold us every now and then; surely we deserve it sometimes. But be an equal opportunity scolder-in-chief, without equivocation. White folks and others have a lot of "splainin'" to do too. To chide Africans for their "victim mentality" and devalue the devastating effects of enslavement on African Americans, in a seeming effort to make others more comfortable is, at best, disinguous and, at worst, insulting and demeaning to Black people. We look to our President to work on problems, rather than spend so much time pointing out the symptoms of our problem.

Memo to the President: After your visit with Officer Crowley and Henry Louis Gates, please keep the invitation to the White House open for all the other brothers and sisters who are profiled, abused, insulted, assaulted, and mistreated by the police. You're gonna need a whole lot of beer and chips, so stock up now, sir.

Better still, Amefika Geuka, Founder and Headmaster of the Joseph Littles Nguzo Saba School in West Palm Beach, Florida, is walking to Washington, D.C. on behalf of African centered education. He would love to visit with you, Mr. President. How about inviting him to the White House to rest his feet, sip on some lemonade, and have a conversation about the education of our children? Maybe you could walk the last mile with him; maybe he could even spend the night at "our" White House.

Raising the Stakes

Powers keep on lyin' While your people keep on dyin'
World keep on turnin' Cause it won't be too long...
Gonna keep on tryin' till I reach the highest ground.
Stevie Wonder

In case you haven't noticed, the level of hateful language against Black people has escalated during the past couple of months. Also, purchases of guns and ammunition have increased exponentially during that same period. Talk show hosts are taking more liberties with their acid-tongued, venom-laced, political rhetoric, and we are seeing more heinous acts of violence across this nation. Both symbolically and substantively, images of what is yet to come are before our very eyes every day; yes, the stakes have been raised to new heights. Have you been paying attention?

On the economic front, things are getting worse. Have you checked out the unemployment rates in various states across the country? They are as high as 17% in some of counties in Ohio, where I live. That means, as we all know, that the unemployment rate for Black people is double and in some areas even quadruple that of the national average.

Housing, jobs, business growth, economic exclusion, and economic apartheid are all very present in today's world. It's almost to the point of dog-eat-dog at this point, especially when it comes to economics, and you know what that means: The big dog eats first and the big dog eats the most. As Nelson Rivers of the National NAACP says, "We need a big dog, but to have a big dog we have to feed the dog we have."

That's exactly what's happening in our economy. The big dogs are being fed while the rest of us look on salivating with envy. Banks are being bailed out. Automobile companies are being rescued from the brink of disaster. War financiers are still busy making money. Politicians are fat and happy with their cushy salaries and pension plans. College Basketball coaches get $30+ million contracts while the college players can't even get a free lunch.

Symbolically, the lowest tactics are being used to divide and conquer the masses. Fox News against MSNBC News, with anchors who are totally engrossed in political claptrap. Partisan politics abound, Obama's olive branch to the Republicans notwithstanding. Dick Cheney paints a doomsday picture for the media; Limbaugh does his usual thing, castigating those with whom he does not agree, spouting and pouting, and his typical name-calling antics; he even called Tavis Smiley a "dunce."

Subliminal messages abound, from Tea Parties to Gun Shows, from peace tours by the President to Global Race Conference boycotts by the President, from Iraq to Afghanistan, from North Korea to Iran, from paying homage to the Queen of England to currying favor with the Potentates of Turkey, from bowing to the Saudi King to bowing down to the Prime Minister of Israel, from the good old days to the New World Order, from the dollar to the euro to the "Amero." We have seen it all in just 60 days. Whew!

The most significant symbolism was that of the young man from Somalia who was brought to the U.S. for his role as a "pirate." A teenager, between 16-18 years of age, having voluntarily boarded the U.S. warship to negotiate a deal to end the standoff, was brought to this country in chains. Chains! How's that for symbolism? It was not as though this guy was going anywhere; it was not as though he was going to fight back and hurt one of the FBI agents who accompanied him; it was not as if he was a mass-murderer. He is a young Black African brought to this country in chains and paraded before the cameras for the world to see, not how bad he is, but how "bad" we are. How ridiculous is that? And, as I said, how symbolic it is that a Black African in 2009 would be brought to these shores in chains?

Yes folks, the stakes have been raised to dizzying heights. We have always been at risk, but that's even more evident now. All the guns and ammo are certainly not for target practice and deer hunting. All the assault rifles are probably not to kill invading Chinese, Russians, Venezuelans, Cubans, Iranians, or North Koreans. Maybe it's those fearsome Haitians the NRA crowd is worried about.

As the unemployment rate escalates, watch for responsive acts of violence. As the talk-show hosts arouse the fears of the "American people," watch for acts of violence against the easiest targets of them all: Black people. Check out your history notes on the 1863 Draft Riots. Don't want to go that far back? Check out Tulsa in 1921.

There are some sho-nuff nut-cases out there just waiting to explode and unload on someone for "taking their job," or for electing "that Black guy" as President, or for increasing taxes, and spending too much. It doesn't take much pressure to move a hair trigger, so watch your back. Meanwhile, understand that the stakes have indeed been raised, and just because there is a "Black" President it does not mean that Black people are any better off substantively, and as I think about it, not even symbolically.

Consequences of Political Greed

My car got repossessed this morning
Harder times I haven't seen in years
Able to throw me a life preserver
'Cause I'm about to drown in my own tears
Standing on shaky ground—The Temptations

In what some are calling the worst economic environment in several decades, and after witnessing some of the most egregious acts of economic irresponsibility and dishonesty committed over the past eight years, we now have to contend with even more. Political leaders, men and women we elect and pay quite well, many of whom become multi-millionaires while in office, are making rules and regulations that will adversely impact our lives for generations to come. When they can find time in between their junkets and parties, some of our politicians are busy at work, or is it just "busy-work," trying to make us believe they are truly interested in our future. What a joke! And it's definitely on us.

Along with their cronies in the private sector, our elected officials, again, all while receiving their income from taxpayers, are too heavy-laden with the burden of getting rich and fattening their own coffers to consider us for a change. They get the best of healthcare, but want to deny us that same benefit. They do not have to pay into the Social Security System, which many say will not be solvent when the next generation retires, but we must put our money into it. They stand by and watch billions spent (and stolen) on the war in Iraq, a war we entered based on nothing but lies, and now they act so pompous and self-righteous, as though Halliburton never existed.

What kind of conscience must politicians have to do the kinds of things they do to the people they are supposed to serve? We rail against the financial sector, the executives who steal billions, and rightly so, but we cannot overlook our politicians and the things they do to us rather than for us.

You folks in Louisiana, South Carolina, and Alaska, for instance, should be riding your governors out of town on a rail in response to their refusal of YOUR share of the federal stimulus money. For their own political expediency, for their own political advancement, with aspirations of moving to the national stage, where they can do even more damage to the people for whom they work, these three governors are thumbing their noses at their constituents. They are ignoring the economic pain and strain among the people in their own states, their neighbors; and they want to be national leaders?

What's more, after Katrina in Louisiana and considering the educational status of children and the unemployment rate in South Carolina, you would think those two governors would have a modicum of compassion. As for Alaska's governor, well she is so far off course and so wrapped up in trying to run for national office in 2012 that she has totally lost her mind – along with those who support her.

It is shameful, irresponsible, and downright criminal for some politicians to still be in office after the shenanigans they have pulled. It is even more irresponsible that we continue to allow them to stay in office. They treat us like dirt, ignore our real needs, turn deaf ears and blind eyes to "the people," and then come around during the next campaign and tell us what they've done for us, asking us to vote for them again. And we do it!

I get so sick of seeing them on television, with their self-righteous speeches, their condescending language, their make-believe concern for "the people," and their holier-than-thou façades.

Millions are suffering in this country, from the Bush administration's thievery in Iraq and turning a surplus into a huge deficit. Millions continue to suffer now from the greed of bankers and corporate executives who commit malfeasance and get paid millions as a result. Our children's children will suffer from our trillion dollar deficit and what is now an $18 trillion national debt that we will pass on to them. Where will it end?

The State Dinners, the parties, the social affairs, the free trips, the best healthcare, the best retirement programs, and all the other perks our politicians have at their disposal should at least give them pause to consider us for a change. I guess they think they will not be affected when this country collapses. Maybe they believe that when "the people" get fed-up we would never think of coming to take their stuff. I wonder if they have ever heard of Maslow's Hierarchy of Needs Theory.

On the news we see our President and his wife engaged in an economic *tête-à-tête* with world leaders and the main thing reported is whether they made a *faux pas* by touching the Queen of England or by Michelle Obama being sleeveless at an affair or by Barack Obama joking with the Queen. You would think she was the Queen of America or something. We are hurting on this side of the ocean; and we should be worried about British etiquette? Give me a break!

Corruption, greed, deceit, pandering, condescension, lies, disregard, and arrogance from the highest levels of leadership, all running rampant in a nation that claims to be founded and based on Judeo-Christian principles, blatantly smacks of contradiction and moral decay. Every political speech ends with God Bless America! As much as He has already blessed us, God must be saying the same thing: "Give me a break!"

Buying Black – The Empowerment Experiment

Their water is not wetter;
Their sugar is not sweeter;
Their ice is not colder.

You have probably heard or read about John and Maggie Anderson, who live in Oak Park, Illinois, just west of Chicago, and their year-long initiative to make all of their purchases from Black owned businesses. This couple should be commended for such an effort and the sacrifices they made to conduct their "Experiment." They are exemplary of what we can do to achieve true economic empowerment. The Andersons, their tremendous sacrifices notwithstanding, are doing what Marcus Garvey and others espoused; they are showing what can and should be done by conscious committed Black people all over this country.

As usual, the detractors are calling them "racist and divisive." Some even commented that they would "now" only support White businesses. Isn't that amazing? I wonder what these same folks call Black people who have for years supported White owned businesses.

No one ever complains about the many China Towns, Greek Towns, and Jewish enclaves that promote and, indeed, provide mutual support to their businesses and consumers. I have never heard anyone call these people "racists" and "separatists" or responded to these ethnic economic enclaves by saying they would only buy from White owned businesses. Instead, Whites and virtually everyone else support the business owners in these enclaves. In fact, we celebrate their "entrepreneurial spirit" and characterize them as "educated and informed consumers," "self-supporting" and "hardworking" citizens.

Now that John and Maggie Anderson have started their quest to spend as much of their money with Black owned businesses, some are characterizing them as villains and racists rather than forward-thinking concerned individuals who are trying to empower not only Black people but this country as well. Black folks did not invent nor do we practice racism; we only react to it. For this effort to be characterized as racist is disingenuous short-sighted, ignorant, incendiary, and just plain stupid as far as I am concerned.

It is a real shame that this couple would have to endure any negativity for doing what is right; but it comes with the territory. Because $850 billion moves through Black consumers' hands each year, more than 90% of that amount going to businesses owned and controlled by others, it is no surprise that turning a significant portion of that money inward to Black businesses is frightening to the establishment.

Because Black people have been looked upon, and in many cases conducted ourselves as mere consumers rather than producers, any effort put forth since 1964 (Integration) has been squelched. But whose fault is that? If we would take more control of our dollars, by making them have some sense, it would not matter who said what about our efforts to leverage our collective income into real wealth in our communities.

As I noted in my interview with Mr. Ted Gregory, writer for the Chicago Tribune, regarding what was first called the "Ebony Experiment," this is not the first effort of its kind, but it is unique in its experimental aspects. It could also be unique in its sacrificial aspects, in that the Andersons have to drive long distances to make many of their purchases from Black businesses. Prior to integration, there were Black cooperative buying programs, Buy Black Campaigns, Double-Duty Dollar campaigns, and other initiatives, right in our communities, that brought Black consumers and business owners together in support of one another.

Maggie Anderson, who hails from Liberty City (Miami, Florida), an all-Black community in 1950's, which thrived on mutual business support among Black people, is now doing her best to revive the economic spirit of her childhood community. As I noted earlier, their sacrifice has not come without naysayers and outright "haters." According to the Tribune article, among the responses received by the Andersons was an anonymous letter mailed to their home accusing them of "unabashed, virulent racism." The writer stated, "Because of you, we will totally avoid black suppliers. Because of you, we will dodge every which way to avoid hiring black employees."

See what I mean? That kind of thinking is totally misplaced and hateful. But with $850 billion on the line, there is no telling what kinds of reactions and retaliation this family will get from ignorant, one-sided, and narrow-minded folks who want to maintain status quo when it comes to business development and growth among African Americans.

With all of the hurdles and obstacles they face, this paragon of a black couple has made a commitment and is following through on that commitment, which is, on its own merits, very commendable, especially when it comes to doing something positive for Black people. They truly deserve our support. Drop them a line or an e-mail and tell them you appreciate what they are doing, and then get involved by starting your own Black buying "experiment" in your city.

Through the Andersons' efforts, guided by their advisory board of Juliet E.K. Walker, George Fraser, and yours truly, Black owned businesses will be discovered by other consumers, minds will be changed about buying Black, and consciousness will be raised among Black consumers. I trust that everyone else who reads this will consider John Anderson's words: "Focusing the estimated $850 billion annual black buying power on black businesses strengthens those businesses and creates more businesses, more jobs, and stronger families, schools, and neighborhoods."

Stimulate your own economy

"The principal affliction of poor communities in the United States is not the absence of money, but its systematic exit."
Michael Shuman, <u>Going Local</u>

Of all the ways being recommended to stimulate the economy, very few are directed toward the fact that, like politics, economics is local. The tried and true method for stimulating our local economies is by mutually buying from and selling to one another. You have heard it all before, what has become an aphorism in the so-called Black community: "The Black dollar doesn't circulate even one time among Black people before it leaves the Black community." Whose fault is that, y'all?

If we would somehow turn that cliché into a myth, by acting upon its truth alone, we could stimulate our own economies all across this country; and we would not be sitting around waiting for the politicians, who have already proven how inept and greedy they are, to pass a stimulus package that won't do diddly-squat for the collective empowerment of Black people.

How can we keep more of our money among ourselves? Glad you asked. Support and grow our own businesses instead of everyone else's. Teach our young people how to create jobs through entrepreneurship rather than merely how to "get a job" that belongs to someone who couldn't care less about their future security.

"But we need something we can do right now, Jim." Here is something, and it is quite timely. Who is preparing your tax return? If there is a Compro Tax Service in your town, or another Black owned Tax Preparation Company where you live, then PLEASE go to them and get your taxes done. For God's sake! What could be easier? What makes more sense than this simple but empowering way to contribute to our own stimulus package? Like death, taxes are inevitable, but some of us would rather run to every Tom, Dick, and Harry to use their services instead of using our own Black firms. How sad!

Compro Tax, the largest Black tax firm in the country, should be overwhelmed with business every year, and not just from Black people, but from all other groups as well. They are professionals and, more importantly, they have proven time and again that they are conscious when it comes to financially supporting our communities. The corporate office in Beaumont, Texas, recently completed construction and opened a convention center: The Compro Event Center.

Designed and built by Black architects and builders, wired by a Black owned computer and technology company, staffed and managed by Black folks, catering provided by Black owned companies, and supported by other Black entrepreneurs who rent the retail spaces that are attached to the convention center, the Compro Event Center is the model for other Black businesses to follow. Because of the foresight and consciousness of its owners, Compro Tax has demonstrated yet again that it is willing to invest in the community by putting its money here its mouth is. How about an event center in every town that has a Compro tax office?

During its grand opening in December 2008, esteemed Professor and Psychologist, Dr. Na'im Akbar and the talented young "Master Teacher" from Atlanta, Chike Akua, followed by the "Networking Guru," George Fraser, were the featured speakers at the weekend "Christening" event. Inviting folks like these conscious brothers and sisters to speak at our events is another way to "keep our dollars circulating among ourselves."

So, find a Compro Tax office and let them do your taxes; and don't fall for the heart-rending commercials with Black TV spokespersons. Where are these companies when the tax season ends? What are they building in your neighborhood that will provide a job or a contract for your people? Leave them alone and support your own. Create your own economic stimulus.

Here's another way. Support the education of your children by doing what Oprah did for the school in Atlanta. Her check for $365,000 was a drop in the bucket for Oprah, but many drops into the buckets of our local African-Centered schools, put there by Black people who want our children to be properly and consciously educated, can go far to improve our lot. Determine what your particular "drop in the bucket" is and send a donation; the future result will surely be a self-supported economic stimulus for our children.

I get so tired of hearing us complain about not being able to do things for ourselves. Surely there is something you can do to stimulate your local Black economy, or even that of a city in which you do not reside. Just look around, make the commitment and follow through on it by supporting your own businesses and educational institutions. You may not be an Oprah, but I believe that we have a lot of little Oprah's who can, if only we would, combine our individual dollars and provide an economic stimulus for Black people, locally and nationally. Try it; it just may become a great habit.

The Excuse Game

Adult to child: "Do as I say, not as I do."

"Every child has lost every excuse." Those were the words of

James Clyburn of South Carolina, Majority Whip in the House of Representatives. He spoke those words on BET of all places, in response to Barack Obama being elected President of the United States. As soon as I read his statement, I thought, "Uh Oh, here we go." Now that we have a Black President all bets are off, and all is right with the world; we have reached our highest pinnacle. "Every child," as Clyburn said, which obviously includes every Black child, can no longer be excused for not achieving.

Let's delve into Clyburn's "no excuse" world of an Obama Presidency. While we are at it, let's find some adults, maybe even some U.S. Representatives, who no longer have excuses for their behavior.

The most recent heinous act against a Black man was committed in plain sight of several witnesses and captured on camera. Oscar Grant, lying on his stomach, hands held behind his back, and with one cop's knee on his neck, was summarily shot and killed by a cop who had little regard for the life of a young Black man. But since we have a Black President, I don't want to hear young men in Oakland come up with excuses for not wanting to go along with the system, despite the possibility of being on their way to school and getting shot by an overzealous police officer.

Black children no longer have the excuse of being "steered" to low level education programs because they come from a "poor" neighborhood; they cannot offer the excuse of being targeted as low performers or "hyperactive," thus, requiring them to be put on drugs to keep them calm. Black children can no longer rely on the excuse of not having enough to eat in the morning, or having to sleep in a cold house because the heat was turned off, or not having the adult examples they need in their immediate lives, not from a distance, to guide them along their way. They now have Obama, so no more excuses.

No more excuses for the disparities that exist in our criminal justice system, our social service system, our educational system, and our political system. No more excuses for any child who sees corporate executives and slimy politicians fatten their pockets from the public coffers, and feast at banquet tables fit for kings and queens. No more excuses for the child who cries at night or cowers in fear of being the next Oscar Grant. Yeah, right, no more excuses.

How about the so-called responsible adults who run this country? Are they now out of excuses? Do they now have to take more ownership for their lives and the lives of those for whom they work? Can they still make excuses for not standing up and speaking against injustice, against disparity, and against the crimes we see every day in the public and private sectors?

Has every adult run out of excuses for allowing millions of children, who no longer have excuses, to go without adequate health care? Now that we have a Black President will every adult be held accountable for his or her actions? Will part of the "change" we raved about be adults acting like adults rather than like self-indulgent children who have no regard for anyone but themselves?

Like Representative Clyburn, I also went through a few things in the fifties and sixties as a result of prejudice and racism. I saw the same things he saw, and I also wondered if we would ever have a Black President. Now that we have one, my attention is not so much on the children as it is on the adults. How can we say they no longer have any excuse, especially when many of their excuses can be traced to our neglect of their needs – regardless of who resided in the White House?

Why didn't we tell them that Frederick Douglass and W.E.B. DuBois could have been President were it not for this country's racism? Why not share with them the fact that Barbara Jordan and Shirley Chisholm could have run this country? Why didn't we eliminate their excuses when Reginald Lewis bought Beatrice Foods for $1 billion dollars? Or, when Oprah became a billionaire? Why didn't we tell them "no more excuses" when Ken Chenault assumed the highest level at American Express Corporation? It is sad that some Black people, especially those in my age group, place so much emphasis on politics rather than on economics.

Yes, we have a Black President, but that fact will not eliminate all excuses among our children until it eliminates all excuses among our adults. When our children see more responsible adults, they will be more responsible. The status of the Obama family alone does not, will not, and cannot eliminate all excuses for every child. If that were the case their excuses would have been eliminated long ago by the likes of Booker T. Washington, Harriet Tubman, and Sojourner Truth. Or by other Black "presidents" of companies, like Maggie Lena Walker and Madame C.J. Walker, Ed Gardner and John Johnson, S.B. Fuller and Joe Dudley, Ann Fudge and Suzanne DePasse, Berry Gordy and Robert

Holland, Jackie Mayfield and Dr. Walter P. Lomax.

It is only now that we have a Black "U.S." President, a political leader rather than an economic leader that we say to our children, "No more excuses." When Black politicians, who have "good jobs, great health care, and benefits of public office, speak about the intrinsic value of a Black man rising to the top of our political hierarchy, I wonder what it says about their own value to their constituents. I wonder if that also eliminates <u>their</u> excuses for acquiescing to sub-standard economic and social conditions among Black people in this country. I wonder.

Let's rid ourselves of potential.

The human race is a herd. Here we are, unique, eternal aspects of consciousness with infinity of potential, and we have allowed ourselves to become an unthinking, unquestioning blob of conformity and uniformity--a herd. Once we concede to the herd mentality, we can be controlled and directed by a tiny few. And we are.
David Icke

In a recent conversation, the "potential among Black folks" came up. Surely you have heard it discussed before, and many of you have even engaged in philosophical, statistical, rhetorical conversations on our "potential." I don't know about you, but I am tired of Black folks having all the "potential" in the world. I am tired of all the talk about how great our "potential" is to change, to become, and to achieve. Discussions on the "potential" of Black people remind me of similar discussions about the "power" Black people possess in this country.

Like "power," potential is only realized, or brought to fruition, if it is utilized; otherwise, how would you know you had potential if you never used it? Batteries have power, or so we believe, right? But how do we know they have power until we put them into a device, turn it on, and see a light, or hear a sound, or feel some movement? Those batteries could sit for years and never realize the power within them, the "potential" within them to do their job.

Thus, when the discussion of Black power comes up in my circles, which some say we do possess, I always ask: How do we know we have power, especially political and economic power, if we never use that power to make the headway we need to make in this country?

It's the same with this thing we call "potential." The dictionary uses words like, "possibility," "capable of," "latent," "prospective," and "would-be" to define it. Do these words sound like action? Do they appear to be words on which we should hang our collective hat? Should we continue to be content with having "potential?" My answer is an emphatic, "NO!" We must act on our potential, not sit on it like it's some kind of honorable throne.

Case in point: Around midday on New Year's Eve, a sister in Chicago called me to ask about a mutual friend whose wife died on Christmas Eve; the funeral was scheduled for New Year's Day. I had been in touch with the brother and knew about the situation, at least all but one very important development, which the sister shared with me. The family did not have all of the money necessary to pay the burial expenses.

We see this all the time among our people, for various reasons. In this case, the deceased sister could not be insured because of a preexisting physical condition. But the reason did not matter, especially when I learned that if the balance of the money was not paid by that same evening around 4:00 PM, the funeral would be cancelled and our dear sister's body would have to be removed from the mortuary.

The sister who called me is a member of the Nationalist Black Leadership Coalition, (NBLC), formed under the Black Back Black Movement, which is significant in how this scenario played out. I contacted the husband to find out what was needed, and I got instructions on how we could assure the needed funds got to the funeral home by the deadline. I then made several calls to other members of the NBLC and solicited their support.

Not one of them questioned me beyond how to get the money there in time and how to make sure it made it to the right person. Not only did we need to raise several thousand dollars in a short period of time, we had to make sure it got to the office in time – that same day!

I am proud to say that I attended the sister's home-going today, and I am also proud to say that several NBLC members, conscious brothers and sisters from across the country, did not allow themselves to suffer from "paralysis by analysis." We cared and loved enough to act, to live up to our collective "potential," and turn that potential into a true demonstration of what we can do when we put our hearts and minds to the task.

Brother Amefika Geuka, former Headmaster of the Joseph Littles Nguzo Saba School in West Palm Beach, Florida, always teaches us what Marcus Garvey taught: "There is nothing in the world common to man that man cannot do." It is highly unfortunate that even something as simple as raising money for our own brothers and sisters, certainly one of the "potential powers" among Black people, oftentimes is proven under the worst of circumstances. Someone has to die, or someone has to lose their home, or someone has to get sick for us to realize our "potential" to do good things for one another. (See: YouTube, "The Marcus Garvey Concept, by Amefika Geuka)

But I will not throw cold water on what we did for our brother and sister in their time of need. That's what the NBLC is all about, not sitting back admiring all the "potential" among Black people; we're about destroying our "potential" by turning it into positive action. We're about leaving footprints, not butt-prints, as Ken Bridges used to say.

Yes, relatively speaking, it was a small gesture. It will not get the headlines Oprah received when she recently gave $365,000 to that school in Atlanta. But it warms my heart to know that a few Black folks used our meager resources to help someone else. Another piece of "potential" among Black people bites the dust.

2010

Paying the price for squandering resources

"Waste not, want not."
"A fool and his money are soon parted."

The cases of two Black multi-millionaire NBA stars who now find themselves in dire financial straits follow a long line of misguided, uninformed or ill-informed, unprepared, and self-absorbed brothers (and some sisters) who squandered their financial resources. It is sad to see Kenny Anderson and Antoine Walker suffering from the consequences of their ineptness, ignorance, and cavalier attitudes when it comes to their money and their fame.

Of course they are not the first and, unfortunately, they will not be the last; but it hurts no less to see them go through their trials. It also hurts to see that same level of behavior displayed by others among us who have plenty, some of whom will end up in the same place as Walker and Anderson.

In my last book, <u>Black Empowerment with an Attitude – You got a problem with that?</u>, there is a note on Antoine Walker's penchant for expensive items, and how he was robbed of one of his prized possessions: A $55,000 watch! He was also robbed at his home in Chicago. Could it have been partially due to his flamboyant lifestyle? Bentleys, Mercedes, three multi-million dollar homes, $10 million "invested" in properties mismanaged by one of his boys, and the obligatory entourage of hangers-on and shysters all contributed to Walker's demise.

It's difficult to sympathize, and impossible for me to empathize with a guy who made $110 million playing ball and additional money from endorsements. However, to see him now, playing for the minimum and trying to pay his $21,000 per month restitution to the court, is quite sad.

Kenny Anderson's case is similar in that he frivolously spent his money on material possessions, failed to listen to his financial advisors, and ended up losing much of what he had. Anderson is said to have

57

earned $63 million in NBA, but he also apparently needed 10 cars in his garage, and all the other accoutrements of the high life.

Like MC Hammer, Anderson and Walker helped a lot of their "friends" by "lending" enormous sums of money to them, which was never repaid. The good thing that is often overlooked is the fact that these guys also paid out large sums of money to take care of their children.

You can read about these cases for yourself; here's my point: About 20 years ago (1995), I wrote an article titled, "Plantation Education." I pointed out some critical issues related to collegiate athletics and the way our young men are treated as they help earn millions for their respective colleges. What we see, not only in the two cases mentioned herein but in many other instances among Black athletes, is a lack of Black consciousness, lack of knowledge and understanding of Black history and culture, little or no knowledge of personal finance, lack discipline, and their failure to develop and nurture relationships with a classmate or two who could guide them legally and financially before they sign those multi-million dollar contracts.

The other major point of that article was the comparison between the enormous sums of money paid to the coaches, the highest of which now is around $4 million a year, to the restrictions against the athletes getting paid for their skills. Coaches cut lucrative deals with athletic gear firms and get so many perks on college campuses that you would think they are gods.

If someone buys the student a dinner or pays for a bus ticket for him to go home, the student is in jeopardy of losing his scholarship and maybe even losing his opportunity to move on to the professional ranks. Read the story of the Fab Five at the University of Michigan, about how their talents and styles were financially exploited by shoe and apparel companies, while they had to scrape money together to buy a few snacks every now and then.

Many Black athletes, while they are in college and even beyond, are merely ATM's for folks who care very little about them and their families, that is, as long as the cash keeps rolling in. The NCAA, while it earns billions from television and sponsorships, could make changes to help our athletes before they graduate, but it is too busy counting its own money to care about them.

The ramifications of our young millionaire athletes not having a consciousness is the proliferation of non-black agents, accountants, and financial advisers that prey upon them, and the athletes' penchant to hire them rather than their own brothers and sisters. An awareness and knowledge of Black history and culture would arm our young brothers against self-destructive behavior. Relationships with college peers, who have expertise in finance, business, law, and accounting, would lessen the instances of rip-offs by shady characters.

Kenny Anderson and Antoine Walker comprise just the tip of the iceberg. Their cases are not unique; we have seen this situation in boxing, the film industry, the music industry, and virtually across the board when it comes to many of our brothers and sisters.

This scenario certainly needs to change, so I guess this is a "shout-out" to all of you young super-rich athletes and entertainers. If you are presently in school preparing for and hoping for a call from the NBA or the NFL, please understand first that there are only a few hundred of those privileged positions available. Suppose you don't get that call? Prepare yourself for that as well.

In addition, if you do get that call, make sure you have your act together. Please don't get caught up in the material things. Understand that you only have so many opportunities in life, and make sure that you use some of your resources to empower Black professionals and Black owned businesses. That's what other groups do all the time, and by doing so they have created and are maintaining their own collective infrastructure and safety net.

A rising tide lifts all boats.

"Should you find yourself in a chronically leaking boat, energy devoted to changing vessels is likely to be more productive than energy devoted to patching leaks."
Warren Buffett

You've heard the saying; it was made famous by John F. Kennedy to suggest that an increase in a particular region's wealth would enhance the overall wealth of the entire country. Ronald Reagan and his minions came along and used the same aphorism to suggest that an increase in individual wealth, namely through tax cuts, would result in a "Trickling-Down" of prosperity to the poor (Supply-Side Economics). Now we hear the phrase being uttered by President Barack Obama – I wonder what he means by it.

Whatever the intent, original, twisted, or revised, there is an overriding truth in the phrase: A rising tide lifts all boats, that is, if you have a boat, it has no holes in it, and it is in the water rather than in dry-dock.

Unfortunately, this tired phrase is used to justify the ridiculous amounts of annual compensation for some folks; it is used to support what most of us know is a false outcome; and it is put forth as a beacon of light for poor people, hope that as soon as the rich get richer everyone will do better. Looking at today's economy, I think we can see the fallacy of that contention.

Folks on Wall Street, after making their way around the monopoly board a few times, passing "Go" and collecting hundreds of billions of dollars and numerous "Get out jail free" cards along the way, are being paid embarrassing amounts of money. The annual bonuses given out by investment banks and other financial institutions are more than most of us will earn in a lifetime. I guess they bought a lot of boats with that money; oops, I'm sorry, I mean yachts,

Another saying became popular during this latest rip-off of society by corporate thieves: "Too big to fail." We assured not only that they would not fail but that they would succeed. We assured that the tide would indeed raise their yachts, while our little dinghies sprung leaks and started to sink. The rising tide became a tidal wave for us.

I don't know when we are going to stop falling for the games being played on us by our government and their corporate shysters; but I hope it's very soon. The eloquence of their cute little sayings placates us and soothes our emotions. Their phrases go down in history while we go down the tubes. When will we learn that it's all about them – not us?

Here's the deal, once again for the umpteenth time. No one is going to save us but us. We are all we have. Economics, like politics, is local. You have to own a boat in order for it to rise with the tide. So, let's move forward on those basic principles. Let's lower our penchant for nice sayings and decrease our emotional investment in politics. Let's get real, brothers and sisters, and raise our awareness and activism around collective economic empowerment.

The economic assumptions inherent in a rising tide lifting all boats are flawed to say the least; and we have seen them in action. This latest use of the phrase will be no different, especially if we do not adhere to the first principles of economics: Ownership and control of income producing assets. Until we not only acknowledge that time-tested truth, but act upon it as well, please be aware that a rising tide can also drown us.

The Bi-Polar Electorate

"The difference between a democracy and a dictatorship is that in a democracy you vote first and take orders later; in a dictatorship you don't have to waste your time voting."
Charles Bukowski
"Majority rule only works if you're also considering individual rights, because you can't have five wolves and one sheep voting on what to have for supper."
Larry Flynt

November 2010 once again revealed the "insanity" that Albert Einstein referred to in his famous quote: doing the same thing over and over and expecting a different result. For decades voters have elected folks who, once they get sworn in, do absolutely nothing for the voters and everything for themselves. We elect politicians who deliberate and legislate against us rather than on our behalf. And we keep doing this strange mating dance ad nauseam.

Why do so many of us keep falling for the same old tired game every election? Politics is all about self-interest; that really says it all. The things we see in politics today should tell us, in no uncertain terms, that if we do not play this game to win our self-interests will never be met.

Overall, the political arena dominates our collective psyche; it fills the airwaves of radio stations; it is plastered on our walls via big screen

TV's; it is served up hot and fresh each morning in our newspapers; and every month dozens of major magazines deluge their readers with political opinions and prognostications from one election to the next. Immediately following one election, the next one gets underway.

Can't we see what these folks are doing to us? If the result of political participation were commensurate with the attention given to the process, we would be far better off than we are now. Unemployment would not be as high. Banks would be lending money to small businesses rather than hoarding it, especially after "we the people," bailed them out. There would be no question that Social Security would always live up to its name by being absolutely "secured."

Take Alan Simpson (as Henny Youngman used to say, "Please" take him). President Obama appointed this guy to help straighten out some of the mess in D.C., and he comes out and disparages Social Security and those receiving it. Simpson also castigated U.S. Veterans for receiving benefits that are rightly and justifiably theirs. If Simpson and his cronies in D.C. were forced to participate in Social Security, instead of living large on their fat-cat retirement benefits, that we pay for, they would not be so quick to tinker with it; it would always be secure.

What sense does it make for us, the electorate, to provide jobs for most of these do-nothing-but-campaign-for-the-next-election politicians while they do nothing to keep us employed? We are indeed a bi-polar, schizophrenic, manic depressive electorate. We vote for one party, and in two years some of us are ready to switch to the other party, even though both parties either take us for granted or couldn't care less about us. That is, except when they need our individual votes.

The fact that some candidates spend millions of dollars to be elected to a job that pays $125,000 - $200,000 annually, should tell us something. The fact that DC lobbyists earn an average of $300,000 yearly should tell us something. The fact that the two parties cannot agree on anything speaks volumes. The fact that the House of Representatives and the Senate together cannot get one thing done without acrimony and gotcha tactics lets us know that it's not about us, the bi-polar electorate; it's only about them and their puppet masters.

Thomas Sowell is quoted as saying, "It is hard to imagine a more stupid or more dangerous way of making decisions than by putting those decisions in the hands of people who pay no price for being wrong." This is exactly what we do, and we go from manic to depressive every November in which there is an election. We had better change our politics and stop supporting folks who do not support us. We put them in charge of our lives, our destiny, and even though they continue to kick dirt in our faces, we just keep on paying their bills and sending their children to college.

We must be more self-directed and not be led around like a bunch of lemmings by career politicians who are directing money into their pockets and keeping it away from our pockets. Maulana Karenga said, "Self-determination stresses the quest for control of the politics, economics, and cultural institutions and processes of our communities, and to exercise and receive rightful representation and an equitable share of the resources of society. It also requires a political consciousness and responsibility which result in unity, social activism, and building institutions that house and advance our interests as a people."

Votes cast from a position of economic strength open doors politically and gain reciprocity for those casting those votes. Just look at other groups that are advantaged by politics, i.e. Jewish people, gay people, etc. We must take an honest look at our economic vs. our political history, and understand that economics trumps politics every time. Vote? Yes, by all means, but make it count by collectively leveraging it to get more "quo" in return for your "quid."

Maybe we need to revisit Gary, Indiana, 1972, and start our own political party, because the three we have today are certainly not looking out for Black folks' interests. I also think we need a big dose of election year lithium for our obvious bi-polar condition because, politically speaking, we are sinking fast.

Riding the bench in the economic Super Bowl

"If winning isn't everything, why do they keep score?"
Vince Lombardi

On the national scene, money is being tossed around by the billions and sometimes by the trillions, from the Washington political elite to the super-wealthy and corporate bigwigs via tax breaks and bailouts. The national deficit is around $1.5 trillion and the national debt is $14 trillion (2010). Banks and other financial institutions, in addition to pharmaceutical and insurance firms are livin' large. And the big boys on Wall Street are gearing up for their annual blockbuster bonuses, the average of which is $1 million per employee! Money, money everywhere, and not a dollar for us. It's the economic Super Bowl, folks, and we are sitting on the bench.

We have been relegated to permanent underclass status, as Dr. Claud Anderson told us we would become if we did not act. We have little influence, much less any real power in political and economic circles. In this current economic Super Bowl, even when we get a little ahead, the political referees are always there to throw the penalty flag on us for being off side or, in other words, for being out of our place.

Take the recent approval (finally) of the Black Farmers' lawsuit against the USDA; despite it being settled in the 1990's, it is still being held up, even though the perpetrators of that misdeed were found guilty. Black farmers and their families still suffer as a result of blatant discrimination by the USDA, and yet folks like Representatives Michele Bachman of Minnesota and Steve King of Iowa are railing against the settlement as "pure and complete fraud" and "slavery reparations."

This guy Steve King said, "The fraudulent claims might be, well, Johnny, yeah, he was raised on a farm, but he wouldn't help his dad, he went off to the city and became a drug addict. But now his daddy's died, and Johnny wants the $50,000 that comes from the USDA under this claim." King's and Bachman's words go deeper than just a negative reflection on themselves; they also speak volumes about those who elected and reelected them to the U.S. Congress.

So much for those two idiots. We have billions of dollars going to corporate interests and lobbyists while veterans of war are denied a measly $250 check? Active duty soldiers are given a measly 1.2 – 1.9 percent pay increase. Senior citizens, for the second consecutive year, will get no cost of living allowance in their Social Security checks. Senate Republicans reject the proposed $7.4 billion health care fund for the 911 emergency workers, some of whom are now dying of lung cancer as a result of their heroism. What a bunch of guys we have in

DC, huh? Money, money everywhere, but not a dollar for vets, seniors, and "heroes."

Yes, for a select and relative few the economic Super Bowl is well underway; and for many of us, the best we can do is watch the game, either from the bench (with no hope of getting in), the sidelines, the stands, on television, or we can read about it after the game is over. There will be no losing team in this Super Bowl; the celebration will go on for months in both camps. Dollars will continue to flow into their coffers while we, the Proletariat, remain at the mercy of political court-jesters manipulated by the hidden hand of the greedy and corrupt.

Understanding that in poker you have to play the hand you were dealt, I also understand that a good bluff works every now and then; no need to fold every bad hand. The latest boondoggle for the super wealthy, in the form of tax breaks, is yet another illustration of the continuous and disgraceful kowtowing to a few folks who already have more money than they could ever spend in two lifetimes. In juxtaposition, this latest compromise is also illustrative of an old saying that goes something like this: The measure of a country is in how it treats the least among its citizens.

The sheer hypocrisy being displayed by politicians vis-à-vis those revered as war heroes, veterans, the long term unemployed, and senior citizens, is sickening, shameful, and beyond comprehension. The politicians' complete lack of compassion and concern for those who need help the most can only be characterized as reprehensible – and that's putting it mildly.

But the Super Bowl is underway, folks. And while most of us cannot afford the price of admission, the game will continue nevertheless. When will it end, you say? No one knows for sure, but one thing is certain: It will end. The clock will run out and the celebrations will come to an end. The more important question is: What will we do in the meantime? My recommendation is what it has been for years on end: Organize our own economic Super Bowl; select our own team members; make our own rules; create and execute our own collective economic initiatives.

We must stop being economic benchwarmers waiting to get into a game in which we have no chance of playing, much less winning.

Economics is local too

"The history of African-American repression in this country rose from government-sanctioned racism. Jim Crow laws were a product of bigoted state and local governments."
Rand Paul

The economic problems we face are right in our own backyards. Unfortunately, until our problems reach crisis level we are content to engage in spirited conversations and philosophical diatribes about the likes of Tiger Woods, a multi- millionaire who could not care less about the economic plight of Black people. We live vicariously through super rich entertainers, many of whom would not even stop to shake hands with us if we met them on the street. We get lost in the euphoria of having a Black President, arguing about his issues and his battles in DC, rather than dealing with our own in hometown USA.

With Black unemployment hovering between 35%-50% in our neighborhoods, with what many are calling "economic apartheid" when it comes to inclusion policies that simply exclude Black businesses and employees from construction projects, and with the myriad of other economic issues facing our families on a daily basis, we must change!

I don't know about you but I am not too concerned about the economic situation of millionaires and billionaires, much less their social lives. I am not concerned about whether Oprah stays on TV or leaves; I am not worried about million-dollar athletes being traded from one team to another; I am not anxious about which woman Ray J chooses, who the Kardashians are marrying or sleeping with for the moment, Michael Vick, "T.O.", Tiny, or any of the millionaire Housewives of Atlanta or the Preachers of L.A.

Lil' Wayne going to jail and having to get eight root canals before doing so is of minor importance; it is economically irrelevant to Black people that week after week, night after night, BET gives out awards like they are penny candy. Worrying about the Congressional Black Caucus selling us out is fruitless, especially since it has been doing so for years. What's the point of circular discussions, desperation, and angst about Washington politicians, when your house is on fire?

Pretending everything will be all right because we have a Black man in the White House is, as Mike Tyson would say, "ludicrous." Other than a warm and fuzzy feeling, what have Black folks gotten out of it? These and similar issues that capture our attention are nothing but diversions – but maybe that's what some of us need to keep from having to deal with the terrible reality of our own lives.

Why should we major in the minors as Banks, drug companies, and health insurers are raking us over the coals? Exorbitant fees and excess charges are the order of the day, and corporate greed is running rampant. Medical prescriptions are out of reach for those who need them most, and health insurance companies are raising their rates by 39%, cutting back on payouts to doctors, and denying life-saving treatments to toddlers. All of this in the face of huge profits, outlandish bonuses, and ridiculously high annual salaries for the very persons who received billions of dollars from the government.

Where is the local help? How do we profit from the TARP funds, the Stimulus money? How can we reduce usury interest rates, sky-high credit card fees like $60.00 for "not" using your card? What do we do about banks, insurance companies, and drug companies that are ripping off customers and making it doubly hard on the "little guy?"

If there ever was a time for local empowerment groups, that time is now. If ever we needed local cooperative purchasing programs, the time is right now. If we ever needed to build strong, unwavering, and resolute coalitions among our organizations, we sure need to now.

So what's it going to be, folks? Fight or flight? Stand up and be counted, or lie down and be counted out? Put up or give up? We must make a decision NOW. And that decision must be executed locally at first. If we get our local act together by showing that we are serious about our future, by refusing to be mistreated by banks and other business entities, public and private, we will be well on our way to being able to make an impact on what happens nationally.

At a time when we cannot afford the price of a ticket to see our athletic heroes and our beloved entertainers, we scrape together our dollars and support them anyway. Time was when aristocrats sat in the stands and watched the poor people engage in contests. Now we have poor people in the stands watching the rich play.

While national politics will affect us sooner or later, local politics and surely local economics affect us every day. Taking mental excursions to celebrity never-never land every now and then is all right, but it must be balanced by the reality of our own situation. Change will not occur simply because it ought to; it will only come when we make it so. Our actions on the local level, or the lack thereof, will determine our overall economic destiny.

Pray for President Obama to do what is right and for misguided celebrities to use some of their wealth to enrich the lives of others. And work to improve your own life locally – bloom where you were planted. At the end of the day, that's what matters, because economics, like politics, is local.

Introspection

"I don't think we spend enough time in reflection and introspection. We don't know who we are as individuals in this culture anymore."
Naomi Judd

What has this country become since Barack Obama was elected President? Or, has it always been this way? Where have all the evil, vicious, malcontents been hiding for 100 years? Or, have they been here all the time? How is it that we have not achieved that state of nirvana so many talked about on January 20, 2009? Or, is it really unreachable?

In the immediate aftermath of the election, after the dust had settled, the hoopla had died down, and the euphoria had dissipated, we can take a real honest look at ourselves. Do we like what we see?

Politically speaking, I am not surprised by the shenanigans of the so-called "far right" and "far left" wings; but it is a bit disconcerting to see some of the so-called progressives and centrists getting their shots in as well. It simply begs the question: Have we really come as far as we say we have? And, brothers and sisters, that answer is a resounding "NO!"

On the economic side of the coin, Black folks are still fighting for survival, now along with many others in this country, for employment, inclusion, and business support. We are still being "dissed" by the banks when it comes to loans, interest rates, and credit card fees. Our bailout, long overdue, has yet to come and probably never will come.

Socially, although many pretend to be in a state of mutual respect and brotherly love, we are still at odds with one another due to inequity, suspicion, and fear. One hundred and fifty years after Black people were so-called "freed" disparities continue to exist, institutionalized by various entities, and many are still advocating for "race dialogues" between whites and Blacks. You would think that Black folks just arrived here rather than being in this country since it started.

We know the situation that exists in the areas of education and criminal justice. So what ties it all together, this web of discontent and despair? It seems to me, based on what is taking place among the so-called leaders of our society, along with the big-wig movers and shakers, it all boils down to a scarcity rather than abundance mindset. Too many folks are out simply to get theirs and to get as much of yours as they can. The poor are competing for crumbs and, with their zero sum mindset, are afraid that if you get a dollar or a job it takes a dollar or a job away from them.

Where will it end? Will this country change before it collapses under the weight of its own greed, injustice, intolerance, and hate? I don't know if we will make it or not, but by the looks of things I do know we have a long way to go, and we better get busy turning this battleship around.

Our representatives, those we elect to help us, are bilking us. They have the best of everything but would deny us even a smidgen of relief. They go into office, in many cases, just as broke as we are but leave as millionaires, by working the political system for their own enrichment rather than looking out for our interests. We, the electorate, should examine ourselves, do some introspection, and then make appropriate changes to reverse our self-defeating actions.

Corruption, excess, self-indulgence, and greed rule the day, much akin to some of the great empires we read about in history. Evil acts are being perpetrated against good people, such as Shirley Sherrod, the U.S. Department of Agriculture employee who was summarily fired for what amounted to helping a white farmer. Isn't it strange that no one has been fired for the years of discrimination against Black farmers, which has resulted in a $2 billion punitive award (who knows when it will be paid)? Sherrod gets fired for a positive comment, and for decades other USDA employees keep their jobs while blatantly discriminating against Black farmers. What a country, huh?

We are in the belly of the beast. And we had better get our act together before the vaunted "United" States go down the proverbial tube. How? Form solid blocs of non-party affiliated voters who are willing to break the chains of past political loyalty, and vote for candidates that publicly support Black interests—and they are willing to put their support in writing. Look inside yourself, Black voter; like what you see?

Black businesses still left out

"The GOP convention that pumped a projected $150-million into the economy of the Twin Cities back-handed black owned businesses in that area by excluding them from convention related contracts. This stiff arm even extended to reneging on pledges to post minority businesses on the convention's website as preferred vendors."
Counter Punch, September 2008

Since this country began Black people have been excluded from participation in opportunities for wealth-building. Of course, despite the obstacles placed before our forebears they made it on their own in many cases. But for the most part they were hamstrung by restrictions that prevented them from achieving economic empowerment on the same level as Whites. While I don't think that can be argued on any intelligent level, it's still probably good to cite a few examples.

First of all, if you owned a plantation and received free labor it goes without saying that you would prosper and those providing the free labor would not. The post-Civil War pleas for reparations to formerly enslaved Blacks notwithstanding, our ancestors were "freed" without a way of providing for their families, that is, except to continue to work for their former enslavers, as General Gordon Granger suggested in his General Order on June 19, 1865, in Galveston, Texas.

Then along comes the land rushes, the most notable of which was in Oklahoma. On May 18, 1889, William Willard Howard wrote in

Harper's Weekly, "In 1889 the opening to 'white' settlement of a choice portion of Indian Territory in Oklahoma set off one of the most bizarre and chaotic episodes of town founding in world history."

It was, according to the above quote, "choice" land for whites only. For Blacks it was no land, which meant no wealth. As for ownership of businesses, when Black people founded their own towns and began setting up business enclaves, well, you know what happened in Tulsa's Greenwood District in 1921. Black Wall Street was burned to the ground by angry Whites.

Fast forward to our capitalistic system and ponder the reasons for the many economic disparities that exist between Whites and Blacks, considering the fact that both groups have been in this country since it began. Yes, slavery is a huge factor, but blatant discrimination, and an unwillingness to remediate the problem, then and now, account for much of the disparity we have today.

The railroads, the steel industry, the aerospace industry, and even the semiconductor industry required and received federal assistance in the 19th and 20th centuries, similar to what the auto and banking industries received in the massive stimulus package of 2008-2009. Those are two more examples of Black people being left out and pushed further behind economically. This latest recession has hurt Black people the most. Our unemployment is the highest; our net worth is the lowest; and as usual, we are still the last hired and first fired.

Of course, if you haven't noticed by now, no one is coming to save us. But that does not mitigate the fact that we are so far behind because of exclusion from the basic wealth-building strategies that aided many Whites in this country. Professor Juliet E.K. Walker, in her seminal work, <u>The History of Black Business in America</u>, wrote the following summary of our predicament.

...after two centuries of supporting White American businesses and after reaping the economic benefits of Black slave labor until 1865, the government owes a great deal to Black American business. Indeed, the position of Black business relative to White business has changed little from before the Civil War to after the Civil Rights era, both in participation rates and gross business receipts.

Walker goes on to cite the lack of fairness among banks in issuing loans to Black businesses, discrimination against Black businesses when it comes to subsidies, redlining by real estate companies and banking institutions, and "special programs" that have only set Black businesses back even further.

She writes: *In the post–Civil Rights period then, the federal government has failed American Black business. And preferential treatment, the government's traditional remedy for acts of discrimination, is not the answer to the question of how the government will improve Black American business. A better answer is that Black American business should be provided federal support equal to that provided White American business.*

As the 1992 U.S. Commission on Minority Business Development emphasized, "There appears to be no reason in logic why 99% of the businesses in this country are forced to squabble over 20% of the federal purchase dollar, when a select 1% continue to capture their 80% market share largely undisturbed."

Politricks in full effect

Politricks is the word "politics" altered to convey the empty-campaign promises often experienced after politicians get elected. Politricks sums up the vast difference of how politicians seem when they campaign versus when they reign.

Urban Dictionary

It is utterly amazing to me that so many people in this country fall for the games, the outright corruption, and the tricks played by many of those whom we elect to public office. I mean, it's mind-boggling! First we complain about what we are not getting from them, then we reelect them, and then we start complaining all over again. Our solution: Elect some new politricksters who do the same thing the old ones did.

The 2010 mid-term election caused some to put on sackcloth and ashes, especially when they heard about the proposed cuts in Social Security, and maintaining tax cuts for the super-rich, topped off by the refusal of Congress to extend unemployment compensation. Talk about not having a horse in this race, the poor and the jobless were not even inside the racetrack venue.

Since it seems we don't have the political savvy to change this endless political charade that always ends up hurting Black people the most, and considering the fact that some of our own politicians are caught up in the political cesspool of corruption, greed, and apathy, maybe we should just pack it in. Black folks are losing at politricks, and as Malcolm once said, that makes us "chumps."

The latest salt-in-the-wound, blatantly arrogant, and disrespectful move was that of John Boehner and Mitch McConnell. These two politricksters broke with longstanding protocol by refusing an invitation to meet with the President of the United States, an accepted practice by virtually every politician since this country began. Their actions followed the "You lie!" outburst from Joe Wilson during the President's State of the Union Speech in 2009.

And then we have the Black Caucus, about 40 or so Black politicians, many of whom are caught in Washington's traps of personal enrichment, corruption, or just plain old nonfeasance in office. No benefit for Black constituents there. To add insult to injury, there will be no Black Senators in the 2010 Congress; not that having one did any good anyway, but since we fall for political symbolism over substance, we can count that as a huge loss as well.

Moreover, a barrage of insults have been thrown at our "first Black President" by the likes of Michael "Homeboy" Steele and other so-called Black conservatives, topped off by none other than Sarah Palin and her lemmings. This former governor of Alaska, who quit that job and now wants to be President says, "I believe I can" beat Barack Obama in 2012. When you finish laughing, remember: Bush won, didn't he? Reagan won, didn't he?

Palin's daughter's participation on "Dancing with the Stars" and the outrage Black folks expressed at her beating out Brandy, only tells me that some of us are way out of touch. The fact that we are willing to waste time discussing and being angry about a meaningless television show, suggests we are disconnected from our own economic empowerment. No, she can't dance. But if it were not Palin's daughter we would not be as offended. The Palins are pulling in the cash while we worry about a dance contest.

And just to show who is really running things, Bristol Palin is now featured in a campaign for abstinence; she is being held up to young people as a paragon of restraint when it comes to premarital sex, of course, after she had her baby out of wedlock. What a country!

Listen folks, and especially you, Mr. President. This country loves a gunslinger; we had Bush for eight years, didn't we? He always walked around with a ready-to-draw swagger, and he was not afraid to fire his guns any time he thought he was threatened. And before Bush, Clinton was a gunslinger too, thumbing his nose at tradition and doing what he wanted to do because, in his own words, "I could."

Obama's swagger, his bouncing down the steps of Air Force One without holding on to the side rails, and his unflinching demeanor under fire, will continue to mean nothing unless he is willing to fire his weapon, especially on behalf of Black people. To hell with a second term; he should respond in-kind to his attackers by using his Executive powers to get something done.

He should abandon the three-point shot and start throwing down some Daryl Dawkins Chocolate Thunder dunks on those boys. If you're going down, go down fighting, a la Claude McKay. Forget all the touchy-feely gestures and the Rodney King mantra. Black folks are drowning, Brother President. You and the Black Caucus would not be in office without us; so what are y'all gonna do in the next two years? As for me, I am sick of politricks; so if all you're gonna do is keep talkin', I suggest you start walkin'—toward the door.

Positive cash flow in Afghanistan

Following are reflections on the madness of more war in 2010. Was it all really worth it? Yes, Bin Laden is dead, deserved punishment for 911, but now we have even more terrorist groups that hate us and are willing to die in the process of trying to kill us. How do you defeat people who are not only willing to die but eager to? What do you do to them? Kill them?

Why are we sacrificing more lives in a war that has no identifiable victory in sight? They say we will leave when we "win," but what does that look like? Do we really believe we can "win," and do we think the Afghan people will miraculously change to our way of thinking and our way of doing things when we leave? You would think that nearly 5,000 lives lost in the Iraq war, which was based on a lie and cost taxpayers nearly $1 trillion, would be a pretty good hint for us to stop the current madness in Afghanistan. So, why are we still there?

Osama Bin Laden, as far as our intelligence can tell, if he is still alive, is somewhere in Pakistan; Hamid Karzai, the President of Afghanistan, is corrupt and living very well with all the cash being dumped in his country; and, as was the case in Iraq, billions of dollars are being wasted each week as we continue to use more than 100,000 soldiers to fight against a relatively small group of Al-Qaeda, or is the dreaded Taliban?

Here's the bottom line: As usual, the arms dealers and the other usual suspects from the Iraq war are the beneficiaries of the $2 billion per week price tag of this war. No-bid contracts abound, and the cash is flowing like Niagara Falls into the coffers of the same folks who "lost" $9 billion in cash in Iraq, money that still has not been accounted for.

Can you imagine what $2 billion per week would do for our economy right now? It was recently reported that the U.S. created 1.4 million jobs during the past year – in India, China, and other nations – not in our own country. What's up with that? How many jobs could we create in 52 weeks with $104 billion?

All of this in the face of political hypocrites standing with hand over heart praising the young men and women who are risking and losing their lives in our latest quagmire. They say how much they appreciate and honor the soldiers for their service to this country, but they refuse to pay them for their service, and they silently stand by as many soldiers who are blessed to return home find themselves homeless and mired in poverty. So much for honoring their service to this country.

War is and always has been about profiteering and cash flow for a chosen few. Obviously the war lobbyists and the companies that profit from the deaths of our soldiers are stronger than any of us could ever imagine. They control this game and the war is not over until they say it's over. We railed against George Bush for Iraq; now Barack Obama has recommitted to the war in Afghanistan because as he once said, "that's where we should have been in the first place." That was then; this is now. Why are we there now?

Our economy, at least for most of us, is in very bad shape. Many are suffering financially, physically, and psychologically. Millions are unemployed without even the hope of going back to work. Gasoline is now on the rise again, reaching nearly $4.00 per gallon in some areas. (It's interesting that no one is speaking out against this issue to any large degree, the way they did when Bush was President) One in five mortgages are under water or upside down, meaning homes are not worth what is owed on them. All of this and we are stuck in Afghanistan spending $2 billion a week on a war that has no victory in its future.

These wars have cost twice as many lives as those that were lost on 911. We have spent inordinate amounts of money and lost even more lives looking for one man. We now have a virtual army of permanently wounded, psychologically impaired men and women, without legs, arms, and sight, returning to us with tremendous needs that should be our top priority. They get mostly lip service in return for their sacrifices, but should be the primary recipients from our war chest.

There is a definitely positive cash flow in Afghanistan, and it's flowing to the well-oiled war machine driven by the warmongers and their political puppets. Too bad it is not flowing to American people. How is your cash flow, Black America? Are things going good for you? How about you young soldiers out there? Have you found a home yet? Has some of that cash flow reached you yet? What about senior citizens? No cost-of-living increases for you two years in a row. You doin' all right?

The folks that run this nation are obviously more interested in and supportive of folks in other countries, especially where there are interests like oil, opium poppy plants, gold, and diamonds. Many of our citizens suffer every day while foreigners live like kings and queens at our expense in blood and treasure. The words, "Thank you for your service," coming from some people are meaningless and insulting to the men and women who died and were maimed because of political lies, deceit, and greed.

What a farce! What a shame! What a disgrace! Get out of Afghanistan NOW! And use that $2 billion a week to help the people of this country. Now that's a novel idea, isn't it?

Strategic alliances create stronger businesses

"We must demonstrate our capacity to cooperate among ourselves, before demanding cooperation where the resources of others are at stake. Business is the ultimate test of our ability to cooperate. Somehow we must learn this fundamental lesson. It will be costly; there will be some loss in the process, but we must keep it up until we have developed within the race a group of people of definite capacity and unquestioned integrity, who can lead the way to larger achievements for the benefit of the whole race."
R.R. Moton, President, National Negro Business League, 1928

It seems so difficult for Moton's message to sink in and be implemented by many of our business owners. You would think that during the last 82 years since he spoke those words Black folks, collectively, would have built hundreds of business associations, thereby commanding a much higher percentage of business revenues than we do today.

Moton, and others of his time, were passionate about working together, pooling resources, and cooperating with one another. They knew that if we would survive and thrive in this country as business persons, and if we would empower ourselves as consumers, we would have to work together in support of one another.

The same principle applies today, probably even more so. For example, all across this country Black people are battling to be included in construction projects in a meaningful and significant way. Despite Black tax dollars being spent to help fund building projects, e.g. stadiums, convention centers, highways, schools, Black construction workers and Black contractors have to fight tooth-and-nail just to have the opportunity to even bid on such projects.

Special policies have to be written, and strictly enforced, to attain even a modicum of Black participation. We always seem to be the "included" rather than the "includers." That reality speaks not only to closed-door policies, exclusion, and discrimination; it also speaks to what R.R. Moton was saying back in 1928: our unwillingness to cooperate among ourselves.

Unfortunately, some of our brothers and sisters operate in a scarcity mode rather than an abundance mode. Sadly, some of us are willing to sellout as front companies and pass-through companies, thus, allowing the "includers" to maintain status quo when it comes to the lack of meaningful "inclusion." Even worse, the percentage (payoff) received by the front or pass-through company is minimal and the Faustian deals in which these business owners agree to participate further contribute to Black unemployment and the continued lack of growth among Black businesses.

Blacks in America are too far behind in the economic race and too near last place all along the economic continuum to continue this way of doing business. We must establish and grow more businesses, invest in income producing assets, and form alliances with one another, in order to improve our lot both nationally and globally. Yes, we can brag all day long about our annual income of $900 billion, but those dollars will never make sense if we fail to aggregate them in support of true economic empowerment for Black people.

We can complain all we want about the lack of inclusion, which is a legitimate complaint in most circles, but while we fight against exclusionary practices we must also accept our own culpability in this issue. Much of what we fight against can be stopped by our own power to control ourselves. We always have the choice of doing the right thing or doing the wrong thing. I trust we will choose what is right, not only individually but collectively as well.

What we are experiencing in today's economy is what Yogi Berra called, "Déjà vu all over again." What can we do about it? Be the "includer" rather than the "includee." Form alliances, partnerships, and joint ventures with other Black companies that will increase your total capacity, expertise, and finances and enable you to control various projects, if not own them.

It makes all the sense in the world for Black owned companies to work together to compete for a larger portion of public and private contracts, considering that what was emphasized in a 1992 report by the United States Commission on Minority Business Development is still true today: *"There appears to be no reason in logic why 99% of the businesses in the country are forced to squabble over 20% of the Federal purchase dollar, when a select 1% continue to capture their 80 percent market share largely undisturbed."*

Development is the key; but most Black firms, rather than getting together with others and going after larger projects keep operating alone and, while complaining about being left out, they are not working on controlling the game themselves.

A great example of collaboration can be found in the archives of the Cincinnati Business Courier, which has several feature stories on a Black firm, Jostin Construction, Inc., that put its own investment team together, hired other Black companies and Black workers, and had major control of a several significant projects. And guess what else the astute, business-savvy, and conscious president (Albert Smitherman) of the company did. He collaborated with a Black church that owned some 30+ acres of prime land; he put a development deal together from which the church did quite, quite, (Did I say, "quite"?) well for itself. Do your research and get to work creating your own game of inclusion.

If each of us would give more consideration to the collective rather than the individual, as R.R. Moton suggested, when the deal makers come knocking at our doors, rather than bending over, we will stand tall.

America – The new third world?

While America is the wealthiest nation in the world, and has the most billionaires in the world, not a single U.S. city ranks among the world's most livable cities. Meanwhile, despite our nation's vast wealth, 14.5 percent of U.S. households were "food insecure" as of 2010, and as of 2011, 1.5 million American households were struggling with "extreme poverty."
C.J. Werleman

I thought I had seen it all during the aftermath of Hurricane Katrina when thousands of people waited for days at the convention center for a drink of water, where some of them died in the hot sun and the rancid water, where thousands more were holed up in the Superdome in conditions that rivaled foreign prisons, and where many who were looking for food in order to survive were accused of looting and subsequently shot down like stray dogs. I thought I had seen it all when people were herded off to places unknown, into other stadiums in other cities where, according to Barbara Bush, things were "working very well for them." I thought I had heard it all when those affected were referred to as "refugees."

Well, little did I know that I had not seen nor heard it all. An event in 2010, one that really caused me to think about this country and the government entities that control it, occurred in Atlanta's East Point, where an estimated 30,000 people showed up to get housing assistance vouchers. In addition to the 62 persons who were injured in the crush, the scene was exactly the same as the ones we see on television in far off third-world countries.

Folks standing in the hot sun with babies and small children, reaching their hands out in hope of getting a sheet of paper that would provide assistance to them. That reminded me of the many times I have seen crowds of people reaching out for food, water, flour, and other items in India, Africa, and more recently in Haiti after that devastating earthquake. Only this time it was in Atlanta, Georgia.

This time it was not a result of an earthquake, tornado, or hurricane. This time it was not a result of some tyrant who commandeered all the riches of his country and left the poor on their own. This time it was sheer desperation, fear, poverty, and what I would deem as a total disregard for human dignity on the part of those who organized such a horrible event.

You would think that someone would have said, "Hey guys, it's too hot, and there will be too many people trying to take advantage of this for us to simply go to a parking lot and stand on cars to hand out vouchers." You would think that someone would have considered the risks of having folks stand in record heat for hours, pushing one another, and vying to be one of the chosen few to receive a voucher.

Just what kind of country has this become? Have we reached the tipping point in our society where the gap between the haves and have-nots is insurmountable? Are we so unconcerned about certain segments of our society and unmoved by their plight that we would cast them aside? Have we moved to the edge of self-destruction as a society?

Throughout history all empires have fallen. Are we witnessing the beginning of America's demise? The arrogance displayed among some in this country, outlandish wealth and greed juxtaposed against abject poverty, and the disregard for the "least among us" are foreboding signs of a disintegrating society. Can you imagine sections of this country suffering in third-world conditions? We don't have to imagine it; it is happening right now.

What shall we do? As many have said before me, beneath everything you will find economics. Black people especially must come to a better understanding of that principle and act upon it by collectively working our way out of this quagmire. Regardless of what happens in the government or big business, we must work together to empower ourselves and move away from the futility and danger of waiting for government officials and corporate moguls to "do right by us."

Take it from Malcolm X: "We must be re-educated to the importance of controlling the economy in which we live, by owning and operating the businesses in the community we live in and developing some industry that will employ our people, so we won't have to boycott and picket other people in other communities to get a job. We must understand the importance of spending money in the community in which we live."

Consider this quote: "Being poor doesn't always mean being without resources. Anacostia is one of the poorest neighborhoods in Washington, D.C., yet the total income of all its households is $370 million per year. Most of this money quickly departs in the hands of landlords, business owners, and bankers who live in more upscale parts of town.... The principal affliction of poor communities in the United States is not the absence of money, but its systematic exit." Michael Shuman, Going Local - Creating Self-Reliant Communities in a Global Age (2001)

Third world neighborhoods, right here in our country, are wake-up calls for us to change the way we conduct our affairs, especially our economic affairs. Teaching our dollars to have more sense will go a long way to prevent despicable events like the one we saw in Atlanta. I pray we get it together before it's too late. The clock is ticking, brothers and sisters.

2011

Black America is imploding.

Misdirected energy is wasted energy.
"If you are not part of the solution, you are part of the problem."
Eldridge Cleaver

In the words of a citizen of 1st century Rome, "I smell smoke."

Our position in this country is pretty apparent. You know the stats; they are released every month or so and paint a dreary picture of our status when it comes to incarceration, education, health, employment, net worth, income, life expectancy, and overall political and economic empowerment. With all of this going for us, you would think we'd be spending a great deal of time on initiatives and strategies, both individual and collective, to improve our bleak situation.

Instead of circling our wagons we seem to have formed a circular firing squad, and some of us are firing away. We are killing one another by selling our souls to the devil and by selling our people down the river for a few dollars, which allows the real enemy to sit back and ignore us when it comes to reciprocity in political circles and in the marketplace. We are at one another's throats over critiques of the President, and we are caught between "Barack and hard place" as two "news" organizations, Fox and MSNBC, give us a steady diet of Obama bashing and Obama praise, respectively.

We have Cornel West and Tavis Smiley kicking Barack Obama in the behind and taking flak from Al Sharpton, Melissa Harris-Perry, and Steve Harvey. President Obama socked it to the Congressional Black Caucus with his "stop complaining..." comments which, as Smiley and others noted, were not said to the Jewish, Hispanic, and Gay groups. Sharpton scolded the Ohio Legislative Black Caucus, telling them they, "got too comfortable" and "too low down to stand up for (themselves)." And Black critics of Sharpton are saying he is more symbolism than substance.

Then there are the so-called Black conservatives, led by the likes of Clarence Thomas, Herman Cain, Allen West, and Michael Steele. (But who knows what he is these days, since his Republican buddies took his job?) These guys and a few gals are incessantly lobbing grenades at Obama and other Black folks with whom they disagree. They even lambast Blacks who, through no fault of their own, find themselves at the very bottom of our society.

Clarence Thomas is quieter than usual these days, probably busy trying figure out why he didn't know about that $700,000 his wife was paid by the Heritage Foundation. Allen West said Obama is "the dumbest person walking around in America right now"; he also said the President "should put himself in harm's way" when he goes to war zones.

To top it all off, we have Herman Cain, the Great Black Hope for the Republicans. He is putting in his time as the current "front-runner" for the presidential nomination in 2012. Of the many times I have seen him on TV, and even recently in my hometown, Cincinnati, Ohio, I have never seen another Black person around him, at least not in camera-shot. Nonetheless, Herman is holding his own as he drops H-bombs on Obama, grinning all the way to the bank.

In the last Republican candidates' debate, Herman took a lickin' and kept on tickin'. His famous "Nine, Nine, Nine" Plan was trashed not only by his colleagues, as he called them, but it has been highly criticized by many others as a plan that will not work and will not be passed if he becomes President. I guess a lot of his critics are German because they are saying, "Nein, Nein, Nein" to Herman's plan.

Reminiscent of Booker T. and W.E.B. and later Garvey and W.E.B., along with T. Thomas Fortune and Monroe Trotter, to the more recent sibling rivalry skirmishes between Sharpton and Eddie Long over George W. Bush's invitations to the White House, the Urban League and the NAACP over Bush attending the former's convention and ignoring the latter's, Black folks are again taking sides. We are dividing ourselves into hostile camps, firing at one another and taking ourselves out, which is surely a prescription for continued failure.

I am not suggesting that we should all think alike and act alike; I am not saying that we should not criticize our Black President; I am not saying that individual opinions don't count; but I am saying that there has to be someone among us who is intelligent enough and has enough collective influence on Black people to stop our suicide mission. But I could be wrong.

Our choices as regards our current economic and political activism in this country - and in the world - will lead us to one of two broad outcomes: Complete assimilation or collective empowerment. As my first book was titled, Economic Empowerment or Economic Enslavement – We have a choice, it is up to us, brothers and sisters. We can determine our fate or we can choose to acquiesce to a system in which we, as the number three group in this country, got very little when we were number two.

From my vantage point, both historically and on a contemporary basis, we are imploding. So much so that outsiders have no need to concede to any of our demands for parity. Societies fall from internal strife, and if our current actions continue, Black folks in America will succumb to the same fate.

No job – No tax cut

Every morning about this time
She gets me out of my bed a-crying
Get a job

After breakfast every day
She throws the want ads right my way
And never fails to say
Get a job
The Silhouettes, 1957

All this talk about tax cuts is falling on deaf ears for the more than 14 million unemployed folks in this country. I'm sure many of them are saying we gave the Wall Street bankers their bailout; we extended tax cuts for the one-percenters; and we continue to send billions to other countries to help them out of their financial woes.

So where is the help for the unemployed and the people who have been evicted from their homes, many of whom are now living in cars and even worse? I am sure they are asking themselves when their relief will come. Tax breaks don't mean a thing if you don't have a job.

Extending the unemployment benefits is the least our government can do, but living wage jobs would be much better. It is so sad that we have turned into a two-tiered society, the "haves" who want even more, and the "have-nots" who can't get a decent job.

What is our government doing? The latest disclosures of net worth, salaries, and millionaire status among members of Congress are truly eye-opening; or should I say "eye-popping and "jaw-dropping"?

Recent stats pointed out that one-half of the members of Congress are millionaires. In addition, the median net worth, excluding home equity, of House members more than doubled between 1984 and 2009, to $725,000 from $280,000, according to an analysis of financial disclosures by the University of Michigan's Panel Study of Income Dynamics. Meanwhile, the net worth of the median American family dipped to $20,500 from $20,600, The Washington Post reported.

As Marvin Gaye said, "What's going on?" Certainly everyone should be able to earn as much money as he or she can via honest means, but it seems to me this system is all jacked-up now as it pertains to folks making financial decisions that drastically affect poor people, while they are living lives of luxury unaffected by those decisions. Isn't there some kind of moral imperative in this scenario somewhere?

Are we so enamored by politicians, so enthralled by the emotions of politics, so engrossed in the symbolism of politics, and so caught-up by the hype of politics to notice what is happening to us? How is it that we elect folks to lord over us, to make rules for us, and to preside over us, and all the while they are getting richer and richer and we are getting poorer and poorer? Something is definitely wrong with that picture.

Look at Black people in this country and how we relate to the political system. Since Obama was elected we have heard cries of neglect, oversight, marginalization, and even abandonment of Black folks by his administration. We have engaged in discussions on whether we can say anything critical about Barack as it relates to where Black people stand in the latest political landscape. It has been suggested that we should just sit back and take it because, after all, he is the "first" and he can't do or say certain things on our behalf. Mistake!

Bob Law, national radio personality and community activist in New York City, recently wrote an excellent article in which he cited, "It was on May 7, 2011, that the National Institute for Latino Policy announced that the White House initiative for Educational Excellence for Hispanics swore in several new commissioners and held their inaugural meeting at the White House convened by Executive Director Juan Sepulveda. However Blacks are told that it would be unfair to expect such an effort on behalf of Black students since the President is the President of all Americans. In accepting that logic, Blacks may be the only group in the nation reluctant to pursue a strategy that will address the very real needs of their own group." What that says to me is that same old Black mantra, "By and by, when I die..."

Closer to home is a more important issue: What do Black folks get from local Black politicians? The same thing we say about Obama can also be said, in most cases, about our local royal ruling class. Many of them make a decent living, have good pension plans, get large expense accounts, and all the other accoutrements that come with being elected to public office. On the other hand, Black people and poor people seldom get to share in the fruits of their labor. It's the same as the national scene: High unemployment, which means tax cuts offer nothing in relief for those without jobs

And so it goes; politicians talk about our need but we continue to need the things they talk about. Until work is plentiful again, all this rhetoric about tax cuts for the "working" people will continue to fall on deaf ears among the unemployed.

Teaching our dollars to have more sense involves pooling them in efforts to gain greater economies of scale and the ability to bargain for what we purchase. Pooled monetary resources can also assist us with starting new businesses and growing the ones we have, thereby, creating jobs for ourselves. To continuously rely on the government to provide for us borders on insanity. They can give all the tax cuts they want, but the residual effect on Black people will be minimal, unless we expand our economic base through business development and mutual support.

Watch out for political retreads

This is in remembrance of the comedy that was the Republican presidential campaign of 2011. What a cast of characters, and they couldn't wait to run against Barack Obama in 2012.

It's bad enough that the Repubs are offering a bunch of retreads, retards, recycled rejects, remakes, and reruns to be our next president, but to insult us even more, Newt Gingrich is the "new" front runner! It was not enough that Bachmann is ignorant; Romney is a monumental flip-flopper, which borders on being an out and out liar; Perry is more suited for Saturday Night Live than President; Cain is a philanderer and an arrogant liar; Santorum is a self-righteous loser in his own state; Paul, who makes a lot of common sense, especially on the subject of war, is bordering on senility; and Huntsman, who is the most intelligent, reasonable, and qualified of the bunch, is in last place. Nooo. Newt, who has many of the same negative traits as the others, especially the flip-flopping, has made his comeback. He's baaack!

What a group of candidates the Repubs are offering up for the highest office in the land. And now they want folks to accept the likes of Newt Gingrich as their standard bearer. Admittedly, he leads in the polls, but I often wonder who responds to those polls. Of course, I am sure there not many Black respondents other than Tim Scott of South Carolina, and Allen West of Florida. Other than those two, who are the folks who want Newt for their President? No doubt it's those who remember and liked his shenanigans in 1994.

Newt recently went to South Carolina and spoke at an event hosted by State Rep, Tim Scott, and attempted to mitigate his past and make a case for being the Republican nominee. He also spoke to a crowd in that state, saying he made $60,000 for each speech he gave and suggested he did not need the money he made as an "historian" for Freddie Mac. Heck, he was already rich, so how could anyone say he was really a "lobbyist"?

This guy is a joke, but the joke is on us, folks. Newt is playing his pied piper flute all the way to the bank, and maybe into the White House. Don't laugh; Bush was selected and elected twice! And after being paid

$100,000,000.00 since he was put out of Congress, you know we will have to pay Newt big bucks during his stint as POTUS.

These are certainly strange times, but to bring back the likes of Newt Gingrich, the "Bomb Thrower," has me scratching my head and recalling Marvin Gaye's call to consciousness when he said, "Makes me wanna holla."

Having written several articles on the Newtster back in 1994-1996, and having seen his rise and his fall from grace within his own party, I am amazed at what the electorate will settle for these days. His personal issues aside, there was enough on the political side to indict him and cause his cohorts to say, "Time for you go, Newt."

Now, after all the bombs he dropped via his "Contract on America," especially on Black America, there is a possibility he will be the next leader of our country. It's almost too gruesome to imagine. In a couple of old articles on Newt, I warned, admonished, shouted, scolded, and begged us to prepare for the initial strafing that would take place and the subsequent "Newtclear" bomb that would be dropped on Black people by the modern-day Dr. Strangelove, Newt Gingrich.

In 2011, I issue the same warnings, despite Newt saying he has evolved into a better person, which I pray he has but I still don't want him as President. Let him take some of that $100 million and help those he hurt over a decade ago; then maybe I will believe his purported metamorphosis. Meanwhile, we had better batten down the hatches and get into our bomb shelters because the bomb thrower is back.

Following is a quote from one of my editorials in 1994: "So look out Black America. There's a change a-comin'. The Enola Gay has been pulled out of the Smithsonian and loaded up. It's going on a 'search and destroy' mission. Newt will be the pilot, making passes over Los Angeles, Houston, New York, Chicago, Detroit, Baltimore, Philadelphia, Southeast Washington, D.C. and, yes, Atlanta too. He'll be dropping his 'Newtclear' bombs on the poor and the underprivileged. Try to stay clear of the fallout, and stock up on your supplies; you'll need them. Dr. Strangelove is back."

Man, I am sure glad he didn't win.

Please pardon the interruption.

Busy, busy, busy, "I don't have time." Slow down; life goes by fast enough without the rush.

Considering the fact that Black people are so entrenched in the distractions of this world, I think it's appropriate that I beg your pardon, Black America, in order to get a few important points across. Although for years I have sounded the economic alarm via my newspaper column, four books, and numerous speaking engagements, it saddens me that we have failed to act upon the messages of our ancestors and contemporaries.

There is still a need to "capture" our attention when it comes to economic empowerment. Seems we have to be tricked, embarrassed, and beat-up before we start running for true freedom. So, can you spare a few moments to read this missive, Black America? I beg your pardon for the interruption.

Pardon the interruption of your sports conversations, brothers and sisters, but you are in big trouble. The players, coaches, and team owners have their millions and are very secure; your team is not even in the game.

Pardon the interruption to your anger or euphoria, and your inconsequential rhetoric on Libya and other nations; Black folks in the U.S. are unemployed in some areas as high as 50%. You are still being discriminated against when it comes to access to business, contracts, capital, and justice.

Pardon the interruption of your obsession with Will and Jada splitting up, Kanye and Jay Z's new album, and Tiger's golf game, multi-millionaires every one of them. You are trying to pay your rent, hold on to your homes, and feed your families.

Pardon the interruption to your wondering who will win the dancing and singing contests on television. You are doing the unemployment line-dance ("Now walk it out, y'all") and singing "Stormy Monday" Blues in response to your current economic condition.

Pardon the interruption to your unceasing and loyal dedication to making everyone else in this country wealthy by buying their stuff and boycotting your own. Even with nearly $1 trillion in annual aggregate income, the wealth of Black people is 20 times less than that of whites.

Pardon the interruption to your fascination with other folks' hair. You pay hundreds of dollars for someone else's hair, as if God didn't know what He was doing when He gave you yours.

Pardon the interruption to your penchant to have the best of everything, even at the highest prices. You are so silly to brag about how much you pay for things, while others brag about how little they pay for the same items. You love to go to bars and order whatever Champagne or Vodka some rapper might be drinking – even at hundreds of dollars per bottle. Only top-shelf for Black folks, despite the fact that you don't make or distribute most of the products you purchase. Thorstein Veblen's "Conspicuous Consumption" concept ain't got nothin' on you.

Pardon the interruption to your shooting and robbing one another. It's not enough for you to be under assault by outsiders, you feel compelled to take out your frustrations on yourselves rather than work together for your own benefit. Young people running rampant, wielding guns and having no trepidation at firing them at one another, at the police, or anyone they come across, speaks volumes about the overall condition of your families, your leadership, and your collective internal integrity.

Pardon the interruption of your meaningless conversations about Republicans and Democrats, Liberals and Conservatives, MSNBC and Fox News, and your preference of one talking-head over the other. They have their six and seven-figure salaries and can "talk" about your problems all day long. What do you have, and where will all the talk get you?

Pardon this interruption to your complacency, your apathy, your fear, your doubt, your perceived helplessness, hopelessness, and powerlessness. Pardon this interruption to your stream of consciousness, your psyche, and your apparent overwhelming desire to shut out reality.

Pardon this interruption to your indifference and unresponsiveness to the life and death issues you face. Pardon this interruption to your proclivity toward the temporal, trivial, and the trifling things of this world. Pardon this interruption of your inclination to allow the silly and symbolic to take precedence over the serious and substantive.

Pardon this interruption of your desire to continue majoring in the minors and getting caught-up in practices that matter little in the larger scheme of things.

Yes, pardon the interruption, Black America, but I just had to shake you once again; I just had to try to awaken you once again. I love you too much to let you stay in your comatose state, a state of inactivity and numbness. I care too much about our children's future to sit back and not speak out about our condition and not get involved in initiatives to improve our situation. I respect our elders and ancestors too much to ignore their sacrifices for our economic freedom, some having died "on their way to freedom." Are you on your way?

So, once again, pardon my interruption of whatever you are hiding from or running from or afraid of. I hope you will forgive my intrusion into your fantasy world. But most of all, I hope you will move beyond the mundane and heed this call for appropriate action to economically empower yourself and our people.

Black folks lose again and again...

"When you look at this final agreement that we came to with the White House, I got 98 percent of what I wanted. I'm pretty happy."
John Boehner, Speaker of the House

If Boehner got 98% of what he wanted from the debt ceiling deal, what did the other side get? I haven't heard the opposing side give its percentage yet. Of course, there was Representative Emmanuel Cleaver, who said the deal was a "Satan Sandwich." The quandary here is that if 98% of the deal was pleasing to the Repubs, does that leave 2% for the Dems? And if that's not true, and the Dems say they got 98% of what they wanted, or even 50%, it means that both parties wanted pretty much the same thing. You can't have more than 100% of anything.

I wonder how this debt ceiling deal makes most Black people feel. Are you fired-up mad about it or do you think it was pretty good? Considering the latest statistics on the net worth gap between Blacks and Whites, overall, we should understand that we are in deeper trouble than we were before the deal. But, many of us were asleep about ten years ago when the net worth gap was reported to be about 10 to 1 in favor of White households. Now that it's 20 to 1, with Black households having a median net worth of $5,766.00, and 35% of our families having a zero or negative net worth, we are all riled up.

Top off that news with the latest debt ceiling deal and the highest unemployment rate in the nation and what we have is a real serious problem folks. But you already knew that I'm sure. We will now see cuts in federally subsidized student loans, Head Start, and food stamps, in addition to the loss of more than 300,000 jobs. Black folks won't be left out of that equation.

The Brookings Institute issued a report written by William G. Gale, Senior Fellow, Economic Studies, pointing out: "It does not seem fair or reasonable to impose virtually the entire cost of this part of the fiscal burden on poor and middle-class households, but that is exactly what this bipartisan act of Congress and the White House does. Without tax increases in either part of the current deal or in the foreseeable future, there is no way to get the well-off to pay anything close to their fair share of the fiscal burden. The top 1% own 33% of the wealth and receive about 15% of the income in the country. These shares have risen over the past 30 years. They are being asked to bear none of the burden of closing the fiscal gap."

The report goes on to say, "…the plan imposes the full cost of deficit reduction on low- and middle-income households, gives the wealthy a free pass, and bodes poorly for future negotiations, which, like it or not, will require tax increases or draconian cuts in entitlements."

All right, Black folks, you got stroked again. The deal went down and you didn't get jack from it. In fact, you will have to bear much of the financial burden for the deal. So now, what's it gonna be? Will you continue to buy into the symbolism of politics and its effect on your emotions? Or will you finally take appropriate action to empower yourselves economically and free yourselves from the yoke of economic oppression and exploitation?

Will you continue to be more concerned with catching the latest episode of the Basketball Wives, as they call one another the b-word over and over, or will you at least make an attempt to be informed on economic solutions to our problems?

Will you rest in the refuge of now being able to see a Black man in the 6 o'clock slot on television, making butt prints in your easy chair, or will you get busy making footprints on the path that leads to economic freedom?

Will you continue to subscribe to the mantra, "Jobs! Jobs! Jobs!" asking the guv-ment to create them, you know, the same way it created jobs with the stimulus package, or will you start making your own jobs by growing Black businesses?

The folks in Washington are hardly concerned about our moanin' and groanin', our whinin' and cryin', and our yellin' and screamin'. They couldn't care less, and they have shown us time and time again. Why do we keep asking them to do what we know they won't or can't do? Why can't we see we've been played again? Are we really that stupid? Do we need to be hit upside the head with a sledgehammer in order to take care of business for ourselves?

On August 27th there will yet another march in Washington, and on the 28th they will dedicate the made-in-China Martin Luther King monument (Another example of our dysfunction when it comes to economic empowerment; carved from Chinese granite by a Chinese sculptor.). The songs will be sung again, the speeches will be given again, the tears will flow again, the chants will be yelled again, and the prayers will be prayed again. A few Black folks will be exalted, and the peons will look on from a roped-off distance "feeling good" once again. And after it's all over, Black folks will lose – again. That is, if we fail to stop all the rhetoric and emotionalism, and take appropriate action to end our losing streak in the economic empowerment game by teaching our dollars to make more sense.

High Noon Economics – Who really suffers?

"When elephants fight, it is the grass that suffers."
A proverb among the Kikuyu people, a tribal group in Kenya

In today's parlance I guess we could expand that proverb to say, "When elephants and donkeys fight, the grassroots suffer." Isn't it intriguing to watch the politicians squabble over raising the U. S. debt ceiling? The posturing, the pontificating, the postulating, the predictions, the placating, and that's just the P-words we can use to describe their insincere, uncaring, condescending attitudes toward an issue that up until now has been almost an automatic move by Congress.

Under George W. Bush the debt ceiling was raised five times, thereby increasing the national debt from $5.9 trillion to $9.8 trillion. Several of the politicians who are railing against raising the ceiling now voted all five times to do the same thing under George W. What hypocrites! And common folks, the grassroots folks, voted for these knuckleheads. How stupid is that? Now they are fighting and we are on life support.

How can voter approval of Congress be 13%, the lowest in the history of the Gallup Poll, while many in Congress have been there for decades? This reminds me of another quote: "It is hard to imagine a more stupid or more dangerous way of making decisions than by putting those decisions in the hands of people who pay no price for being wrong."

So where does the real problem lie? Who is really at fault here? We have seen politicians like this current bunch do the same things year after year, causing their constituents to suffer. Yet we vote them right back into office. We have stood by and watched those we elect say and do nothing to improve our economic situation while they wallow in wealth and all the perks that come with being our "representatives."

What we have here is a stand-off, one that will probably go to the eleventh hour when both sides will come out say how it was their idea, their efforts, that "saved" the day for the country, or they will hunker down in their positions, and we will sink further into economic depression.

This country is rapidly moving toward a two-tiered society in which one group has tremendous resources and the other group has few or no resources. If economic catastrophe occurs and hyperinflation takes hold, those who have will be able to load up their wheelbarrows with money and buy that proverbial loaf of bread. After all, corporations have hoarded the trillions of dollars they received or heisted in the past two years or so; they won't have too much of a problem, which is why the politicians can afford to posture and threaten one another. They won't suffer; we will.

Those without resources will suffer tremendously during an economic catastrophe. Yes, we can do wonders with a pot of beans and some cornbread, but what about the long run? In our current economic state people are breaking into homes to steal a couple of pounds of copper piping that they can sell for about $2.00 per pound.

Two things for your consideration, especially you politicians: First, our children's future is in a tug-of-war right now; they are the ones who will surely take the hit for the games you are playing now. They are in schools where teachers were laid off and activities cut in response to budget shortfalls. They are in colleges across this country, mounting up student loans, which comprise the latest "bubble" just like housing and Dot Com's. When they graduate they will be faced not only with paying back tens of thousands in loans but also with very dire prospects for obtaining a job with which to do so. All of this while you play political games with their future.

Second, when politicians take office they proudly take their positions to be sworn in. Many have their families around them and someone special to hold the Bible upon which they place their hand and swear or affirm some boilerplate verbiage about their duties. I have to believe that after the pomp and circumstance, after the "swearing in" ceremony, after the celebrations and accolades have been given, and after the congratulatory glad-handing, most of politicians never sit down and open that Bible to see what it says about their obligations and responsibilities. That Bible collects dust for the next two, four, or six years waiting for them to stand again and swear again that they will do what is right by those who elected them.

While, admittedly, it is hard to do, we pray for these political hypocrites who are in leadership positions; we pray they will not only pose for their photo-op with the Bible but they will also do what it says with regard to those over whom they rule and for whom they make decisions. Don't just put your hand on the Book; turn the pages once in a while.

May this high-stakes game of economics come to an end soon, and may those who are playing it come to their senses before it's too late. This is not merely about the debt ceiling; it is about the future of this country and economic foundation upon which our children and grandchildren will stand. They are the ones who will suffer from this latest elephant-donkey fight.

Need a job? Exxon is hiring.

During the $4.00 and $5.00 per gallon period in 2011, oil companies were raking in the profits, and much of the common household budget was allocated to pay for gasoline. We had to get to work and had no other choice but to pay, whatever the price was. Yes, some folks formed car pools, and some bought motor scooters or rode bicycles, but overall billions of dollars were spent on family transportation that year.

Exxon, as well as Shell Oil, Conoco-Phillips, Chevron, and British Petroleum are all hiring. All you need to do to work for them is buy their gasoline. Every time you "filler up" you are essentially working for the oil companies, whether you want the job or not. It is rapidly getting to the point where those of us who need fuel to get to whatever jobs we are so blessed to have are simply working to pay for transportation to those jobs. Thus, these oil companies that are seeing as much as a 69% increase in their profits and paying their CEO's annual salaries of as much as $21 million, ostensibly have all of us in their workforce. The problem is that they don't have to pay us; we pay them instead. Now, that's a good deal.

Now that Osama Bin Laden has been killed, will the price of gas go down? Do you think we will leave Afghanistan and Iraq, and stop our involvement in Libya? Will we refuse to get into a conflict with Syria, Iran, Yemen, and Egypt? And finally, since Osama was taken out by a couple dozen men, with a logical assumption that he could have been killed that way a long time ago, did all of the soldiers who died in Iraq and Afghanistan give their lives in vain? Things to think about.

Virtually everyone agrees that there will be some kind of retaliation for the death of the FBI's Most Wanted man. The logical inference would be to believe that if a skirmish in Libya can cause gasoline prices to increase beyond $4.00 per gallon, a series of retaliatory acts will elevate those prices through the proverbial roof. Osama's plan was to destroy the U.S. economically, to drive us into debt and eventually bankruptcy. He could now be reaching out from his watery grave to continue his assault on our economy, first with gas prices and then with the devaluing of the dollar and the ridiculous amounts we have spent on the ensuing war after 911. Like I said, the employment line is open at your local gas station, folks. Go get your job.

Even more serious is the looming specter of hyperinflation. All of the economic issues impacting our daily lives have the potential to cause the "perfect storm" in this country and, sadly, we are oblivious to it all. We spend much of our time discussing these issues but little time acting upon them – at least that's what's going on in my neck of the woods. Ignorance abounds as some of us blissfully stroll into a future laden with a myriad of economic uncertainties and pitfalls.

The U.S. has spent between $1.5 trillion and $4 trillion dollars on wars during the last decade. Our current debt is $14 trillion, and our deficit is $1.5 trillion dollars, give or take a few hundred billion. We are assisting other countries, even those that are working against our interests, while U.S. families are suffering every day trying to make ends meet, especially putting gasoline in our cars to get to work. This makes no sense at all, but we are obviously too reticent and timid to do anything about it. We are too caught up in the political drama and rhetoric to make the sacrifices necessary to change our dire situation.

We should be full steam ahead with refusing to make gas purchases from certain stations in our local areas and leverage lower prices from those we do support. We should be sharing our resources by moving in together and supporting our own businesses to a much greater degree. Since we have to buy gas at some point, we should find ways to save some of our money by working together.

As the saying goes, "Drastic times call for drastic measures." Are you really hurting enough yet to do what is necessary for real change? Or, are you willing to allow things to get worse without even trying to curtail our downward spiral? I heard someone on the radio say, in response to soaring gasoline prices, "The administration is 'investigating' why the prices are going up so high." That comment was made to console the listeners and, whether intentional or not, to keep us "hoping for a change" in our economic predicament as we continue to pull up to the pump and go to work for the oil companies.

Gasoline in Kuwait is a few cents per gallon; that's the country whose behind we saved from Saddam Hussein. In Venezuela the price is .12 cents per gallon. In Russia the price is only $2.10 per gallon. Is it because they drill and refine their own oil? If so, why is the oil that we drill and refine in this country sold on the world market at OPEC prices and end up costing us nearly $5.00 per gallon? And pardon me if I take no solace in the fact that folks in the Netherlands pay $6.50 per gallon for their gasoline.

We are being ripped off big time, and it's up to us to respond in kind. There are several things we can do if we are willing to make individual sacrifices for the benefit of the collective and for our future generations. Right now, there is little evidence that we are so inclined. So, be sure to pack a big lunch when you go to work for Exxon; it's going to be a long shift.

It was not until mid-2014 that gas prices started to decrease significantly. Now in early 2015 they are headed back up again. Iran and Israel may be the cause this time. Oh well, here we go again.

Circle the Wagons!

"Protect yourself at all times, and come out fighting."

LeBron James, after losing one of his championship series, took an arrogant but truthful shot at his critics for saying he choked. He said most of us will "wake up tomorrow with the same problems and the same life we had yesterday." To expand on his critique, the less fortunate will face rising prices, inflation, foreclosures, unemployment, college loan defaults, and trying to pay for a fill-up in order to get to work or operate our small businesses.

We can live vicariously through athletes and entertainers if we want to, but at the end of the day, as Mr. James stated, we will "have to get back to the real world at some point" while he will be relaxing on some island.

We should be able to see by now that no one is going to save us; we must save ourselves, and we must do that by working closer together in support of one another. Put away the selfishness, the pride, the ego, the zero-sum thinking, and the HNIC syndrome and get to work, collectively, doing what must be done to survive in this ever-increasingly desperate and disparate society.

On the political front, Black people are watching the game not from the sidelines but from the bleacher seats and the nosebleed section, hoping for a play on our behalf, one that will tilt the game in our favor. While "Demopublicans" and "Republicrats" fight it out in Washington, deciding how much longer we are going to suffer through their latest economic squabbles, we wring our hands and take sides on radio and television talk shows. We get into heated discussions and vehemently argue our national political point-of-view while ignoring our local political issues.

Do you remember the words of Peggy Joseph of Florida, at a rally for Barack Obama in October 2008? She said, "I don't have to worry about putting gas in my car; I don't have to worry about paying my mortgage; if I help him (Obama) he's going to help me." Even with the ensuing election of our current President, that was such a naïve and, quite honestly, an ignorant thing to say. I know it emanated from the hype and emotionalism of the moment, which is exactly our problem with politics, especially now that we have a Black President. Emotions only make us "feel good"; they do not make politicians "do good."

The current plight of Black people in this country is worse now than it was two, three, four years ago. Yes, we feel good about our President, but good feelings won't fill up our gas tanks nor will they pay our mortgages. Gary Younge, the Alfred Knobler Journalism Fellow at The Nation Institute, wrote an excellent article titled Obama and Black Americans: The Paradox of Hope, in which he said, "But for all the ways black America has felt better about itself and looked better to others, it has not actually fared better. In fact, it has been doing worse. The economic gap between black and white has grown since Obama took power. Under his tenure black unemployment, poverty and foreclosures are at their highest levels for at least a decade." He continues, "…almost every other Democratic president has failed in a similar way."

We know the mitigating circumstances under which Obama took over the Presidency, but that still doesn't help solve our local problems. Fact is, we rely too much on national politics by thinking Washington will solve our local economic issues.

Younge went on to say in his article, "Obama should do more for black people—not because he is black but because black people are the citizens suffering most. Black people have every right to make demands on Obama—not because he's black but because they gave him a greater percentage of their votes than any other group, and he owes his presidency to them. Like any president, he should be constantly pressured to put the issue of racial injustice front and center." I agree with Younge's position, but I also understand that whatever Obama does for Black folks will take time, and we cannot afford to wait for him.

It's way past time for us to circle our wagons and protect ourselves. How? Establish and grow our businesses through consumer support, leverage, strategic partnerships, and good management practices. We must adopt one of the goals of George Fraser's FraserNet movement: To increase the number of Black people working for Black businesses. Economist, Thomas Boston, also admonished us to do the same. And while we are at it we should leverage our votes too, instead of giving them away without reciprocity.

Teach our children the basics of entrepreneurship, which will allow them to access the opportunities therein, whether they own a business or not; if they begin to think like an entrepreneur they will be better at whatever career they pursue. Entrepreneurship should be taught in all of our schools.

Start local chapters of the Collective Empowerment Group, formerly known as the Collective Banking Group. By pooling our resources, via our churches, and leveraging our collective membership, you know, the way Sam's Club and AARP do, Black people could have a very positive impact on our local economic situation.

Finally, circling our wagons and protecting ourselves – and our children's future will demonstrate our willingness and ability to work together, define ourselves by our example, and grow our own internal economy for far more than just the relative few Black folks we see on the news, in the papers, and on television.

Serving Mammon

"Thousands of contractors who got stimulus money to do such things as build roads and provide social services owe more than $750 million in back

taxes, according to a federal investigation." This was the lead point in an article written by Jennifer Liberto for CNN Money. The article goes on to say, "More than $24 billion in stimulus money went to some 3,700 contractors who still owe the federal government taxes, according to the report released Tuesday by the General Accountability Office, Congress' watchdog agency."

Do you remember the highway signs that bragged about stimulus money being used to put America to work through "recovery and reinvestment"? Yeah, right! So much for that charade. Billions of dollars paid out to contractors to rebuild roads, few if any Black contractors, at least in my neck of the woods, and now we see that many of them cheated the government out of payroll and corporate income taxes. Stimulus? For whom? Did you get a stimulus yet?

Elderly people on Social Security have gone two years without receiving a cost of living increase; unemployment is off the charts, especially for Black people, which is more than 16% now. Losses in housing values have robbed the so-called middle class of much of its wealth; the oil barons are robbing the people blind and lying to Congress while receiving record profits, testifying that they are not "out of touch" with us every day common folks and our economic plight.

While the politicians play their games, pontificating on the evils and virtues of oil subsidies, this nation is drowning in a sea of debt, which causes most of us to question if and how we will be saved. As for those subsidies; here's a solution. The boys and girls in Washington could send each adult driver an equal portion of the subsidy and we could spend it on gasoline. That way, our pain at the pump would be eased and the oil companies would get their subsidy money anyway. That makes too much sense doesn't it? The government's answer is to "investigate" high gasoline prices, and Exxon's answer is to produce an "I feel your pain" TV commercial to educate us on oil sands in Canada.

Wall Street firms that are "too big to fail" have gotten paid; banks that intentionally made bad mortgage deals got their money; health care and insurance companies got their money; and selected contractors got their money, through highway work and two wars, one of which we did not need and the other of which should be stopped immediately, now that Bin laden is dead. All of this prosperity for a selected few, gained by keeping the majority in abject poverty.

Here is the worst part of this country's legacy of avarice: Juxtaposed against soldiers needlessly dying in Iraq and Afghanistan and coming home to poverty is the hypocrisy displayed by so-called patriotic politicians who are the first to say we should "honor" our service men and women. They pin medals on them, attend homecoming parades for them, and make tear-jerking speeches at their gravesites, but they pay them meager wages for their service.

Consider this idea: Pay soldiers at least as much as the politicians who sit in their cushy office suites "playing war" games are paid. That way, the patriotic rhetoric and that condescending statement, "Thank you for your service to our country," will really mean something. Of all the folks involved in war, it should be the troops who are compensated the most. Aren't their lives worth it? Soldiers serve the country; greedy politicians and corporate execs serve mammon.

As some of us know, serving "mammon" is a dangerous thing. Just in case you don't know that, read Matthew 6:24. Today, in our world of "get all the mammon you can get" by any means necessary, it's sad to see the examples being laid before our children. Corporate moguls sit before Congress with their weak responses to questions; lying and cheating are on display by politicians and lobbyists who are only interested in grabbing as much cash as they can; and flaunting of material things by celebrities and athletes, all on a backdrop of poverty, natural disasters, and economic inequity, will surely prove to be the demise of our society.

Too many people in this country are unwilling to take a real stand against the corruption and greed we see every day. And too many people in this country are willing to serve mammon instead of God. Considering that reality, how long do you think this society of ours will last?

Sending out an S.O.S.

I remember hearing Black Conservative, J. Kenneth Blackwell, tell an audience that the difference between the two political parties is this: If you were drowning in the ocean, 100 feet away from a ship, the Democrats would throw you a 200 foot rope, but they would drop it. The Republicans would throw you a 50 foot rope, because the swim would do you good."

For years now we have been involved in movements, events, and initiatives organized for the purpose of saving Black people from the ravages and vestiges of historical discrimination, disparity, and disenfranchisement. We have had meetings, conferences, forums, and seminars whose purpose was to provide a roadmap to true freedom for Black folks. Our public discourse, in large part, at least among the so-called "conscious" among us, has been centered on self-reliance, political and economic empowerment, and self-determination. Reflecting on the results of our rhetoric, I offer the following insights and, if I may, recommendations.

In light of the fact that Black people have no real voice in the political process, not with the President, not with the Black Caucus, and not even with many of our local Black politicians, it seems to me that we must do as the folks in the Tea Party did – start our own party and let our voices be heard via that collective. And, because politics is local, as Tip O'Neill said, we must act on a local level to appropriate the benefits we need to survive and thrive in our own neighborhoods, by electing Black folks - and others - who have our best interests in mind and are unafraid to act on our behalf. If the Black vote is as important as everyone says it is, then why aren't we leveraging it to the extent that Black people get something back for it?

On the education front, we see an increased assault on our young people after we turned them over to be educated by a system that cares nothing about them. Read Michelle Alexander's book, <u>The New Jim Crow</u>, and get a real handle on what is happening when it comes to schools, jails, and Black folks.

Economically, Blacks are in deep trouble. We have the highest debt and the lowest net worth. We have the highest unemployment and the lowest savings. We have the interest rates and the lowest asset base. We have the highest dependency and the lowest self-sufficiency. We demand the most and supply the least. In many cases around this country, if a crisis arises, Black people could not feed ourselves for a couple of weeks; we could not take care of our children's needs; and we could not provide assistance to others. We have no infrastructure to deal with crises, thus, we would all be isolated in our own cocoons individually trying to fend for ourselves.

We are too busy watching "reality" shows and living vicariously through celebrities, worrying about who will win dance contests, and what the joke of the day is, to take just a little time to deal with the problems we and our children face in this society. Maybe they're just too overwhelming and depressing, too daunting, for many of us. We talk a lot, but our actions do not reflect our own collective "reality" show.

At the end of the day, Blacks are going to have to save ourselves; we are going to have to take care of ourselves. Those of us who are near the end of our activist road still have much to offer in the way of counseling and direction, and we must make every effort to do that. You younger folks have the energy and the intellectual capacity to effect significant positive change in local communities, and you must do that. I have counseled several younger men and women about authentic leadership and how, if they work together, they can take the lessons of the past and obtain a reasonable level of political, educational, and economic control in their cities.

The keys are cooperation and a willingness to use individual resources for the benefit of the collective. We must learn to support one another more as we stay in our individual lanes of expertise, and be open-minded enough to submit to one another's leadership when the situation calls for it. Put aside ego and understand that everyone has something to offer and no one has all the answers. We must learn the difference between what Dr. Nathan Hare calls, "Black Leaders and Leading Blacks" and not fall for the ploy often played by dominant media as they prop up a couple of Black folks on the news shows and suggest they speak for all of Black America.

This S.O.S. is sent out to Black people as a desperate call for drastic change in the way we not only look at things around us but how we act on the critical issues of our time. This S.O.S. is for young, strong, committed, and unafraid brothers and sisters to take the helm of the Black Ship of State and steer us away from the impending rocky shores toward which we are heading.

To borrow a line from Charles Dickens' book, <u>A Tale of Two Cities</u>, depending on what we do, this could be the "best of times" or it could be the "worst of times" for Black people. If we would just get a stronger grip on our dollars and our votes, we could win the battle—not the war, but this battle. We have an army of strong, intelligent, and otherwise well-equipped soldiers. What's it going to be? Fight or flight?

War! What is it good for?

"Oil"
"Natural resources"
"Land"
"Greed"
"Power"
"Money!!"

That question was posed in a song by Edwin Starr during an earlier generation, and we are asking that same question now. Well, it's good for raising the price of oil, gasoline, and diesel fuel, isn't it? It's good for hypocritical politicians to rail against the same actions they refused to challenge when their guy was spending a billion dollars per week in Iraq—5000 Americans dead because of a big lie. So now we ask what good is this latest war. The answer: "Absolutely nothing," just like Edwin Starr refrained back in 1969, that is, unless you are a war profiteer.

Yes, here we go again with this never-ending charade of managing the world, dethroning dictators we don't like, interfering in another country's internal affairs, getting in the middle of a civil war, and the resulting benefit of that old stand-by: price gouging. Taxpayers are footing the bill for the wars and the results of wars. We are suffering through one of the worse depressions in history while our heads of state are slashing budgets in an effort to balance them on the backs of the poor and so-called middle class. And we believe Libyans have it bad?

Remember when fuel prices were sky high a few years ago? We blamed George W. Bush, suggesting he could make a few calls to his Saudi buddies and get those prices down to a reasonable level. Who are we to call upon now? Oh yes, that's right, Barack Obama. Funny, I haven't heard him speak out about the high price of gas lately. He should have paid Hugo Chavez a visit during his trip to South America to make a deal on some Venezuelan fuel.

How about those vaunted reserves we keep hearing about. Economists say that all we need to do is hint we will use them and the price of gas will fall precipitously. Here's an even better question. Why didn't the folks who run this country buy a couple of billion dollars' worth of oil when it was $40.00 per barrel and add it to our reserves. Isn't oil a futures commodity? Such puzzling issues to wrestle with these days, all while we are slowly but surely drowning in our own mess

The real kicker is the fact that Libya's share of the world's oil market is a mere 2%. How can prices at the pump rise by 75 cents in such a short period of time simply because the people in Libya rebelled against their leader? Could it be manipulation, or maybe just greed? In case you haven't noticed, we are being played like a saxophone in the hands of Charlie Parker. I wonder how long we will take it. I wonder how high the price has to get before we take some kind of collective action.

I don't know about you, But I am sick and tired of the convenient wars, the lies, the hypocrisy, the billions spent (or stolen), and most of all, the lives lost or destroyed because of oil. Now we find ourselves in Libya, "liberating" the people from a guy who has been in charge for 42 years, a guy who lately had become our "friend," a guy who has been doing the same thing the same way for four decades, and now we are insisting he leave because he is mistreating his people. I wonder why we haven't insisted he leave years ago. This country is a real piece of work.

They say Kaddafi is killing his own people, so we have to go in and stop that. Yet we stood by and watched Rwanda and the Sudan. We watched North Korea and Iran. And now we are watching Yemen and Bahrain do the same things. What's the difference?

Our sanctimonious approach to other countries where internal violence occurs is something to behold. Our memory is very short however. Kent State, Fred Hampton, Amadou Diallo, Kenneth Walker, and Roger Owensby, just to name a few. And, if you go back to the 1920's, what about the hundreds of Black folks killed by government supported white citizens in Tulsa, Oklahoma's Greenwood District, better known as Black Wall Street?

Yes, the hypocrisy abounds without shame. The money keeps rolling in and the ignorant consumers keep falling for the same Three-Card Monte trick that fills the pockets of the affluent and keeps those less fortunate wondering how to pay for a fill-up. It used to cost me about $11.00 to fill my gas tank back in 1997 or so. Today that same amount of gas for that same car requires more than $50.00 to fill 'er up. Yes, I still have that same car (375,700 miles and counting).

The bad news is that forecasters say we are definitely looking at $5.00 per gallon gas next year. We know the politicians will not stop the senseless wars, so what are you prepared to do about this economic crisis? I still say that until consumers change our behavior the rip-offs will continue.

One-day national demonstrations are cute but ineffective. Let's get real; our action has to be on a local level. Organize a critical mass of consumers and start talking to a local gasoline chain about cutting your members a deal, and only support those who support you. Start your own gasoline war, and you'll know what it's good for.

The Collective Empowerment Group

"There are reports that in some sections the Black man has difficulty in voting and having counted the little white ballot he has the privilege of depositing twice a year. But there is a little green ballot he can vote through the teller's window 313 days each year and no one will throw it out or refuse to count it." Booker T. Washington

Economic leverage is the most powerful tool available in a capitalistic society, and the Collective Empowerment Group (CEG), formerly known as the Collective Banking Group, has provided glowing examples of that truism for two decades. Echoing and implementing the "green ballot" strategy of Booker T. Washington, the C.E.G has used the strength of its hundreds of thousands of members to leverage reciprocal benefits from banks and other businesses. By coming together across all superficial boundaries, and not being constrained by egos, its members have demonstrated economic empowerment among Black churches and their congregants.

Now, moving into its next phase of development, the group has expanded its vision and its reach. The CEG is designing and executing initiatives that speak to and deal with the whole person by including in its mission a head-on assault on the myriad of issues that plague our communities. Health issues, political issues, criminal justice issues, employment issues, as well as economic issues are all on the table for the CEG, because the Church is the most effective vehicle to bring the change that is sorely needed among our people.

Historically the Black Church attended to most of the needs of Black people in this country. Many schools were established, businesses were started, benevolent societies began, children were taken in, the homeless were attended to, and the disenfranchised were comforted all by the Black Church. Why not today? Considering how much money Black churches deposit into banks every week, as well as the interest paid on church buildings, topped off by all of the folks who sit in the pews every Sunday and the staggering amounts they spend at various businesses, Black churches should rightly be at the front when it comes to economic empowerment.

The CEG has been at the front since its inception, and that's why we should all follow its example by establishing a chapter in our respective cities. I am proud to say that we started our chapter in Cincinnati in 2009; we are not where we want to be yet, but we are certainly far beyond where we used to be, especially when it comes to working together and using our collective economic strength.

We hosted our first annual economic empowerment event on February 26, 2011, during which Pastor Jonathan Weaver, Founder and National Spokesperson for the CEG, delivered the keynote address. We conducted workshops on Financial Fitness, Legacy Building, Debt-Free Living, and other pertinent topics. We also used the event to recruit even more local churches into our chapter.

If you have been a regular reader of my column you already know about my full support and advocacy for the CEG. Having collaborated with its members for years now, I am so pleased that our local ministers have taken up the gauntlet and committed to build a strong CEG Chapter. As I have said many times over, it is not a panacea, but it sure beats what most of us have going for ourselves when it comes to economic empowerment.

Look around, brothers and sisters, and tell me you don't see what is going on in this nation and around the world. Economically, socially, politically, and in the education and health arenas, we are suffering. But our fate is only sealed if we fail to stand up and do something about it—collectively. The President, the Congress, our local political officials, and most of those upon whom we have been taught to depend are not coming to save us. That's our job.

The assault on the poor and the so-called middle class has begun. Layoffs, gasoline price gouging, stagnant wages, food costs going through the roof. Have you made plans on how you are going to fight back? Or, have you just resigned yourself to defeat with those tired words, "There's no use trying to do anything;" "The man is not going let us do that;" and "They gonna do what they wanna do anyway." The question before Black folks is, "What are we gonna do?" Or, to make it personal, "What are YOU gonna do?"

Stop complaining about what the churches are not doing; celebrate the good work many of them are doing. The CEG is a model that has worked and is still working. It has shown the power of leverage via the only continuous and consistent act of pooling Black dollars by Black people: Church contributions.

Take a giant step toward your own salvation here on earth by starting and building a strong chapter of the Collective Empowerment Group. There is power in the Collective.

Just who are "We the People"?

"I am an invisible man. I am a man of substance, of flesh and bone, fiber and liquids - and I might even be said to possess a mind. I am invisible, understand, simply because people refuse to see me."
Ralph Ellison

Lincoln's words, included in the Gettysburg Address, "...and that government of the people, by the people, for the people, shall not perish from the earth," take on an esoteric meaning as we look at today's political situation. A brief look at politics will show anyone with an ounce of sense that "we the people" have not, do not, and will not run the U.S. government. The silly name-calling among politicians, the bought-and-paid-for members of Congress, the lack of progress on anything related to our economy, the absolute lack of concern for the poor, the elderly and veterans, the kowtowing to Wall Street puppet masters, and the total aloofness of those whom "we the people" sent to Washington are blatant examples of how screwed up our political system has become.

Just whom was Lincoln referring to when he spoke his famous line about "the people"? One thing we know for sure is that he was not talking about Black people, and I would venture to guess he was not talking about poor White people either. And that whole thing about the government being of, for, and by "the people" is in no way applicable to us, which leads to the logical conclusion that "we the people" must mean those who have the most money.

So where does that put Black people when it comes to the current economic state of this country and its future? What does it say about our political clout? Do "we, the Black people" and "we, the poor people" have a dog in the hunt as regards economic security, political influence, and/or power?

Can you wrap your mind around $2 billion being spent by the two Presidential candidates for the right to occupy the White House for the next four years? How about the billions of dollars in bailouts for banks and investment firms? How many of you have attended one of those political fundraisers at $20,000 per plate?

When I think about the fact that the bank bailout fund earmarked $50 billion for those whose mortgages were underwater, yet only $4 billion was used for that purpose, I cannot help but think that we are being played. But what else is new, huh? As a result of the bailout, the "too big to fail" banks are now even bigger; if one of them fails now its sheer size will drag the entire economy down the drain with it. Maybe that's why the Department of Justice has not prosecuted Goldman Sachs. Banks can now do whatever they want to "we the people."

When it's all said and done, all of the vitriol, sarcasm, and lying back and forth will result in more millionaire politicians holding on to their money and making every effort to cut into yours. We will see no relief prior to the election because the two parties are squabbling and posturing for votes and dollars right now. There will be no solution to unemployment, the housing market, tight lending policies, Medicare, the national debt and deficit, and all the other fiscal ailments that have beset us, simply because the folks we sent to Congress are more interested in keeping their jobs and all the accoutrements thereof.

Meanwhile, Black men are incarcerated at an unprecedented rate; they are shooting themselves in the head with guns that were undetected during two searches, all with their hands cuffed behind their backs; they are still being shot (30 times, or was it 46 times?) by six police officers in Saginaw, Michigan, for cursing and holding a knife. I suppose they shot him because they didn't want him to hurt the police dog they threatened to let loose on him.

I don't claim to know much, but one thing I am certain of is that politicians, no matter what stripe, are not going to do anything about the conditions we, the Black people, face. I believe it was Marcus Garvey who said, "All the shoes have been shined and all the cotton has been picked." He went on to suggest that Black people were no longer needed by white folks, therefore, if we did not change our ways when it came to business development we would indeed become obsolete.

No matter how you look at it you cannot deny that our system of government is broken. A stranger might ask, "Why would you keep putting the same people back in office, especially considering how they treat you when they get elected?" Good question, isn't it? So I ask again: Just who are "we the people"? Another thing I know for sure is that, it sure ain't us.

2012

The African Connection

Years ago my friend, Jenny Laster, told me that while visiting Ghana, I believe it was, she asked one of the men showing her around, "Why did you allow us to be taken away from our country?" He replied, "Why haven't you come back?"

Have you noticed all the current efforts to promote business opportunities in Africa? Have you wondered how now, all of a sudden, so much emphasis is being placed on Africa by politicians? Have you seen and heard about conferences and initiatives taking place across this nation that stress the importance of business connections with the Motherland? Why is this happening now? Why is Africa so vital to our economic interests now?

In my book, <u>Economic Empowerment or Economic Enslavement— We have a choice</u>, I cited an article in Black Enterprise Magazine (April 1996) that featured African American business opportunities and relationships in Africa. After reading the article I thought of the irony of a continent, rich with diamonds, other minerals, and vast natural resources, populated and owned by Black people, our ancestors, just sitting there waiting for us to come back and take care of business.

Moreover, during that same period of time (1994) nearly one million Africans had been slaughtered in Rwanda, and the United States under the leadership of Bill Clinton, refused to intercede because "we have no interests there." I am sure they were talking about economic interests rather than human interests.

Despite the fact that Africa, the place where time began, the first place God put man and gave him everything he would ever need, the place where diamonds and gold are in abundance, the place where other natural resources flourish, and the place where commerce and trade were established, it is only now being put forth publicly as an "opportunity" by our government officials.

A U.S.-Africa Business Conference was held in Cincinnati to "showcase U.S. business expertise to African clients and to highlight trade and investment opportunities in Africa to U.S. exporters and investors. Johnnie Carson, the Assistant Secretary of State for African affairs, was there to talk about those opportunities. In an interview, Carson stated, "For American companies, Africa provides a fast-growing consumer market, and forecasts anticipate Africa will have seven of the 10 fastest-growing economies over the next five years." That was around the mid-1990's.

Hillary Clinton also chimed in on the African economic opportunity issue at the African Growth and Opportunity Act Forum, by calling Africa the "land of opportunity." In a Cincinnati Enquirer article, Africa was called, the "last economic frontier."

Ironically, or sadly, Africa, having been there all the time and having contained all the riches and opportunities imaginable, was not very important to our national interests when hundreds of thousands were being murdered; but now it's deemed the "last" economic bastion of the world. One correction: It was also the "first" economic bastion of the world.

Notwithstanding King Leopold's veiled attempt through his International African Society to "civilize" the continent, and the Berlin conference in February 1885, in which European countries cast lots for various countries in Africa, with the exception of Ethiopia who fought against them and won, it is now being held in high esteem by the U.S. powers-that-be.

Although China, Lebanon, and other countries have been investing in Africa for quite some time, believe me, the U.S. will now be in the fast lane trying to catch up and even surpass them in their efforts to cast more lots for Africa's resources. Question: What about Black Americans? For many years now Blacks have known about the opportunities that are now being paraded before us; Black leaders like Booker T. Washington and Marcus Garvey, in addition to many more, advocated for African-African American business relationships, but we failed to take them seriously and follow through. Now we face being left behind and last to the table again.

In my book, I quoted Dr. Morris Jeff who, in responding to the question, "Why did our families allow us to be taken away from our homes and brought to America?" said, "Maybe we were sent here." He went on to posit that African Americans are the ones who, after gaining all of the knowledge we have today, are supposed to return to Africa and help develop that continent. While others are just now trying to make an African connection, we have had one for centuries. What will we finally do with it?

An Unhappy Median

Black folks are stuck in the medians of economic super highways, unable to cross to either side for fear of being run over and killed.

Although there is still a debate between those who say "Happy Median" and "Happy Medium," despite the latter being correct, there is no doubt that in today's parlance "median" is the topic of conversation; but, it definitely is not a happy median. To the contrary, the topic on the minds of many in this country is the decrease in median income and net worth, and that's making a lot of people very unhappy.

The 2012 article from the Pew Research Center, titled, The Lost Decade of the Middle Class was depressing. To no one's surprise I am sure, it pointed out the dire straits of the so-called middle class, citing that median household income had dropped 5%, but even more important was the fact that median household wealth had gone from $129,582 to $93,150, a startling 28% decline.

All of the rhetoric about the "middle class" leaves me wondering what politicians and statisticians think about the poor or lower tier people in this country. Most of the conversation and concentration is on the middle class. Of course, the upper class is well taken care of and, according to folks like Paul Ryan, it's only significant when poor people get freebies from the government, not Wall Street bankers and major corporations.

Mitt Romney's assertion about the poor having a safety net, therefore, he was "not worried" about them, paints a very graphic picture of the antithesis of what this country should be about. Who was it that said we should be judged on how we as a nation treat the least among us? I wonder if the folks in charge think that by ignoring the poor they will just go away.

We will hear much about the middle class and how both parties plan to help that group of people, but I'd like to know what their plans are for the poor, some of whom were pushed out of the middle class due to loss of jobs, housing foreclosures, or a reduction in the value of their homes. A story in USA Today in September of 2011, titled, Typical U.S. family got poorer during the past 10 years, stated, "The share of people living in poverty hit 15.1%, the highest level since 1993, and 2.6 million more people moved into poverty, the most since the Census began keeping track in 1959." The article went on to say, "Median income for black households fell 3.2% to $32,068"

The term "Unhappy Median" points to the seriousness of the problems facing this country, especially among Black and poor people. And right now no one is addressing this ever-expanding group of citizens. President Obama "can't" say anything in support of Black people, and Mitt Romney doesn't "care about the poor." Where does that leave us? Well, as usual, it leaves many of us on the sidelines, watching the game and even cheering for one side or the other, in spite of our unhappy state of affairs.

As for that "safety net," chew on this statement by the Center on Budget and Policy Priorities: "While the increase in poverty primarily reflects developments in the economy, weaknesses in the safety net particularly in the temporary federal unemployment benefits program also contributed to it."

A great deal of the crime in this country emanates from the economic position of some who commit the crimes. I suppose only when we have seen enough killing among young folks, who are willing to get money or things they value by any means necessary, will we see a significant change in how we address the issue of poverty.

Statistics and rhetoric obviously will not solve the problem. To show how silly we are when it comes to our own economic security, we vehemently complained about the Shackle Gym Shoe, so much so that it was taken off the market. But that new $315 pair of LeBron James gym shoes will surely be the rage of the marketplace, mainly the Black marketplace.

Determining median household income and net worth are great exercises for the statisticians, economists, and politicians; but to those at the bottom of the economic spectrum things are in a most unhappy state. Regardless of what happens in November 2012, we will wake up the next morning and find ourselves in the relative same situation, and it will persist until we decide we have had enough. Then and only then will Black economic empowerment move to the forefront of our psyche and take the precedence it deserves and should have had for decades.

Black people must change the way we see and participate in politics, yes, but first and foremost we must reverse our downward spiral when it comes to how we spend our money. If our income is dropping, and even if it is static, doesn't it make sense for us to hold on to it for a little longer? Isn't it reasonable and rational for us to refrain from frivolous purchases of expensive trinkets and whatever clothing item happens to be in vogue at the time?

Wouldn't it be prudent and wise to teach our dollars to have more sense, even if we do not have sense enough to change?

Invest in your business and watch it grow.

No one is going to finance your dream for you; put some of your own skin in the game before asking others to.

Often we hear that most small businesses fail because of a lack of capital. We hear the tales of woe, and some are quite true, of entrepreneurs who did not make it because they simply did not have enough money to fund their business. They failed because they could not get a loan from the bank. They failed because of cash flow problems.

While all of those reasons are legitimate and valid, in many cases small businesses fail because of improper planning and marketing, as well as a lack of adequate research. Too many business owners are unwilling to invest some of their own limited resources in the very things that will make them successful. Further, sad to say, too many of us are unwilling to hire other Black professionals to advise us on things such as accounting, legal, marketing, and other very necessary functions to any successful business.

That's too bad, but I suppose it's why less than 5% of African Americans are entrepreneurs. According to the last economic census in 2007, Blacks owned 1.9 million nonfarm U.S. businesses. These Black-owned firms accounted for 7.1% of all nonfarm businesses in the United States, employed 921,032 persons (0.8% of total employment) and generated $137.5 billion in receipts (0.5% of all receipts).

In 2007, there were 106,824 Black-owned employer firms; these firms employed 921,032 persons, had a total payroll of $23.9 billion, generated $98.9 billion in receipts, but accounted for just 5.6% of the total number of Black-owned firms and 71.9% of Black-owned firms' gross receipts. The average revenue for Black-owned employer firms in 2007 was $925,427.

In contrast, 1.8 million Black-owned firms had no paid employees. These non-employer firms generated $38.6 billion in revenue, accounted for 94.4% of the total number of Black-owned firms, and 28.1% of gross revenue. Average revenue for Black-owned non-employer firms in 2007 was $21,263.

This scenario, coupled with the rate of failure among Black owned businesses, strongly suggests a need for better management of those businesses. Just as importantly, the data indicate a tremendous need for growth and job creation among Black businesses.

The value of proper marketing and advertising cannot be overstated when it comes to the success of a business, especially a small business. For some reason we seem to shy away from spending money on advertising, marketing, and research. In many cases we even fail to allocate money for these services in our initial budgets. That's a prescription for failure— or, at a minimum, a business that will not likely reach its full potential.

The handwriting is on the wall for the workers of this country. Downsizing, rightsizing, re-engineering, or whatever you want to call it, are the orders of the day. Business ownership and mutual support are keys to the success of Black people in this country. We must be willing to support one another's businesses, and we must be smart when starting new businesses.

Place high priority on getting the proper assistance with your business plan. Hire a Black professional to guide you through the maze of research, management, and marketing needs. Yes, we know how to do those things too.

Advertise your business in the proper medium, and please use Black owned media to do so, as well as other means of getting the word out about your business. In other words, do something that will benefit some other Black businessperson. Marketing? Don't be afraid of it, and please don't deny the opportunity for a Black marketing professional to write your marketing plan and to execute a portion of that plan, if the need arises.

Research! Research! Research! Before, not after you jump into business. Just because you are a great cook does not mean you can run a restaurant. Spend some of your money researching your market to determine the need for your product or service, as well as what your competition is doing.

You know the saying: "Everybody wants to go to heaven, but nobody wants to die." This is the case of many people wanting to be entrepreneurs; few are willing to do what it takes to be successful.

Let's create and maintain strong and thriving Black businesses. Let's use one another's strengths and expertise to make our businesses grow. Let's work together, cooperatively, to make a better future for our children, teaching them how to make jobs rather than take jobs. We can only do that through business development, and we can only develop viable businesses by learning more about entrepreneurship.

Recognize and understand the rules of the entrepreneurial game, and learn to play them well. Money follows good planning and good management, no matter what color you are.

Misguided Priorities

"The most important area for the exercise of independent effort is economic. After a people have established successfully a firm industrial foundation they naturally turn to politics and society, but not first to society and politics, because the two latter cannot exist without the former."
Marcus Garvey

Centuries ago Black people in America came to realize that to survive in this foreign land they had to make it on their own. As enslaved Africans, with talents and skills necessary for building the wealth of this country, they never had to be concerned about their employment rate –

it was always 100%. What they did have to worry about was how they could someday free themselves from the yoke of bondage and get paid for their talents and skills.

Our ancestors figured out very quickly that if they had money they could buy their way off the plantations and become free men and women. They understood the value of their skills and knowledge, and began to "negotiate" with their enslavers for the right to have a little piece of land on which they could grow crops for themselves and sell a portion to others.

As our ancestors accumulated money from their entrepreneurial initiatives, they were able to purchase their freedom and that of their family members and friends. The entrepreneurship skills inherent in those enslaved Africans came to the fore, and set in place the priority of economic empowerment among Black folks in this country. They knew that ownership and control of income producing assets were keys to their success.

I often wonder what they would say to us today regarding our failure to place that same priority on our economic empowerment. Under the worst of circumstances, they worked hard to gain the economic footing needed to care for their families and send their children to school. They did what they had to do, that is, use entrepreneurship to elevate themselves to levels that would eventually lead to flourishing Black owned and operated enclaves across this country.

Today our priorities have changed almost to the point of ignoring the very basis of existence in this capitalistic society. The rules have not changed since our ancestors learned them and passed them on to us through their demonstration of individual and collective pursuit of economic freedom. In general, it seems we have become a complacent bunch of mentally enslaved people, driven by emotional speeches, paralyzed by the passion of what could be rather than what really is, and captivated by the success of others while ignoring our own lack of success.

What have we become, and what will become of us? It's simply a matter of priorities, folks. It's a matter of keeping the main thing the main thing, as our relatives did way back when. The main thing in this nation is economics; in second place is politics, and everything falls in line after those two. Chew on this: "Although poverty conditions for Black America have improved, the rates are still staggering when compared to that of all Americans." Black Demographics.com

As we move closer to the election, I see excitement, commitment, and energy especially among Black people to get out the vote, which is commendable to be sure. However, that same energy is missing when it comes to economics. If Black people would muster the same enthusiastic activism when it comes to empowering ourselves economically, we could carve out a niche in the marketplace and take a permanent seat at the table of commerce.

If we continue to get "fired up and ready to go" around politics and fail to bring that same level of engagement to the economic fight we will forever be relegated to the bottom rungs of this society, and politicians will only call upon us when it's time to cast our votes. We really need to change our thinking and our actions and get back to the same economic principles incorporated by our enslaved ancestors.

In this era of political infatuation, vicarious living, escape TV, and nonsensical diversions from reality, Black people are in special need of proper priorities. Yes, we have done well in some circles; just take a look at the current issue of Black Enterprise Magazine. Yes, we have made significant strides in the corporate and entrepreneurial worlds; but we have a long way to go, a long way to even get back to what our people did in the 1700's, 1800's, and early 1900's.

We have grown more dependent than independent; we have allowed our emotions to control us, thereby, allowing others to control our thinking, our actions, and our priorities. We have rejected the words of Marcus Garvey, and we have failed to heed the warnings and lessons of our forebears. We must do better, and then we must teach what we have learned to our dollars.

Cashing in on the "Lootery"

Money isn't always the answer to all of life's problems. In fact, sometimes money can create even more problems – as, it seems, is too often the case for lottery winners. It's not uncommon for lottery winners to end up with

even less than they had before their windfall and sometimes they even end up with nothing at all... many lottery winners lose their way and blow their winnings on exorbitant luxuries and frivolous possessions. Many buy astronomically priced homes, expensive cars, lavish vacations, priceless antiques and collectibles, and costly jewelry. TheRichest.com

I remember when I was about 7 or 8 years of age, the two elderly ladies who lived downstairs from my family would give me a ladies handkerchief tied in a knot with some coins and a piece of paper inside. They would have me walk up the street and give it to another lady about two or three times a week. Of course, I would get a piece of candy or a nickel for doing so. I had no idea at the time that I was their "numbers runner."

Back then it was a game of chance that involved a few pennies bet on a number, which I believe came out each day in the newspaper business section. I think it had something to do with the closing number on the stock exchange or something like that. I can hear the older folks who are reading this and saying exactly what it was and how the winning number was retrieved. I am sure they remember.

Fast forward to the early 1970's I believe, when the states began commandeering the numbers racket, primarily run in Black neighborhoods, and turned an illegal activity into a legal game of chance, called the Lottery, which has evolved into what I call the "Lootery." The few coins in the handkerchief and the hopes of winning $25.00 or so have changed to monthly shell-outs of hundreds of dollars by individuals with hopes of winning millions of dollars. The only thing that has not changed among many Black folks is the dream book that tells what number to play if you happen to dream about death, or the sky, or a trip, or a meal, or a new job, or a car, or a truck, or the devil, or God, or you name it. Whatever the dream, there was a corresponding number attached to it.

The lines formed at the stores and folks started spending millions and billions on "the number" all in an effort to "hit it." Many folks would use their last dollar, their rent money, their bill money, their lunch money, to take a chance because they had a feeling or a certain dream, or saw a certain number somewhere. The funniest thing was the folks in line with their sheets of paper and their long list of numbers to play each week. When they got up to the counter they would almost whisper the number to the clerk. I often wondered why they would do that; I attributed it to a scarcity mentality and the fact that some of us don't want our brother or sister to prosper, thus, we keep our winning numbers to ourselves.

The recent $580 million Powerball jackpot, the largest in history, was the craze of new wave "Lootery" players. Some folks spent hundreds and thousands of dollars on one chance in 175 million to win all that money. Finally on Thursday morning, November 29, 2012, millions of people were tearing up their worthless tickets as their dreams of winning the prize had been dashed. The "Lootery" had gotten them again. Oh well, "I'll get it next time."

I guess it is fun and it feels good to imagine what you would do with a few hundred million dollars and, except for those who hit it big and then live in misery after winning, most people would do some very good things with their windfall. But, in general, the "Lootery" has become a legalized frenzy of transferring hard-earned dollars mostly from those who can least afford it, to high-salaried "Lootery" Directors and others who just love it when those balls start dropping through the tubes. They always win, no matter which numbers come out. Sure some of the money goes to schools, but where is the benefit when it comes to our children receiving a better education? In general, the "Lootery" is just another regressive tax.

Here's my solution to making the Powerball "Lootery" at least a bit more palatable and the chances of winning a bit higher. When the total gets to $100 million, let the drawing be for ten winners of $10 million each. Keep drawing numbers until ten tickets win.

My point is this: If we are going to have $500 million prizes, why not intentionally award that prize to more people? I would love to see ten winners of $50 million, or even 100 $5 million winners, rather than one winner, or even two splitting a $500 million pot. I am sure some of those highly paid "Lootery" Directors can figure it out.

Think about that when you're standing in the next line of "Lootery" hopefuls and dreamers. Who knows? Maybe there can be some changes made in how the prize money is allocated, and you will have a better chance of winning. Oh yeah; remember a "brutha" when you hit.

Experiment in poverty, or political hyperbole?

"When you sit down to eat with a ruler, consider carefully what is before you."
Proverbs 23:1

During his tenure as Mayor of Newark, New Jersey, Corey Booker, now a U.S. Senator, following the example of Phoenix, Arizona Mayor, Greg Stanton, accepted a challenge to live on a $35.00 food stamp budget for one week. Mr. Mayor would add to his resume of shoveling snow and rescuing a woman from a burning house this latest feat that some news reporters are calling an "experiment." Booker's background, going back to his youth, includes other out-of-the-box actions, which are admirable and respectable; however, this "experiment" as some are calling it, will not go down as one of them.

A person who earns more than $13,000 per month going for one week on what is essentially a diet may be a nice news story but does nothing to alleviate the reality of those who are on that "diet" every day. The "bringing to the attention of the general public" angle is worth a 30-second political campaign sound-bite, but it's not like folks in this country don't already know the stigma and trauma and futility of feeding one person, much less three of four persons, on a weekly allocation of food stamps.

The "walk a mile in my shoes" angle may demonstrate some compassion and maybe even some temporary empathy, but after the week is over, and even during the week of rationing food, or as some may even call "fasting," the celebrity goes back to a much better life, as if he or she ever left it at all. Real people on food stamps must stay in that place for much longer than a week.

I don't know Mayor Stanton or Mayor Booker, but I did some research on Booker and found that he has done several commendable things for others during his young life. Also, Booker drew a lot of attention from his run for office against former Newark Mayor, Sharpe James. Booker's public profile was raised again during the last Presidential campaign, when he jumped into the fray by defending the work of Mitt Romney and Bain Capital. Thus, I doubt he needs to use food stamps for a week to gain more attention.

So why is he doing it? Reporters say he is doing it to bring attention to the food stamp problem, to "teach people how to responsibly budget and learn to eat nutritionally on a limited budget." Just how limited, they didn't say. The recommendation along with Booker's actions is that people across the country take part in the challenge as well.

Maybe some need to live for a week on food stamps to know what others are going through; but I don't. Just like I don't need to spend a week in prison to know I never want to be there, I don't need to live on $1.40 per meal to know that people on food stamps are having a very difficult time doing so. As I said, it's nothing more than a diet as far as I am concerned, and many people do that every day without the fanfare and drumrolls.

Folks on food stamps live every day as guinea pigs for the food stamp "experiment." So, is the hype about Booker's one week sacrifice to eat less a publicity stunt, exploitation, or a sincere effort to change the poverty conditions of millions on food stamps? Only Mayor Booker can answer that.

My contention is that living for a week on a food stamp diet, depending upon the reason for doing so, can also be deemed a fast. We are familiar with fasts and the reasons for them, especially those having a religious connection. Moreover, we are instructed to go about our fasts without bringing attention to ourselves, so it will not be "obvious to men" (Matthew 6:16).

Additionally, there are other important points made about fasting in the 58th Chapter of the Book of Isaiah: "Is this the kind of fast I have chosen, only a day for a man to humble himself?...Is not this the kind of fasting I have chosen: to loose the chains of injustice...to set the oppressed free...is it not to share your food with the hungry and provide the poor wanderer with shelter...when you see the naked to clothe him? ...if you spend yourselves in behalf of the hungry and satisfy the needs of the oppressed, then your light will rise in the darkness, and your night will become like the noonday."

Let's not make this food stamp issue just another political advantage for election or reelection. People in this country are suffering, and many who have to eat on the food stamp plan would much rather have an alternative – like a job. We should do what we can to help them, and we should do it not for publicity or accolades, but because it's simply the right thing to do.

Since Corey Booker has been a Senator, I have not heard or seen anything from him that indicates he is sponsoring or working to pass legislation that will ease the dilemma of tens of millions of people on food stamps in 2015. Was his experiment mere grandstanding? Was it a campaign ploy? Was it sincere? Was it just to draw attention to his "nice guy" persona? Did he help a few poor families by buying them some food? Did he teach a class or do a forum on how poor people on food stamps can eat better? Or, was it all just political hyperbole?

> "Life's but a walking shadow, a poor player,
> That struts and frets his hour upon the stage,
> And then is heard no more. It is a tale
> Told by an idiot, full of sound and fury,
> Signifying nothing."
> Macbeth, William Shakespeare

Falling off the Fiscal Cliff

"When government fears the people, there is liberty. When the people fear the government, there is tyranny."
Thomas Jefferson
I have come to the conclusion that politics are too serious a matter to be left to politicians.
Charles de Gaulle
Too bad all the people who know how to run the country are busy driving taxi cabs and cutting hair
George F. Burns

Or will we be jumping from the cliff? Congress along with the President will determine whether we fall, jump, or back away from the cliff. While I trust they will get together and make the right decision, I think we should be prepared for the worst case scenario. How do we prepare? First of all, learn what the fiscal cliff and its implications are for your personal economy. Too often we put ourselves in a position of having to react to things that have taken place while we were asleep, literally and figuratively. We had better stay awake on this one, folks.

In general, the fiscal cliff refers to $7 trillion in tax increases and spending cuts that will take place on January 1, 2013. For most of us, on a personal level, it means that we can say, "Adios," "Sayonara," "Cheerio," "Ciao," and "Goodbye" to that increase in take home pay, called the Obama payroll-tax holiday, we have been enjoying for the past year or so. Most workers would see a 2% tax increase instead because the "holiday" was at the expense of the Social Security tax.

The broader impact on the economy would be dire as well. The Congressional Budget Office (CBO) estimates it would cut gross domestic product (GDP) by four percentage points in 2013, sending the economy into a recession. It also predicts unemployment would rise to 9% with a loss of 2 million jobs. Neither individual workers nor the economy as a whole can absorb that kind of hit.

With a little less than two months to prepare, you probably should be doing what the big corporations have been doing for a while now: Holding on to your cash. They have also been converting their financial instruments to cash. Have you checked out the stock market for the past few days? If the big boys and girls are scared of falling off the fiscal cliff, what should our position be?

We have heard for the past three years or so that big companies have trillions in cash sitting on the sidelines waiting to see what will happen with the economy. They want to be fairly certain of the long term strategies being put forth by the government. They are refusing to spend or invest or lend that money until they feel comfortable. We are complaining about it but that will not get them to release their money back into the marketplace. We complain, while they retain.

Our position should mimic theirs, however. We should not plan to sleep out all night and get up at 3:00 AM to stand in line on the Friday after Thanksgiving (and this year starting at 9:00 P.M. on Thanksgiving Day!) to spend money we don't have, to buy something we really don't need, to impress someone who really doesn't care. We should not use the upcoming "holiday" season to be an excuse for frivolous purchases, and a way to satisfy our instant gratification mindset. We should put off buying all the stuff we usually buy during this time of the year, until we are in better position to do so.

Offers of credit cards, layaway plans, rent-a-couch or a Big Screen TV, and other schemes to get money out of your pocket will intensify over the next few days. Watch out! You may get into that debt now and regret it later, especially if Congress and the President do not solve the fiscal cliff issue. Around January 20, 2013, you will find yourself with more month than money if you are not careful.

While I sincerely do not believe the boys and girls in Washington will allow us to fall, jump, or be pushed off the fiscal cliff, I do believe that whatever they decide and agree on will hurt those at the bottom tier of the economy. Whether it's a regressive gasoline tax, the elimination of tax deductions such as home mortgage, medical, and contributions, or whether they choose to put an end to cost of living increases for social security recipients, folks at the bottom will be negatively impacted the most.

No, it's not fair. No, it's not the right thing to do. No, it's not moral. But, after all, it is always about the money, and you know who wins that fight. So until Black people learn how to refrain from being the best consumers in the entire world, and produce goods and services to a much greater degree than we do now, we had better learn how to respond appropriately to national and international fiscal issues. Keep your money in your pocket, the same way big corps are keeping their cash on the sideline, and hold it until you see what direction this nation will be taken by those in charge of it.

You can get that big screen TV, that new car, and that entertainment system later. Believe me, the manufacturers will be waiting for your dollars next year, and as Jay Leno used to say in his Doritos commercial, "[They'll] make more."

Black Dollar Derby

"And they're off!"

"Gotta have that Big Screen TV" is out of the gate first, with "I wanna X-Box" on the rail and closing fast. But "I like the Wii" is having none of it as he moves up in position to strike. Running in fourth place is "I need a Blu-Ray" with "My New Nikes" in a close fifth. In a surprising move, here comes "Designer Shoes and Clothing" on the outside, moving into striking distance of the lead pack. And bringing up the rear is "I still need that iPad Mini" and "Must have the Windows 8 PC."

As they head down the back stretch, it's "Designer Shoes and Clothing" leading "Gotta have that Big Screen TV" by a length. As they near the far turn, it's a horse race now, as they jostle for position, ignoring the others around them, bumping and even using their whips against the others. Oh my God! "Designer Shoes and Clothing" has fallen and is being trampled by the pack as they race for the finish line.

And here they come down the home stretch, folks! The ground shakes as the thundering herd passes, and their eyes are fixed on the prize, the grand bargains they are seeking. Here they come to the line. It's "My New Nikes" in the middle of the track, followed by "I wanna X-Box" with "I like the Wii" in third. It's going to be photo finish, folks. Fifty yards to go and, what's this? "Designer Shoes and Clothing" is back in the race. I have never seen anything like this before; she is moving up beside the leaders. What a race!

It's a four horse race now, but here comes "Gotta have that Big Screen TV" on the rail, struggling to carry the extra weight. "Big Screen TV" is passing "My New Nikes" and it's a photo finish, as "Big Screen TV" wins by a nose over the tenacious "Designer Shoes and Clothing." What a race, folks, what a race!

And the loser is, YOU!

From November 22nd through December 31st and a little beyond that date, we will make our way to the stores in search of the bargains we treasure. Billions will be spent during that period, most of which will be charged. The analogy of a horse race is quite apropos as we will watch the eager hordes of shoppers "jockey" for the best position to win their race for all the "bargains" offered by the myriad of stores in their locales.

While I am not trying to tell anyone how or when to spend their money, I am suggesting that we take a look at the current fiscal situation in this country and understand how it relates and how it affects us personally. Yeah, Obama won, but he is not going to pay our bills. And this "fiscal cliff" issue still looms on the horizon; if they do not fix the problem, our take home pay will decrease as of January 1, 2013.

So be careful and be safe if you are planning to go to the race track and get in the horse race this holiday season. Understand that there is another race going as well. It's the race by the stores to get your money, either now or later, as quickly and as easily as possible. What's a couple of casualties, a stampede at the door, or even an assault or two? It's all worth it to some, because after everything is said and done, it's all about the money – your money.

As for me, I'm gonna have a Mint Julep and watch the race.

Sowing and Reaping

"Do not be deceived; God is not mocked. For whatever a man sows that he shall also reap."
Galatians 6:7

All the talk about how "minorities" were successful in getting Barack Obama reelected should give us pause to reflect on just how this nation got to this point. Listening to the grieving Romney supporters and the shock they were experiencing brought with it the realization that the 2012 election was a result of things that took place hundreds of years ago.

When this country decided to create its wealth by using free slave labor and then exacerbating the situation with Black Codes, Jim Crow Laws, segregation, lynching, and disparate treatment of Black people, indigenous people, Chinese people, and other so-called minorities, it put itself on a path that inevitably would prove to be antithetical to its stated mission.

The Laws of the Harvest: We will reap what we sow; we will reap more than we sow; and we will reap after we sow. This nation sowed seeds of racism, discrimination, and subordination of entire groups of people. Because of its power to take, to use, to discriminate, and to exact punishment, our country unwittingly set itself up for what we see today: The collective power of so-called "minorities" to determine the outcome of national elections.

This nation of immigrants has demographically evolved and is continuing to move toward what many are calling a "minority majority." As oxymoronic as that term is, the reality is that folks who have been subordinated and mistreated for centuries are growing in numbers and will, in a couple of decades, outnumber what is now the collective White majority. Pat Buchanan warned about demographic and cultural changes, and power shifts among ethnic groups in his book, The Death of the West.

While I do not subscribe to Buchanan's reasoning, I believe much of the remorse we saw and heard on the "morning after" emanated from persons who received their wake-up call regarding the true face of America – what it was and has become. Some call it the "Browning of America." Mix politics with that reality and you get paranoia among the elected and the electorate.

Sow seeds of discontent and discontentment will grow. Sow "majority rule" and reap likewise. The yield will be greater and will come after the sowing, which may be hundreds of years later; but it will surely come. We have come full circle in the U.S. What was sown long ago is ready for harvesting, some good—some bad. That harvest is reflected in our political environment and discourse and in the minds of some who fear the next four years.

So, as Rush Limbaugh noted after the election, "We're outnumbered!" As newspaper headlines announced, "Minorities won [the election] for Obama." As one Republican County Commissioner cited, "We got drilled in the non-white population."

On the "morning after," some Republicans began rethinking their strategy to win elections. They finally realized that neither they nor anyone else can ignore the changes this country is going through, and they cannot afford to ignore the two largest so-called "minority groups" in the U.S. In order to win elections they must now reach out much more to those who have been marginalized for so many years.

Prior to FDR, Black people voted almost entirely Republican. Now we see that more than 95% of Black voters support Democrats. While that is not a prescription for success in either direction by the Black electorate, maybe now we will come to our senses as well by understanding the power of the collective. But that's another article.

The nascent United States, what some called an "experiment," has evolved to another level of discovery, and some dislike the current results of that experiment. Had the experiment been conducted without a biased thumb on the scales of justice, without mistreatment and malice toward those who were darker in complexion, without religious prejudice, without suppression and oppression, but instead with the understanding of the Laws of the Harvest, the latest political outcome would not be about Black, White, Hispanic, and minorities. It would be about the best man or woman winning an election.

We have become so polarized by race, which was sown when this nation was established, that there are those among us who are actually fearful now that another race, long considered inferior and subordinate, has the power to determine the political landscape. Rather than the result of the elections being a simple majority rules scenario, it was interpreted by many as a minority rules sea change, which caused unfounded trepidation and uncertainty. That's simply the reaping that must occur from the sowing that took place previously.

The Democrat/Republican thing has gotten out of hand and has been used by some to further divide races and ethnic groups. Thus, we continue to sow seeds of discord and acrimony. What do you think we will continue to reap?

We cannot live in the past, but we can learn from it. In the beginning, this nation sowed arrogance, superiority, and hate. It is now reaping fear, guilt, and division. Although we have made significant strides socially, educationally, politically, and economically, we must continue to change and, at the same time, embrace the new face of America.

Black Economic Dysfunction

We are financing our economic oppression instead of financing our own economic freedom.

Amazingly, Black folks in this country still don't get it. After all we have been through and after everything we have accomplished prior to and after integration, our relative collective economic position in America has changed very little. In some cases we have digressed in terms of ownership of land, from some 20 million acres of land (31,000 square miles) in 1910; and in our ownership of banks, of which 128 were founded between 1888 and 1934 and 64 Black existed in 1912. As for other necessities like supermarkets, manufacturing concerns, and distribution networks, we are not even on the economic radar screen.

In light of the latest financial news that predict yet another recession just around the corner, and the financial "cliff" from which we will soon fall, as reported on CNN's, Your Money, one would think Black folks are busy getting our economic act together, our history of business ownership and mutual support notwithstanding.

Sad to say, we are still floundering, enamored by the trappings of the "good life" and living vicariously through reality television shows and the shallow personalities thereon. Instead of working on our own economy we seem to be more interested in the economies of others, like the Kardashians who make about $30 million per year, not counting Lamar Odom's contribution. We just love to check in on those "wives" of wherever and listen to their vulgarity and watch their extravagance. We can't seem to get enough of the gossip shows and things that only make others wealthy.

Bob Law once said, "Black folks are just happy because Oprah is rich," as he pointed out how ridiculous we have gotten when it comes to our own collective economic empowerment. He also chided us for just wanting to see a Black man in the White House – that's all, just to know he is there.

Most of the people we follow and nearly worship are multi-millionaires and couldn't care less about us. They wouldn't give most of us the time of day if we saw them on the street. Yet we idolize and follow them in all they do, as we slip further and further behind in rebuilding our collective economic base.

Recent reports cite how important the Hispanic consumer market is, comprising more than $1 trillion in buying power. They also point out that Hispanics are the second largest population group in the U.S. and by 2015 they will be 18% of the total population at nearly 58 million persons. Those of us who were paying attention to Dr. Claud Anderson 15 years ago heard him predict just that. He also warned that if we didn't get anything from this society when we were in second place, we'd certainly get nothing in third place? He begged us to get prepared, but we were too busy helping everyone else build up their wealth and take care of their children. As the saying goes, "It's time to pay the piper."

What can we do now? For starters we can look into a mirror and admit how we have played a role in our own economic demise; and then ask, "What can I do to contribute to our collective economic uplift?" Well, you can establish or get involved in a local effort to empower Black people, whether through education, politics, economics, or all three. You have to take action.

Remember when the lady on the school bus was harassed by students, and a couple of days later more than $660,000 was raised for her through Facebook? That's how easy it is for us to do something collectively to help ourselves, yet we fail to take advantage of successful models that have been and could be implemented to help ourselves.

There was, and could be again, the Blackonomics Million Dollar Club (BMDC) that sent money to 20 Black institutions; we tried to get just 200,000 people to send $5.00 each to a designated charitable entity, but at its height there were no more than 1,000 participants involved. We have the Collective Empowerment Group (formerly Collective Banking Group) that should have a chapter in every major city across this country, but some heads of churches are too egotistical and individualistic to get involved. We had the 10-10-50 Movement, the Nationalist Black Leadership Coalition, the Bring Back Black Movement, and even a Black owned and operated distribution network, The MATAH. Of course there have been many more opportunities that we have shut down for lack of involvement.

Please, let's reverse our economic dysfunction and help create a meaningful, pragmatic, and sustained economic movement. Don't you think our children deserve that as a legacy from us?

Reflecting on the results of our rhetoric

"Talking loud and saying nothing."
James Brown
You are talking so loudly that I cannot hear a word you're saying.

"Talk is cheap!" "Talkin' loud and sayin' nothin'!" Black folks do a lot of talking, rappin', espousing, pontificating, and philosophizin'. No matter the subject, we seem to know all about it and are more than willing to engage the topic at hand. God gave us only one mouth, but He gave us two eyes, two nostrils, two ears, and two hands; we should get the hint that talking should not be the dominant of the five senses.

Talking is what we do after using our other four senses. So why is rhetoric so high on our agenda? Why do we hold in such high esteem a speech, for instance, that brings with it no action? Why are we so captivated by leaders that only talk, albeit very well, but have never established an entity, built a business, or started an initiative related to their rhetoric? Why do we even call these folks "leaders" in the first place? Shouldn't we at least measure them by the results of their rhetoric?

I am so sick of hearing folks who only whine about our problems and never lift a finger to provide solutions. Loquaciousness is very overrated among Black folks. You can hear it on talk radio, callers and sometimes even hosts who have little if any information on the topic, talking on and on as though they know everything there is to know about it. Even sadder is the fact that they give out erroneous information that others take and run with, thereby, perpetuating the ignorance of a certain issue among our people. Their favorite thing is to say what others "need" to do or what "we as a people" need to do, all without offering one thing they are willing to do.

I am also tired of seeing Black folks on television (legitimate news journalists not included) who only "talk" about the issues, usually telling us what we already know, and never having done one thing to contribute to our economic uplift. You ask them for a few dollars to help with a cause or to invest in a Black owned business and you can't find them with a search warrant. Why are we so enamored with these folks? Is it because it requires no work on our behalf other than to simply sit and listen to what they have to say?

Politics is the best example of this phenomenon among Black people. There's nothing like an arousing, emotional, down-home speech to get us wound up. But if all we get is wound up, and the speaker walks away with thousands of dollars for his or her rhetorical gymnastics, wowing the audience with big words and provocative quotes, what good is it? We must demand more from our "leaders" and not let them off the hook so easily.

Another thing we do is call "Town Hall Meetings." Nothing wrong with that, but it sure would be nice if we owned a Town Hall or two in which to hold our meetings. And let's not forget about the charlatan preachers and their prosperity gospel that always ends up providing for them but seldom if ever "trickles down" to those whose dollars enriched them in the first place. Why are we so weak? Why are we so vulnerable to mere rhetoric? Are we so lazy that we simply refuse to "test the spirits" to see if what they say is true? It's one thing to risk your money; it's another thing to risk your soul.

The point here is that Black people cannot afford to be drawn into the euphoria of rhetorical nonsense or rhetorical excellence. We must not fall prey to those who only talk a good game but never get into the game. Before you believe, follow, or praise anyone simply because you heard them speak eloquently or share some information, find out what they have done and/or what they are doing. See if they are using their other four senses to initiate, build, or facilitate something of substance rather than just talking about it or telling you what you should do.

Beware of bloviating rhetoricians and sentiment-grabbing, self-absorbed, self-proclaimed know-it-alls. We need authentic leadership not sideline coaches and Monday morning quarterbacks. Rhetoric alone cannot move us further ahead in this country. Words without action are just words. Information is only power to those who act upon it. Blackonomics requires action.

Pooling our resources

"We must cooperate or we are lost. Ten million people who join in intelligent self-help can never be long ignored or mistreated. The mass of the Negroes must learn to patronize business enterprises conducted by their own race, even at some disadvantage."
W.E.B. DuBois, 1898.

Why does the concept of putting our dollars together for one collective purpose, say, business development, seem so foreign to us? Yes, we do a great deal of talking about it but seldom see the results of having done so when it comes to purchasing foreclosed homes, vacant lots, and businesses in our neighborhoods. We complain about others coming into our neighborhoods and setting up businesses or buying the property, while we continue to support them through our purchasing power. Doesn't make sense does it?

The concept of pooling financial resources is certainly quite familiar to Black people; after all, we do it every Sunday via our contributions to the churches we attend. As a matter of fact, that's virtually the only place Black people pool our dollars to any substantial extent, and the results have been billions of dollars in land, interior finishes, song books, choir robes, musical instruments, internet and phone services, energy costs, and elaborate buildings in many cases. Unfortunately, many of the buildings are what I call "non-performing assets" as they are only used two days per week.

There are many churches that have done outstanding things by pooling their dollars. For instance, apartment complexes have been built, businesses have been started, community multi-purpose centers and senior citizen facilities have been brought on line. Churches have played a major role in economic development by utilizing their Community Development Corporations (CDC's) to build and sustain economic prosperity for their members as well as citizens living in close proximity to the church.

The lessons are there for us, not to mention those of the old African informal organizations called Susus, better known in America as Rotating Credit Associations. First used by Black people and now used by others, Susus have served as the financial stimulus for small would-be entrepreneurs. Many African and Caribbean ethnic groups use them extensively in this country to start and grow their businesses, to purchase property, and to pay off debt.

So why are African Americans so reluctant to pool our money to any great degree outside of the church environment? First of all, many of us simply don't see our church contributions as a pooling of our resources, despite what it says about the early church in Acts Chapter 2, and we fail to recognize the business aspects of where most of that money goes on Monday morning: Banks, most of which are neither owned by Black folks nor responsive to Blacks when it comes to approving business loans in return for the billions of church dollars held in their vaults.

Second, while we sometimes blindly trust those in charge of the church funds to do the right thing, we do not trust one another enough to pool our resources to develop businesses and such. It seems we are too concerned about who will "be in charge" and who will "handle the money," and we listen to that negative radio station, WIFM, "What's in it for me?"

Susus function on trust and honor; they are successful because the folks involved do what they say they will do, which is to make the regular monthly deposits and wait for their turn to receive the entire amount. No jealously, no envy, no cheating, and no disrespect. Just business start-ups, just debt relief, just college educations, just home purchases.

So how can we move beyond the collective economic stagnation in which we find ourselves today? We could take a lesson from the churches and then practice pooling our resources on a different level. Stop simply complaining about vacant lots and empty storefronts; purchase them, clean them up, and open businesses. Stop complaining about "other" folks coming into our neighborhoods and "taking" our money on a daily basis; stop "giving" them your money and try giving it to Black businesses instead. Stop saying "we need" this and that; start saying "let's get" this or that by pooling our resources and taking care of our business for our children's future.

For decades now Black people have talked a good game when it comes to pooling resources, and while we do have some glowing examples of how it's done, we still fall short of practicing what we preach. If we want and need so much economically, heed the words of Booker T. Washington: "Let us act ... before it's too late, before others come from foreign lands and rob us of our birthright."

Cash Flow Projections

"The fact is that one of the earliest lessons I learned in business was that balance sheets and income statements are fiction, cash flow is reality."
Chris Chocola

With all the talk about the economy relative to the rich and the poor, tax inequity, disparities in employment, and high prices for the necessities of life, one very important consideration for Black people in the U.S. is cash flow – both individual and collective. Simply put, cash flow projections tell us how much cash is coming in and how much is going out. Good projections also allow us to get in front of an impending problem rather than having to react to it when it's too late.

Businesses suffer when cash flow projections are improperly planned and "red flags" are not dealt with in a timely manner. Black folks are suffering because our cash flow is jacked–up, which means it continues in a negative mode rather than a positive one. We have much more going out than coming in, and that has resulted in our individual family net worth being less than $6,000 on average. And many of us have a negative net worth, which means even after we die, someone will have to continue to pay our bills.

In business, cash is king; unfortunately, that saying is not being applied in our neighborhoods and households, as we continue to outspend everyone else in this country, handing over our cash to any and every business we can find to support that is, except our own. Cash is the life-blood of any community; if it flows through a community, via locally owned businesses, rather than out of a community, via businesses whose owners live in another community, the result is good economic health for the community.

It is unfortunate that, for the most part, Black folks only talk about "recycling" dollars while failing to actually implement the principle. But all is not gloom and doom; we still have time to change, and we do have a great deal of "disposable" income. Instead of "disposing" our $1 trillion annual income among everyone else's businesses, we must find ways to keep more of it among ourselves for a longer period of time. How can we accomplish that? Business development and business growth.

Entrepreneurship is the way out of our negative economic situation. Yes, we need to establish more businesses, but we must also grow those businesses to the point of being able to employ our people. According to the last economic census, of the 1.9 million Black owned businesses in the U.S., only 106,500 have employees. And to add insult to injury, the number of those employees is a meager and embarrassing 909,000, all of whom are not Black.

If the vast majority of Black businesses continues to be sole proprietorships, our cash flow will stay on the negative side and our net worth will continue to be 20 times less than that of whites. If all we do is complain about being on the bottom, without kicking, scratching, and doing everything we can to move up economically as Malcolm, Garvey, Tony Brown, and many others have admonished us over and over, then we certainly deserve the negative result.

In order for Black cash flow to be positive, it must change its direction. Our dollars must start making more sense. Entrepreneurship is a major component of economic empowerment, thus, we must place more emphasis on it in our homes, our schools, our churches, and in our neighborhood circles.

Currently, Black cash flow projections are not looking positive at all. Our neighborhoods are in economic distress despite having significant cash on hand from week to week. However, as Michael Shuman noted in his book, Going Local (2000), "Being [classified as] poor doesn't always mean being without resources. The principal affliction of poor communities in the United States is not the absence of money, but its systematic exit."

Stronger and larger local businesses, hiring local residents and family members, play a major role in economic empowerment. So too does owning the houses and apartment buildings in our neighborhoods, many of which are on the market at very low prices. These basic economic solutions go a long way toward keeping our cash flow positive and making our self-reliance a reality rather than some nebulous feel-good term we like to use once or twice a year.

Economics is local. If we teach entrepreneurship, start and grow our businesses through support and mutually beneficial relationships, and own the real estate on which they exist and do business, our neighborhoods will become genuine communities once again. More cash should be flowing toward rather than away from us.

2013

Wealthy Black Africans

"As the seemingly well-intentioned French journalist spoke about Africa's scarcity and its limited resources, Nine smiled to himself almost condescendingly. He considered such statements an absolute joke. Africa did not, nor did it ever have, limited resources... Nine knew something the journalist obviously didn't: Africa was the most abundantly resourced continent on the planet bar none."

James Morcan, <u>The Ninth Orphan</u>

Who is the first Black person that comes to your mind when you think of wealth? Probably 99 out of 100 of us think of Oprah Winfrey, followed by Bob Johnson and his ex-wife, Sheila Johnson, and then on down the line with the likes of Michael Jordan, Earvin "Magic" Johnson, and Tiger Woods. Let's not forget about P Diddy (or whatever his name is these days), Jay Z and Beyoncé, Tyler Perry, and Bill Cosby. Sadly, we'd probably leave Dr. Michael Lee-Chin and the Roberts brothers, Michael and Steven, off the list because they choose not to be as visible and flamboyant as the others.

The estimated net worth of the top twelve Black tycoons in this country is approximately $10 billion, with Oprah leading the pack at a robust $2.7 billion. Following are athletes, entertainers, corporate execs, and entrepreneurs - not necessarily in that order, which comes to an additional estimated $10 billion. That's a lot of "jack" as they say; makes those folks who are "only" millionaires look poor.

Now most of us know that Warren Buffett and Bill Gates alone have over $100 billion in net worth; heck, the Mayor of New York is worth $25 billion! What does that tell us about the so-called "wealth gap" disparity between Blacks and Whites that has once again raised its ugly head? What it tells me is that we had better not go for the distraction of trying to get even, which would be an exercise in futility. Closing the wealth gap is a worthwhile cause, but getting even is out of the question.

There is another group of Black folks we should be cognizant of when it comes to wealth: Africans. Those of you who still have images of Tarzan movies in your mind, and those of you who picture Africa as "the Dark Continent" are in for a pleasant surprise. While we know about all the natural resources Africa possesses, despite it being called by some the "poorest" continent, we should learn more about its "official" 54 countries. Pull up some photos of the cities in various countries and you will notice they look just like American cities. Prior to his transition, Brother George Subira would bring large posters of African cities to any conference he attended. I bought one for my daughter when she was very young so she would not grow up like I did, cheering for Tarzan.

To add even more positive information about the land from which we came, there are three men and two women whose collective wealth is more than $37 billion! According to the latest Forbes calculations, Aliko Dangote of Nigeria tops the list with a net worth of more than $16 billion! Mohammed Al-Amoudi, with a net worth of $13 billion, is said to own over 70% of all the oil in Ethiopia and produces 4 tons of gold per year. Mike Adenuga, a Nigerian who made his fortune via oil, telecommunications, and banking, is worth about $4 billion. African females, Folorunsho Alakija of Nigeria, and Isabel dos Santos of Angola, billionaires themselves, also stand out as some of the wealthiest people in the world commanding over $5 billion in net worth.

Our images of Africa and Africans must be couched in reality, not myth and certainly not stereotypes promulgated by those who want us to think Africa is not worth anything. Black Africans are leading the world in wealth creation and growth, and we should be proud of the brothers and sisters who have turned the tremendous natural resources of Africa into billions of dollars for themselves and their families. Notwithstanding other Africans like the Oppenheimer family and its diamond empire, along with other Europeans who benefitted from the Berlin Conference of 1884-1885 to divide Africa, Black folks have made significant strides in the Motherland.

Let's work to change the perception of Africa, especially among our young people, as they will be exposed to the many opportunities therein. As they approach adulthood and begin to choose careers and business strategies, they should have information about Africa so they will not continue to see Africa in a negative light, the way many of my generation were taught. Believe me, the Chinese, Lebanese, and Indians have not missed the opportunity.

Don't hate. Don't rationalize African prosperity with the corruption excuse. Yes, corruption exists, but you don't have to look all the way across the ocean to find it. Just look around here in the U.S. Congratulations to all of those Africans who are taking care of their business and doing quite well at it. They have capitalized on Africa's natural resources, in many cases starting from meager beginnings, and used what they had to become some of the wealthiest people on earth.

Political Poverty Pimps

"In a country well governed, poverty is something to be ashamed of. In a country badly governed, wealth is something to be ashamed of."
Confucius

An article published on nky.com, titled, <u>Running for Senate not job for paupers</u>, cited: "The average household in the United States has a net worth of $69,000, but the average wealth of a U.S. senator is about $12 million, according to statistics from the U.S. Census Bureau and Center for Responsive Politics." To me, it illustrated the fact that we are far removed from the original intent of serving in Congress; no longer are "regular" people going off to serve for a few years and returning home to their jobs as farmers, shopkeepers, and factory workers, and the like.

Washington, D.C. has become a veritable money pit, and candidates are doing and saying some of the dirtiest hypocritical things in order to set up residence there. At the likely prospect of becoming millionaires, it's no wonder those running for office are quite willing to forget about "the people" and get to work immediately to maintain their lucrative jobs in Congress. They spend more time running and campaigning than they do governing, and they end up staying in their positions for ridiculously long periods of time, which is why we have such dysfunction in Congress.

But, there is also a high level of dysfunction among "the people" because we are the ones who elect and keep them in office, despite their horrendous record of working on our behalf. They become multi-millionaires and we keep losing ground economically. You would think, in light of the current debate over raising the minimum wage and the financial issues affecting most Americans, "the people" would do something about the disparity and the utter disregard some of these nouveau poverty pimps have for us.

Now let's be real here. It takes two to tango, right? If some of our elected officials are pimps, what does that make us? You know the word, no need to say it here. Question is, "Why do we allow ourselves to be treated this way?" We are obviously mesmerized by what we perceive as "royalty" and celebrity in this country, but to allow our penchant for person-worship to bleed over into the political arena is very dangerous—and we are seeing the results of having done that for so long. We respond to some of our politicians in ways that mimic idol worship, and pay them quite well in the process.

Since award shows are in vogue now, we should have a Political Players Ball and give an award for the best "playa." They could dress in their best playa outfits—pinstripe suits with red or blue ties, that is, and strut their stuff down the runway while they rattle off their promises and claims, and tell us how bad they feel for the poor and for disabled veterans. Of course, the one who has the most money would have a leg up on the competition and would probably get the most votes for "Political Playa of the Year."

Educator, Amos Wilson wrote, *"The irrational economy of...America, based as it is on irrational consumption, requires a high level of impulsivity and economic stupidity in its population, all the more in its lower classes and subordinated African American population."* Wilson was referring to economic empowerment and its absence within our ranks, but the same principle applies to political empowerment, not only for Black voters but for the entire U.S. electorate. This nation's elite relies and thrives on the necessary "stupidity" of consumers and the electorate to keep them in their positions of power. Political pimps, with an average wealth of $12 million versus $69,000 for those over whom they rule, are definitely slapping us around and making us pay them for doing so. What's that famous line Huggy Bear and other pimps used to say? "...better have my money."

I encourage the bi-polar electorate and the blind consumers to be more aware and active issues. If we act like sheep, we will be treated like sheep. We must stop getting so fired up about politicians who are only interested in having a sweet job as a result of our voting for them. We must stop being so emotional about politics, and start being more practical. We major in the minors and get fighting mad because someone calls our President a name, and we spend an inordinate amount of time allowing talking heads to stir the flames, which keeps our attention diverted from real issues. President Obama is a multi-millionaire too; believe me, he is not the least bit concerned about folks calling him names. He and his family are going to be just fine. What about you and your family?

Stop working for the political pimps; they are supposed to be working for us.

Going from cells to sales

This is dedicated to the folks in jails and prisons. Please share it with them.

According to the 13th Amendment, slavery in this country has not been fully abolished; there is an exception that says if one is duly convicted of a crime he or she can be enslaved. So, if you have been enslaved by either doing a crime or because you are in prison for something you did not do, why not learn how to turn your enslavement into a profit by studying to become a business owner? When you are released you will have your business plan in hand, ready to meet the world of entrepreneurship head-on.

For two decades now I have written and spoken about that "exception" in the 13th Amendment and advocated a literal boycott of prisons especially by Black men, who make up a disproportionately high percentage of those incarcerated in this country. How do we boycott prisons? Just refrain from doing some of the stupid things we do that result in prison time. It's bad enough that we have many who have been wrongly convicted and incarcerated—why volunteer to be a slave? We cannot keep complaining about the "prison industrial complex" while refusing to do our part to put it out of business by refraining from crime.

For those already imprisoned in what has become "Incarceration Nation," why not use the time you have there to research ways in which you can make something or do something and sell it to someone? A few years ago, I wrote an article titled, "Prison Profits." Well, a profit can be generated by prisoners, a profit they can keep in their pockets rather than have it appear on some corporation's P&L statement. If prisoners would build up their brains the way they build up their muscles, they would come out with a new skillset as well as a new body.

Just as our ancestors did during their enslavement period in America, we can do the same. Many enslaved Africans became "Intrapreneurs," as Juliet E.K. Walker describes in her book, The History of Black Business in America. Despite their lack of physical freedom, they leveraged their knowledge, and even their services in some cases, in exchange for a plot of land from which they could earn profits that would end up being used to purchase their freedom, and the freedom of others. They did not succumb to the conditions under which they were held; they made the best of their negative situation by utilizing their time not only to obtain freedom, but also to be prepared for freedom when it came.

We all know it takes money to be free. God showed us that when He told the Israelites to go back and get treasure from Pharaoh. Check it out in Exodus 12, the first case of reparations in history. God knew they would need "money" when they secured their freedom. We must learn from the past and use it to propel us forward to true economic freedom. While in jail and when released from jail, our brothers and sisters must change not only their behavior but their attitude about business as well. All the excuses and reasons for crime notwithstanding, we know the system is against us, but many of us keep engaging it and repeating that process over and over again. Recidivism rates are around 60% after three years of incarceration.

We know there is a cause and effect relationship between poverty and crime, and to the degree that we can shift that equation to our advantage, by teaching our young children and teenagers entrepreneurship, and by starting and growing our own businesses, we should make every effort to do so. It is our responsibility to do what we can, to control what we can control, to stay out of prisons, and then to advocate for the kind of training in our schools that can at least provide the opportunity for business ownership among our youth.

Here I go again, making up a new word: "Prisonpreneur"? A recent CNN segment featured men at San Quentin becoming technology entrepreneurs while in prison, and getting great jobs when they were released. They were taught all the skills of owning a business while they were spending time incarcerated. What a novel idea, huh? Well, it's not novel at all, as I have just shown you with our enslaved ancestors, but now that CNN has lauded it maybe it will take hold throughout the prison system population.

We need to stop being so hard-headed and make the appropriate changes necessary to control our own destiny, rather than turning it over to a prison system that is only interested in making a profit from the work we put in every day behind prison walls. The answer: Work for yourself not for the new slave master, the prison system. Become a Prisonpreneur.

Entrepreneurship is the key to empowerment

"Since our capitalistic system is a competitive system, the black man must learn to compete with his fellowman. He must not only seek jobs, but he must own establishments which will give jobs to others"
S.B. Fuller

One of the greatest entrepreneurs in this nation, Arthur George Gaston, offered these wise words of advice to prospective business owners: "Find a need and fill it." If there is anyone we can look to for an example of how business is done it is certainly A.G. Gaston. Starting out by lending his money to fellow miners, A.G. parlayed his earnings into personal profit with the interest he made. That reminds me of my days in the U.S. Navy when I used to do the same thing. In addition to being paid for pressing their uniforms and shining their shoes, every payday I would lend money to my shipmates, and require the principal and interest be repaid the following payday. I guess I had a little A.G. Gaston in me back then.

What it all amounts to is heeding those famous words. Businesses are primarily built on the needs of consumers, and as I have said before, sometimes an entrepreneur can turn a want into a need with slick marketing and advertising campaigns. Gaston used his fill a need statement to his advantage; it is said that when he died in 1996, at 103 years of age, his net worth was in the tens of millions of dollars—one estimate had it as high as $130 million! He filled needs by starting a burial insurance service, complete with cemetery plots, a construction firm, a motel, a radio station, a business college, and other ventures.

This phenomenal businessman is just another in a long line of Black entrepreneurs who understood what it took to start and grow a business, and they did it quite well, despite the hurdles, discrimination, setbacks, rejections, and failures. From Anthony Johnson, in the 1600's to John and George Johnson in the 1950's and 1960's, to Bob Johnson in the 1980's until the present, Black entrepreneurs have made their mark in this nation, and not only should we appreciate their accomplishments, we should also learn from them.

Another thing we can learn from Gaston's life is how the connection between the civil rights movement and Black economic empowerment worked. Blacks were not allowed to stay in most motels in Birmingham in the 1960's; Gaston built his own motel and allowed MLK and his team to stay there and use it as their "war room." When King was put in jail by Bull Connor, it was Gaston who put up the bail money to get him released. It goes to show the importance of having an economic base from which to fight for civil rights.

In his review of the book, Black Titan, written by Carol Jenkins and Elizabeth Gardner Hines, David Beito wrote, "Gaston's wealth and cordial ties with the white elite gave him a certain amount of clout that others did not have. His favorite methods were quiet negotiation, deal making, and, if necessary, private threats.

He was often effective. For example, the 'White's Only' signs on the drinking fountains in the First National Bank came down after Gaston threatened to pull his account. Many have forgotten the extent to which blacks were exerting economic pressure successfully to bring integration in the decade before the Civil Rights Act of 1964." Beito went on to suggest that the civil rights movement was the by-product of the economic foundation first laid by individuals such as [Booker T] Washington and Gaston.

Isn't it amazing that in spite of the obvious fact that economics runs this country, Blacks in 2013 still place more emphasis and expend more energy on politics and so-called civil rights, than we do on economic empowerment? Booker T once shared that a society does not have to be compelled to associate with a Black man who is educated and has $50,000 to lend. A.G. Gaston took that to heart and used it to his great financial advantage as well as for others.

To all of you future and current entrepreneurs out there, make sure to take some time to study Black business owners, especially those from the late 1800's and early to mid-1900's. S.B. Fuller, Annie Malone, Madam C.J. Walker, Anthony Overton, Sarah Washington, Phillip Payton, Herman Perry, Wendell Dabney, and others, are all examples of what we should be doing today as business owners. Of course, there are many contemporary Black entrepreneurs we must study as well.

Booker T. Washington said, "America will have no internal peace until there has been a grant of full economic rights and opportunities to Black America." We have a role to play in that ideal, brothers and sisters, by establishing viable businesses, growing them, and creating jobs for ourselves. Let's get busy; and remember to "find a need and fill it."

Economic Self-Interest

"In case of an emergency the oxygen masks will drop down; put your mask on first before trying to help someone else." Instruction from flight attendants

"The economic distress of America's inner cities may be the most pressing issue facing the nation. The lack of businesses and jobs in disadvantaged urban areas fuels not only a crushing cycle of poverty but also crippling social problems such as drug abuse and crime… A sustainable economic base can be created in the inner city, but only as it has been created elsewhere: through private, for-profit initiatives and investment based on 'economic self-interest' and genuine competitive advantage." Michael E. Porter, "The Competitive Advantage of the Inner City," Harvard Business Review, May-June 1995.

Yes, nearly twenty years ago another call for a little common sense was put forth regarding the problem of America's inner cities. Today, we have the same questions, the same issues, and many of the same folks running around trying to get elected by offering to change things for the people who reside in what Dr. Ron Daniels calls, "America's Dark Ghettos." We have talking heads misleading us on what it takes to make the appropriate changes necessary for our collective growth, all while their pockets are being filled and ours are being emptied.

We also have shysters and hucksters running from city to city declaring Jobs! Jobs! Jobs! They play on our emotions with MLK quotes, still asking us to keep his dream alive. In other words, they want us to remain asleep while they rake in the dollars from their all-talk and no-results protestations.

What a naïve and childlike people we are to be held captive by folks we call leaders, who have been doing and saying the same things for decades with no commensurate collective benefits for Black people. As Booker T. Washington once said, "There are some Negroes who don't want the patient to get well." We should be ashamed of ourselves. Sure, many Black people are doing quite well, individually, but far more are trapped in a generational cycle of poverty; and while personal choice and responsibility have led to many of their problems, their children had no choice in the matter. They are suffering the most from our dysfunction and lack of common sense when it comes to economic empowerment.

Michael Porter's words are not unique, and his prescription for success is not new. Our forebears demonstrated how to empower themselves economically many years ago, and they did it under the worst of circumstances. They were not perfect; they were not educated; and they were not affluent. But they endured hardships and worked tirelessly with the understanding that it was up to them to take care of their children, and it was their responsibility to determine the direction of their own lives.

The key words in Porter's quote are "economic self-interest and genuine competitive advantage." Black people, especially at the ballot boxes across this nation have abdicated the authority, power, and reasoning we once had with our votes. All too often we simply cast votes, not in our own self-interest, but as though we are voting in some local popularity contest. All a politician has to do to get our vote is hold our baby or show up at our church or eat some Bar-B-Q with us. Politics is about self-interest, the kind that Porter's words speak about and the kind demonstrated by our ancestors. How can your vote be powerful if you simply give it away without reciprocity?

As for "competitive advantage," Black people in this country have several business niches from which we could grow our collective economy. Look at the products we buy, the foods we eat, and the services we use. Look at the high concentration of Black people in various cities, veritable economic enclaves themselves, except right now our dollars are going to someone else's business, and not to our own. One problem is that many of us look at ourselves as being "competitively disadvantaged" and, thus, play into the self-fulfilling prophecy of not having the ability to open, support, and grow more businesses in our own neighborhoods.

Dr. Victor Garcia, a noted pediatric surgeon in Cincinnati, Ohio, took it upon himself to explore the reasons for the ever-growing number children requiring emergency surgery for gunshot wounds; he wondered what he could do to prevent it. He knew a great deal of the crime in our town was the result of poverty, hopelessness, and drugs. He also knew that by creating sustainable businesses in the inner city to employ our youth, at least some would be deterred from crime and drugs. Dr. Garcia understands what "economic self-interest and competitive advantage" are all about and is working hard to bring about change through sound economic principles.

Collaborating with the likes of William Julius Wilson, author of <u>When Work Disappears</u>, Michael Porter, and other local supporters, Garcia established an organization called Core Change, which is dedicated to designing and executing transformative business models within the urban core through which we can have our own Jobs! Jobs! Jobs!

He is definitely working "outside of his lane" in an effort to make a real difference in the lives of our people. But as Michelle Alexander recently reflected on her work on mass incarceration, "I'm getting out of my lane…I need to connect the dots, I hope you're already out of yours."

Protest Profits – Definitely in the Black

I got it! Here's a great idea. In response to what took place in Ferguson, let's walk 130 miles to the capital of Missouri. That will surely get their attention and things will change. Yes, it will cost a lot, but it's worth it, right? Six months later: Has the governor conceded yet? Nah, we're still waiting on his response. Any day now…

Overruling myself, I decided to write a column in which I will mention two items: Skittles and Iced Tea. I cringed every time I heard those words during the pursuit of justice for Trayvon Martin and his family. They became synonymous with Trayvon himself, and were mentioned just as much as his name was mentioned. As far back as March 2012, demonstrations and protests were held, one of which took place in Liberty City, Florida, that featured protesters holding up bags of Skittles and cans of Arizona Tea.

In case you have not yet figured out the connection by reading the title of this article, as Booker T. Washington said many years ago, "Beneath politics, beneath education, even beneath religion, lies economics." And I would add, even beneath protest lies profit. Understanding that nothing happens in this capitalistic society until something is sold, when I read about the windfall profits of Wrigley and Mars, makers of Skittles, that truism hit home even more.

Our protests leave a residue of profit for many companies, some of which is unavoidable, admittedly; but in the case of Trayvon Martin, the protests in which people purchased candy and tea, and even hoodies in many instances, resulted in unexpected, incremental, and welcomed profits by the manufacturers of those products.

It is safe to say that the vast majority of the protest items were purchased from stores that are not owned by Black people, which points once again to the fact they we prefer symbolism over substance. And in Liberty City, of all places, which was once a bastion of Black owned businesses and economic empowerment for Black folks, according to a 1986 INC. Magazine article by Joel Kotkin, titled, "The Reluctant Entrepreneurs," the irony of protest profits looms even larger.

The article cites, "Back in 1957, when Sonny Wright arrived in Miami, business was lively and vibrant in such black inner-city neighborhoods as Over Town and Liberty City. Independent laundries, restaurants, nightclubs, hotels, many of them black-owned, flourished along the main streets of the steamy resort city. 'We had a thriving little business community,' Wright remembers, 'the black entertainers like Sammy Davis Jr. and Nat King Cole stayed in our hotels. Blacks bought from blacks.'"

"[He] continued, 'now all that has changed. Ever since integration, everything is gone, the smart guys went to work for the government or moved to the suburbs. Nobody stayed around. Nobody created jobs in the community. Integration set everything downhill for black business in this town.'"

Sad to say that now protesters of a senseless killing of a young Black man no longer have those Black owned stores in Liberty City and most other cities across this country.

We protest while others profit; we count people "at" our protests while others count profits "from" our protests. Symbolism over substance is killing us. Arizona Beverage and Wrigley/Mars, although innocent and unattached to the tragedy received windfalls from the protests.

Skittles and Arizona Iced Tea had absolutely nothing to do with George Zimmerman killing Trayvon Martin, and yet they have become "symbols" in the aftermath of his death. If young Martin had nothing in his hands that night, would it have made any difference? Would it have made any difference at Emmett Till's funeral if they announced what brand of bubble gum he bought in that store? But folks back then had a little more sense than we do now. They did not rush out and buy the bubble gum and wave it during their protests and mail it to the police chief of "Money," (another irony) Mississippi.

We must understand the role Blacks play in the economics of this country – yes, even in the face of tragedy. We have to keep the main thing the main thing in all that we do, especially when it comes to economic empowerment. If this does not at least cause you to think about our collective actions and the futility thereof in many cases, if it does not make you know that many times our dollars just don't make good sense, then I have failed to do my job. I will keep trying though; you can count on it.

Marching in Place

"Hut two three four
What in the world are we marching for?
Five six seven eight
I don't know, just don't be late"

As we drew nearer to one of the most relevant events in history, an event that has been revered and immortalized by the iconic phrase, "I have a dream!" hundreds of thousands of people were preparing to relive the famous March on Washington. August 28, 1963 was the day that a quarter million people descended on the National Mall and heard Martin Luther King, Jr. deliver his timeless speech that began with an economic theme and ended with a rousing, thought-provoking, soulful call for freedom and equality.

In 2013, many people are excited about marching once again to commemorate that day in 1963, to restate MLK's dream, and hear speeches from civil rights icons. In the last 50 years Black folks have organized more marches than I care to remember. And now we march again, not only to commemorate, but also to demonstrate the failure of our society to fulfill King's dream.

When W.E.B. DuBois departed this country for Africa, according to Gerald Horne, <u>Black and Red: W.E.B. DuBois and the Afro-American Response to the Cold War</u>, he lamented, "I just cannot take any more of this country's treatment. We leave for Ghana October 5th and I set no date for my return…Chin up, and fight on, but realize that American Negroes can't win." DuBois died on August 27, 1963, just one day prior to the famous March on Washington, thus, never getting the news about the 250,000 participants and never hearing King's words of accountability, admonishment, and idealism. I wonder what he would have thought about that day and what he would have suggested we do from that point forward. Keep marching for 50 years? I kinda doubt it.

A half century later we are steeped in the same emotional quandary we started with in 1963; we are bombarded by calls to come back to Washington to repeat what took place in 1963; and we are teaching our children about that day and telling them to "keep the dream alive," to "relive the dream," to "redeem the dream," and to go back and march with us 50 years later.

Have we been marching in place all this time? Should we still be doing the same thing we did back then to highlight the same issues and to convince the same entrenched government and society to accept us as "equal"? Marching in place has taken us nowhere, which is hardly a revelation. By definition, as we learned in the military, it is not supposed to move people forward; rather it is supposed to keep them active, keep their metabolism rate up, and keep their attention right where they happen to be while marching in place. It's how a "commander" controls his troops while making them expend energy, maybe to tire them out before they are allowed to sleep. Sound familiar?

We have been ordered to march in place for years, only to make us weary and tired, which has caused us to go back to sleep after every march. We slept after we marched in Selma, in Birmingham, in Mississippi, in Chicago, in Harlem, in Washington with a million plus Black men, and after we marched to Jena, Louisiana; Jasper, Texas; and Sanford, Florida. We marched to the polls and voted for Barack Obama, and went back sleep. Now we have awakened once again "fired up and ready to go" to do what the President suggested a couple of years ago, "Take off your bedroom slippers. Put on your marching shoes..."

If our history of marching is any indicator, after we march this time we will go back to sleep a short while afterwards. So what's the point? Here's how Dr. Claud Anderson recently put it: "Blacks have been marching for centuries and have barely moved an inch. Marching does not injure the majority society. In fact, it does just the opposite. Black marches reward those who are kicking our butts. Blacks spend millions of dollars on hotels, airlines, restaurants, clothing stores, rental cars, and cabs while attending a march."

I say we have been marching in place. Instead, we should be marching to our businesses and supporting them, marching to our banks and depositing our funds, marching to our schools to educate our youth, marching through our "hoods" and turning them back into neighborhoods and then into real communities. Let's march to our churches and form Collective Empowerment Group Chapters across this country.

Stop being "treadmill activists." And, in light of MLK dying while fighting for an economic cause, if you are going to march in Washington this year, at least fill up at a Black owned gas station, stay at a Black owned hotel, eat at a Black owned restaurant, and charter a Black owned bus. I can hear the moaning, groaning, and excuses now. Sorry for my cynicism, but I wrote the same thing in 1995, prior to the Million Man March.

A Sporting Chance

"Show me the money!!!...I love Black people...Congratulations, Jerry, you're still my agent."
1996 movie, Jerry Maguire

Let me make a "pitch" (pun intended) for Black sports agents. Watching the NBA playoffs and finals is more than an exercise in pulling for my favorite teams; it is also a very frustrating experience for me because I tend to look at most things from an economic perspective.

While Black athletes dominate football and basketball, and have a major presence in baseball, relatively few of them hire Black attorneys, accountants, and agents, thereby, putting as much as 5% of their contract amount into someone else's economy. Black dollars are not making sense.

For years we have seen this intriguing phenomenon. In 1995, <u>Black Enterprise Magazine</u> ran an article titled "MVPs," that shed light on this subject. Mr. R. David Ware, noted at that time for negotiating the largest non-quarterback (Barry Sanders) contract in the NFL, voiced his frustration about the situation this way: "It is so disheartening that so few African Americans are given the opportunity to represent African American players...they wear Kente cloth and talk about pride in their heritage, but when it comes to business affairs, they don't use African American lawyers, agents, or accountants."

You would think African American college graduates would know better. But, in my opinion, they lack a consciousness that would have them act otherwise, and many have virtually no knowledge, or interest for that matter, in Black business history and the role they play in this nation's economic system. They are noted more for their shoe, soft drink, and fast food commercials, rather than their commitments to conscious capitalism. They have become fashion icons instead of paragons of Black empowerment. My suggestion to one of my students who played basketball at the University of Cincinnati was to develop a relationship with a fellow student who was majoring in finance, law, or business, and hire that person as an agent when he turned professional.

Let me pause here and say, I am not using a broad brush to paint all Black athletes (and entertainers). I know many of them are doing very positive things when it comes to supporting African American business persons and causes. So, please, as you read this, just take it as a recommendation for economic empowerment for Black people.

There are too many Black athletes who refuse to hire other African Americans. Considering how much money these guys and gals earn, if they used Black professionals, it would have a huge effect on the African American economy. Imagine how many Black real estate agents could earn commissions on the mansions purchased and sold by Black athletes. It makes no sense for us to keep crying over what we do not have, while we are steadily giving away what we do have to others.

As our young boys and girls are practicing their sport of choice, they should also spend some time learning how to practice collective economics. It is one thing to have millions of dollars, but knowing what to do and not to do with that money is far more important. Just ask Allen Iverson, Kenny Anderson, and Antoine Walker. Twenty year-olds need good advice on how to spend and invest millions of dollars. And they must be exposed to the fact that Black professionals can provide that advice. The *Jerry Maguire's* of the business must get up every morning and thank their lucky stars for Black athletes. As the not so fictional character yelled over the phone "I love Black people!"

I read a magazine article about one of our mega-millionaire ball players buying 22 pairs of shoes from a famous store that many Black athletes patronize. Of course, the store is not Black owned, but what else is new? Anyway, the shoes cost $16,000. Throw in about ten suits for a couple of grand each, and multiply that by thirty other Black professional athletes who frequent the store, and you're talking about a serious positive cash flow. You know how we like to look good. Unfortunately, other groups know it much better than we do, and they sure do take advantage of it. They make it and we buy it, no matter how it looks.

I know there are competent White agents out there, but as Mr. Ware said in the article, *"It's no longer a question of ability, but one of opportunity." Some white agents were crying foul when more African Americans got into the game. In a television special a White agent accused Black agents of "playing the race card" to get Black athletes to sign with them. He suggested Black athletes should select their agents and others who work for them solely on the basis of talent. Ironically, he was asking for a "level playing field."*

If Asian athletes comprised 70% of NBA players, we would see nearly 70% Asian agents. A similar scenario would prevail if there were a majority of Jewish or Hispanic players. Why are we accused of playing the race card when we suggest African American athletes hire Black agents? (I wonder how many White athletes are represented by Black agents.) If we play it right, one day not only will we win the game, but also the set and the match!

A hard head makes a soft behind.

"Caldonia, Caldonia, what makes your big head so hard?"

"Stop that! I'm not going to tell you again." I am sure many of you have heard your parents say those words more than once. Why? Because you always repeated what they told you not to do, right? Now that we are adults ourselves, we who are consciously aware of the state of the Black economy in this nation are saying the same thing to our people. "Stop that!" Stop spending so much and start producing more. Stop creating wealth for every other group and virtually none for ourselves. Stop capitulating to the whimsical and dangerous malaise of "instant gratification." Stop!

The latest piece of information that made me scream at our people when I read it was a well-written article, by Jeneba Ghatt, and featured in the online magazine, Politics 365. The title itself, "Black Spending

Power to Hit $1Trillion by 2015, But Black Wealth is Dropping," conjured up an immediate, "Say what?" and "What the…?" The inference I drew from the title comprised a conundrum, an enigma, a paradox, an oxymoron, an irony, an inconsistency, a contradiction, and just plain out of order.

My penchant for yelling, "Stop it!" has come from two decades of writing essentially what Sister Ghatt delineated in her article. And let me commend Dr. Claud Anderson, Tony Brown, and others who have been yelling a lot longer than I have about the foolishness of Black folks bragging about, or buying into others who brag about, so-called "Black Spending (Purchasing, Consumption, or Buying) Power." It may be power, but only for those with whom we spend our trillion dollars; it's definitely a weakness for us.

Can you see the untenable and downright ridiculous economic position Black people are in vis-à-vis having a $1 trillion annual income versus not having built a commensurate level of wealth with such a great deal of money? What sense does it make to even discuss Black spending power if we are not willing to leverage that $1 trillion into wealth for ourselves and our children? It's similar to how we brag about how "powerful" our votes are, but get very little in return for them.

Here is an excerpt from Jeneba Ghatt's article: "Although Blacks make up 13% of the US population, they own merely 5% of all US firms and only 1.8% of companies that employ more than one person… More than half of Black-owned businesses had less than $10,000 in business receipts in 2002, compared with one-third of White-owned firms and 28.8 percent of Asian-owned firms." Question: What does that say about our support of Black businesses with Black dollars? We have a trillion dollars in income, but embarrassingly low business receipts.

"Stop it! I'm not going to tell you again." That is, until the next time I tell you the same thing, and the times after that, just as any good parent does out of love for their children. But in addition to my continuing to rant and rave about our economic condition, and offer ways to ameliorate our situation, I will continue to encourage folks like Ms. Ghatt to enlighten us. It's the same message with a different messenger, but all in the line of stalwarts from Booker T., Garvey, Bethune, DuBois, Maria Stewart, Elijah Muhammad, to the Harvard MBA Preacher who founded the Collective Banking Group, Jonathan Weaver.

In his own inimitable style, Dr. Claud Anderson, author of Powernomics, responded to the article in part by saying, "Bragging about how much Blacks consume is like a crack addict bragging about how much money he spends to consume crack. It's the producers and sellers of crack that have the power, not the consuming addict. All the crack addict has is a bad habit that consumes brain tissue and wealth. Like the crack addict, we as a race, simply consume what others produce. We have enriched every racial, religious, and ethnic group on this earth except ourselves."

I am sure Claud's parents told him a hard head makes a soft behind, and he is constantly telling us the same thing, calling for us to wake up and have our dollars start making some sense by putting them to work for us rather than for everybody else.

Ms. Ghatt ended her piece by also offering some wise words: "[The Nielsen Report] should be…a call to arms to better educate ourselves on saving and growing money so that it lasts longer than one pay period."

I continue to say, "Stop the madness, folks." It is way past time for us to grow up, despite what was done to us in the early years of this country; it's time we take charge of our own economic empowerment by sharing more of our $1 trillion with one another, first.

"The eagle flies on Friday, and Saturday I go out to play; Sunday I go to church and kneel down on my knees and pray." Yes, they call it stormy Monday. I wonder why. Could it be because we are broke – or, just broken?

A Friend in Need

"You just call out my name
And you know wherever I am
I'll come runnin' to see you again
Winter, spring, summer or fall
All you have to do is call
And I'll be there
You've got a friend"
Carole King

The aphorism, "A friend in need is a friend indeed," is especially relevant to the conversations being held among Black people vis-à-vis our President and our lack of economic progress in this country. The "friend in need" is the collective of African Americans who overwhelmingly voted for Barack Obama but yet find ourselves even worse off economically, as Ben Jealous pointed out in 2013, than we were prior to our "friend" being elected to the highest office in the land.

If you listen to the Carl Nelson Radio Show (1450 AM, WOL in Washington, DC and woldcnews.com), and you should definitely listen, you have heard conversations regarding whether or not Black people should critique the President's actions, or the lack thereof, when it comes to specific Black issues. Mr. Nelson's show is one of the best on radio and the Internet, with very intelligent callers and astute guests who are engaged in action-oriented solutions to the problems we face in this nation. The callers' comments are riveting, passionate, and intellectually stimulating. They deal with substantive and relevant issues that affect us politically, economically, educationally, and socially, which is probably why so much is being said about our President.

On the question of whether President Obama is doing enough for Black people, there are two opposing sides; but more important is Nelson's open forum through which both sides can be heard. Recently callers discussed the economic state of Black Americans juxtaposed against the backdrop of having a Black President. One caller noted that we are too sensitive about critiquing Barack Obama, specifically on what he is not doing for Black people and what he says to us as opposed to his statements to other groups. The brother pointed out that we must be willing to engage our "friend," the President and, in fact, we have an obligation to do so.

The caller ended with a statement related to what I have written about for a while now regarding our involvement in the political game. He said Black people are too emotional about politics, especially now that a Black man is in the White House. Our emotions cause reluctance and even fear of saying anything negative or critical about the words and actions of Barack Obama. In my opinion, the caller was right on point.

Blacks are the "friend" in the most need, and we are looking for our "friend" in the White House to help fulfill some of our needs. When some Black people ask, "Is he a friend indeed?" others get uneasy and uncomfortable. What sense does it make for Black people to celebrate the rise of a Black man to the Presidency but yet receive little or nothing from that Presidency, especially when Black votes played a significant role in making it happen? The answer is "none." But, our emotional involvement in politics keeps us from doing what other groups have always done: advocate for ourselves, especially now that we have our "friend" at the top.

Do Black people have a friend indeed in Barack Obama? As far back as 2004, when I first wrote about then Illinois State Senator, Barack Obama, I warned us to be careful how we dealt with what was becoming a movement to draft Obama as a candidate for President of the United States. Here's an excerpt from that article, just in case you missed it.

"Barack Obama, the new fair-haired child, has recently been crowned as the probable first Black President. But Obama may turn out to be the Tiger Woods of politics. Some say Obama 'transcends race' because he is not the 'stereotypical Black man.' One commentator said, '...he is not black in the usual way.' What in the world does that mean? Does it mean that he is light-skinned and doesn't seem too threatening? Obama is certainly an excellent candidate, but let's not fall for the game, brothers and sisters. If he is deemed 'safe' then what label will be put on the rest of our Black politicians? Besides, even Obama will not set us free. That's our job."

Having written several other articles on the implications of having our first Black President, I am even more convinced that I was accurate in my assessment of how we, Black people, would react to it. In all my years of working, studying, teaching, speaking, advocating, and writing my newspaper column, I have come to know some very basic truisms, one of which is that Black folks must be our own best friends, especially when we are in need. It is dangerously naïve and just plain stupid to place our "hope" solely in a politician, as Jeremiah Wright intimated in 2008.

We must move beyond our discussions of whether Barack Obama is a real friend or a symbolic figurehead from whom we can only derive emotional comfort. We had better change our conversations and start dealing with the realization that we are on our own, and we must act in accordance with that reality.

What do we demand of ourselves?

"Confidence and empowerment are cousins in my opinion. Empowerment comes from within and typically it's stemmed and fostered by self-assurance. To feel empowered is to feel free and that's when people do their best work. You can't fake confidence or empowerment."
Amy Jo Martin

Frederick Douglass' words, "Power concedes nothing without a demand," have been haunting me lately, because of the pressing issues we face in today's political world, the dire economic straits in which many of our families find themselves, and the ever-present social problems Black people deal with every day. The key word in that admonishment is "demand."

Ever since Douglass uttered those words we have used them to determine how and what we must demand from others. Our responses have been external. My question is, "What is our internal response to Brother Frederick's words?" Are we demanding anything from ourselves as we seek power instead of mere influence in this society?

Although we seldom follow through on much of the knowledge passed down to us by our forebears, we sure do like to quote them. I guess it makes us feel good; but as I always say, "There is a big difference between feeling good and doing good." Yes, words make us feel good, but they should also make us "do good" too. Too many of our ancestors have sacrificed too much of themselves for us to merely repeat what they said without following through on what they said.

Thus, the "demand" that Douglass spoke of is magnified to an even larger degree and should be – must be – applied internally as well as externally. Our elder also said, "People might not get all they work for in this world, but they must certainly work for all they get." That statement is more suited for an internal response, which is probably why we don't use it as much as the one that has to do with power.

On an economic level, Black people are deserving of repair, or reparations, as some would say. There is no doubt and no lack of truth about our history in this country as it pertains to the wealth we created for others with our free labor, and the intellectual contributions our forefathers and mothers made to this society. Those contributions, including inventions that are still used today, along with a couple of centuries of free labor, are definitely worth billions if not trillions of dollars, and we should at least have a discussion at the highest level of government, from the President on down, about how to make up for such a wrong. Apologies are not enough.

Beyond that ideal, I believe we must also consider and act upon what Conrad Worrill and Ken Bridges called "Internal Reparations," which speaks very directly to the internal demands we must be willing to make upon ourselves. Are we willing to demand that we support one another? Are we willing to demand that we become the primary educators of our children? Are we willing to demand much more of ourselves when it comes to loving one another, respecting one another, and trusting one another more? Are we willing to demand of ourselves a sense and practice of Black on Black love rather than hate and destruction? Are we willing to demand of ourselves, especially our leaders, a high level of integrity, dedication, and sincerity? Are we willing to stand against the lies, divisiveness, and evil tactics of those among us who are only bent on selfish opportunism?

Those are just a few questions related to the demands we must make on ourselves, individually and collectively. We must be willing to acknowledge our internal faults and deal with them head-on if we want to make educational, political, social, and economic progress. Yes, it will take the backbone of a Marcus Garvey, the resolve of a Harriet Tubman, the fearlessness of an Ida B. Wells, the strength of a Maynard Jackson and Harold Washington, and yes, sometimes even the willingness to make the ultimate sacrifice, as Martin Luther King did.

I end this with MLK quotes and ask you to think about and act upon what he and others have said; and then demand from yourself the internal fortitude to stand against the "wiles of the devil" by doing the right things for the right reasons – all the time.

"History will have to record that the greatest tragedy of this period of social transition was not the strident clamor of the bad people, but the appalling silence of the good people."

"Our lives begin to end the day we become silent about things that matter."

"In the end, we will remember not the words of our enemies, but the silence of our friends."

"He who passively accepts evil is as much involved in it as he who helps to perpetrate it. He who accepts evil without protesting against it is really cooperating with it."

"Our scientific power has outrun our spiritual power. We have guided missiles and misguided men."

Amen, Brother Martin, that sure is right!

Common sense leads to common cents

"Economists who have studied the relationship between education and economic growth confirm what common sense suggests: The number of college degrees is not nearly as important as how well students develop cognitive skills, such as critical thinking and problem-solving ability."
Derek Bok

Some people say "common sense is not common," which may be the main reason Black people are not as far up the economic ladder as we should be. Having been in this country since it started, having provided the free labor that led to the creation of much of the wealth now enjoyed by those in charge, and having built a history of self-help and entrepreneurial initiative since our enslavement, Black people have the strongest case and the greatest need to exercise a little common sense when it comes to working collectively to improve our position in the U.S.

If we use our common sense, we will have more common cents. Using our common sense will cause us to do what other groups are doing, and as our forebears did in this country: pool our resources and support one another.

Common sense tells us to look around and see the dire straits our children are facing in this country and start compiling some common cents to help them meet and overcome their current and future economic challenges.

Common sense teaches us that we must not do anything that will subject us to the misery of incarceration and the profiteering of this nation's prison system; we must give our youth alternatives, especially economic alternatives, to their negative behaviors.

Common sense should teach us that discrimination still exists in financial institutions, and using our common cents we can overcome much of that discrimination by collectively leveraging our resources and supporting our own financial institutions. (When you ask why we need Black owned banks and credit unions, also ask the same about Korean banks, Cuban banks, Polish banks, Chinese banks, and all the others that exist in this country.)

Common sense dictates that we utilize our common cents to fund our own initiatives, first, and then look to others to support them – support them, not control them. Having common cents would also increase our ability to defend ourselves against local political issues that are not in our best interests. Our common cents can be used to fund ballot initiatives, finance the campaigns of candidates who will work on our behalf, and pay for research, analyses, and recommendations that can be used to make informed voting decisions.

Common sense instructs us to pursue our self-interest in a society that is rapidly becoming more polarized. Common sense tells us that we do not control the major political and economic games; but in order to assure a win every now and then we must use our common cents. Economics runs this country; common sense tells us that.

If we use our common sense we will also use our common cents to create and sustain an economic foundation from which to operate and on which to build even more common cents' initiatives. We must use our common sense the way our ancestors did, as they quickly caught on to the system they faced and immediately went to work building their economic resources to purchase their freedom and that of their relatives and friends. Freedom still ain't free, y'all.

Looking back on our progress for the past 50 years, common sense shows us how far we have come relative to the strategies we chose to pursue and the leadership we decided to follow. Common sense says several of our leaders have done marvelously well, but as a whole Black people are still stuck at the bottom of the economic ladder, a ladder with rungs that begin at the halfway point. We must figure out how to get to the halfway point by adding our own rungs to the ladder.

Utilizing our common sense would move us away from individualistic thinking and toward common cents strategies. We must change our minds, raise our level of consciousness, and put positive action behind our rhetoric.

We must be willing to use our individual God-given gifts, to contribute to the uplift of a people who have suffered more horrendous treatment, both physical and psychological, than any people in this country. Common sense tells us that. How else are we going to prosper? How else will we achieve economic empowerment? How else will we be able to positively impact the futures of our children?

If common sense is not common then I guess I can understand the paucity, or lack of common cents initiatives among Black people. But I don't believe Black people are short on common sense. How did we survive in this country? How did we progress in the face of adversity and even death? Why are we still here? How have we retained our sanity? How could there have been a Greenwood District in Tulsa, Oklahoma – and all the other Black economic enclaves across this country?

Our great-grandparents could not have done all they did without possessing a tremendous amount of common sense that, in turn, directed them to accumulate a great deal of common cents with which to take care of their business? So, what's up with us?

Blackopoliticonomics

"Economic, cultural, and spiritual depression stalk Black America, and the price for survival often appears to be more than we are able to pay... "At every critical moment of our struggle in America we have had to press relentlessly against the limits of the 'realistic' to create new realities for the life of our people. This is our challenge at Gary and beyond, for a new Black politics demands new vision, new hope and new definitions of the possible. Our time has come. These things are necessary. All things are possible."

The National Black Political Convention (1972)

As George Benson sang in Moody's Mood, "There I go, there I go, there I go…" making up words again. I couldn't resist this one in light of our penchant to choose sides when it comes to economics versus politics. It seems we cannot understand, nor act upon, the fact that by combining the two disciplines and leveraging the resulting power from such a sensible strategy we could build a stronger base and finally put an end to being ignored and taken for granted.

So I made up this word in an effort to indoctrinate us, to condition us, to program us, or whatever you want to call it, so that Black people can stop being sacrificial lambs led to the political and economic slaughter.

We do not have to choose between the two, but as I always say, if I had to choose I would definitely take economics over politics. Why? Isn't it obvious that while politics runs most of our lives (because we have no real economic base) it certainly does not run the lives of those who are economically empowered?

Whatever Wall Street wants Wall Street gets. The stock market hits record highs; but Black people are sinking lower in net worth and income. Black people are too busy watching the Wives of …, or Scandal, or all of those BET Award shows to recognize the subordinated consumer-oriented role we are playing in the economy. In the words of Sweet Brown, "Ain't nobody got time for that!"

As the war machine cranks up once again, the moneychangers are rubbing their greedy hands together in anticipation of another windfall from supplying the tools of war, the food for the troops, the equipment, the uniforms, and all the accoutrements necessary to dispose of those pesky Syrians and Iranians.

In this country, as the saying goes "He who has the gold makes the rules." Blacks aren't making any rules; we are just playing by them, and being used as grist for profit mill. Sadly, some of us are so entrenched in the political shenanigans in Washington, so enamored by the celebrity of our President and those with whom he socializes, that we either ignore the "weightier" things in life or simply refuse to listen, even though we know that the road we are on leads to destruction.

Just watch the dueling news channels, MSNBC and Fox, and you will get a steady dose of Obama love and Obama hate. He can hardly do any wrong on MSNBC and can seldom, if ever, do anything right on Fox. I often wonder if these newscasters have a life outside of the bashing they do of each other's political parties. Even sadder is the fact that Black people, who have little or no skin in the game, take sides and fight one another over emotional rhetoric centered on who likes or dislikes the POTUS and his policies.

It makes little sense for us to spend 90% of our capital and time on 10% of our problem, as Dr. Khalid Al-Mansour suggested in his book, Betrayal by any Other Name. When it comes to choosing instead of combining and leveraging, Dr. Al-Mansour says, "Blacks feel helpless because they hear so many conflicting voices and so much empty rhetoric. It's easy to throw up one's hands, get drunk, and have another baby. The African American has been hearing about the problem and the solution since he can remember and yet, his condition always continues to disintegrate."

We get a daily dose of political rhetoric and hardly ever take any economic medicine; it's no wonder that many Black people see no way out of our economic/political dilemma. We have chosen political rhetoric over practical tried-and-true economic initiatives to free us from psychological bondage - a prescription that has not and does not work.

The political hacks are doing what they do because they get paid to do it, not because they necessarily believe in everything they promote. Our problem is allowing these jokers to dominate our thinking and our actions, as though what they say, or who they support, or what ideology they promote will move Black people to a position of real power rather than mere influence. And if that happens at all, whatever influence we attain will have to be channeled through them, because they are the political gatekeepers.

As Malcolm said, "...you are chumps..." when it comes to politics; and I say we are pawns when it comes to economics. However, if we combine politics with economics and not be led around by the ears by so-called leaders who only care about themselves, their political connections, and the money they make from selling us down the road, we will be much better off than we are now.

So, turn off the television and start reading more, start learning more for yourself about yourself, and start initiating and participating in efforts, where you live, to combine and leverage your collective economic and political clout – a winning strategy for sure. In other words, start practicing "Blackopoliticonomics."

Vying for the Black vote

"Vote for me and I'll set you free! Rap on brother, rap on."
Ball of Confusion, the Temptations

The push for the Black vote is on. Black folks are back in style. Black is beautiful again! Since the 2012 election, the mantra has become, "Get more 'minorities' to vote Republican;" and Black voters are at the top of that list. Yes, they want to increase their Hispanic support, but the African American vote is ripe and ready to be harvested by just the right message given by just the right messengers. Wow, that sounds familiar; don't the Democrats have that same strategy? They trot out a couple of spokespersons to soothe us with convincing platitudes that have kept us in their corner for decades.

Now the Republican sleeping giant has finally awakened, and it is ready to do whatever it takes to regain Black voters' confidence and support. They have launched a new Black political role model into the limelight; he is an icon among Black people, a hero, Horatio Alger personified, and his name is Dr. Ben Carson. He was the darling of the CPAC convention and is the new love of Sean Hannity's life. Fresh off his in-your-face, Mr. President, speech at the National Prayer Breakfast, Carson has decided to quit medicine and pursue "other" interests. The Republicans are already drafting him for the 2016 Presidential race.

To rub salt into the wound, some Black commentators and columnists are suggesting that Black voters should seriously consider moving from the Democrat plantation to the Republican plantation, and Chairman of the Republican Party, Reince Priebus, has a plan to make that happen; so does Rand Paul. Both of them have said Republicans must get more Black people to remember what their party has done for us, and bring us back into their "big tent." Yes, we are definitely in vogue these days.

The question is: What are we going to do with our newfound popularity? Just like they say in that bank commercial, the same applies in politics. When political parties compete – for your votes – you win. I wonder what the Democrat response will be to this Republican incursion. After 75 years or so of Black voter loyalty the battle lines have been drawn by Priebus, who has set out to do what Michael Steele could not do with "fried chicken and potato salad:" get more Black folks to vote Republican.

Why is it always an either/or choice between Black folks being Republican or Democrat? It seems to me Black people should always be independent and willing to support either or neither party if, of course, that party addresses the interests and needs of Black people, or it fails to do so.

Notwithstanding the opposing arguments regarding what Presidents Lincoln, Eisenhower, and Nixon did for Black people versus what Presidents Roosevelt, Kennedy, and Johnson did, we should base our voting on interests rather than parties. Our unique position and genesis in this country demand political independence rather than political allegiance to anyone or any party. It's all about reciprocity, and the last time I checked, Black people have yet to receive even a reasonable return on our investment in the U.S.

Our American experience is unique. No other group has committed so much to, worked so hard for, fought and died in wars for America, and received so little in return. Other groups did not go through what we went through, and our right to play in the political game was bought and paid for hundreds of years ago. However, this is still, above all, a capitalistic society, and economics rules the day. If we take care of business in the economics arena, the political arena will be easy pickings.

Heed the words of T. Thomas Fortune, Journalist and co-founder of the National Negro Business League: "No people ever became great and prosperous by devoting their infant energies to politics. We were literally born into political responsibility before we had mastered the economic conditions which underlie these duties."

His message is clear. We are not even in the political game because we do not use our political leverage to get what we say we need. All we get back from our "precious" votes is a good feeling, which could be characterized as having sex rather than making love. Black people are in love with our political party; and our party is just having sex with us.

We had better wake up from our infatuation with political parties, and understand that they only want us for one thing: our votes. Of course, they would also like our campaign donations, but we certainly aren't trying to hear that. Black people must be more politically independent, and stop letting the talking heads and so-called leaders, both Black and White, steer us toward one party over the other. We will be more politically effective if we leverage our votes with those who espouse and support our interests. If we can't do that then we should at least be present at both tables in large enough numbers to have a positive impact on each party's agenda. Right now, the reference to Black people being made by either major party is related to our votes, not our progress.

Remember the words of U.S. Representative William Clay: In an article from a 1975 issue of *Ebony,* Clay looked back on the Civil Rights movement and cautioned Black America that a new struggle--one for economic equality--still existed. He wrote: "The new, and indeed racist and shrewd, second-line opposition of institutional America now seeks to overshadow our common interest by rewarding a select few blacks with tickets to the good life, thus dousing the fires of a much-needed potential source of leadership. Perhaps the simple truth is that before, we had a single objective that fused us into one politically-animated mass. Now, in our quest for economic equality, we do not...Your political philosophy must be selfish and pragmatic. You must start with the premise that you have no permanent friends, no permanent enemies, just permanent interests."

Including ourselves in economic inclusion

In order to write the rules of the game and in order to control who plays in the game, we must have ownership of the game.

Thomas Boston, noted economist and author of <u>Affirmative Action and Black Entrepreneurship</u>, called for a strategy that would establish and grow Black owned businesses to the point of having the capacity to employ 20% of the Black workforce by the year 2010. Aptly titled, "Twenty by Ten" – A strategy for Black Business and Employment Growth in the Next Century, Boston's charge was right on point, especially since he wrote it in 1999.

When I read his book, "Twenty by Ten" seemed very doable to me. After all, we had ten years to make it happen, not to mention the fact that if we implemented his plan Black folks would be well on our way to a higher level of economic self-sufficiency. What an idea, I thought to myself; I was certain politicians and businesspeople would jump on that idea and bring it to fruition.

Well, it's been 13 years since Professor Boston called for "Twenty by Ten" and sadly, we are shamefully behind on Boston's idea, and according to a poll I recently read, we are not only behind we are seeking every solution except the one that he put forth in 1999.

The poll to which I am referring was commissioned by Robert L. Johnson, Founder of BET, multiple business owner, and employer of many. Titled "Black Opinions in the Age of Obama," and conducted by Zogby Analytics, the poll brought forth some very interesting responses from Black people, one area of which was Black Employment.

When asked why they believed the Black unemployment rate was double that of whites, respondents' answers included, failure of the education system for minorities and African Americans, lack of corporate commitment to hiring minorities and African Americans, and lack of good government policies.

When asked why the wealth gap has increased by $70,000 over the last 20 years, nearly half (47%) of respondents said that both the lack of jobs and a lack of access to capital were to blame for the wealth gap between whites and African Americans. When respondents were asked if they have ever been overlooked or felt discounted as a serious contender for employment because they were Black, nearly half (47%) said "Yes."

While the answers are all valid and reasonable, I was struck by the absence of any response that suggested what Thomas Boston called for over a decade ago: More Black businesses hiring more Black people. There was a noticeable lack of onus put "on us" when the subject turned to unemployment and wealth creation/retention.

I am not trying to wrap all of our problems into a neat little package called "Twenty by Ten," but I am attempting to point out a flaw in our thinking and a gap in our own responsibility toward Black economic empowerment. Yes, we have need of solutions to the many problems we face, but many can be resolved if we would follow the perfectly sensible business model of starting and growing more Black businesses to the point of having the capacity to hire more Black people.

Yes, the government has a role to play; yes, the private sector has a role to play; but what is our role? I am tired of hearing so-called leaders beg for "Jobs! Jobs! Jobs!" from folks who are too busy taking care of their own to worry about us. It drives me crazy that there is no call for "Businesses! Businesses! Businesses!"

We must get back to common sense strategies for growth of the Black economy, which means we must produce more, or at least just as much, as we consume. And, we must hire more of our people. Others certainly have an obligation to hire us as well, no doubt; but we cannot keep chanting slogans and begging them without, at the same time, building and growing our own employment base.

Dr. Boston noted, "Without question, economic inclusion is the next civil rights frontier…promoting the growth of Black owned business means reducing society's unemployment burden, providing jobs where they are most needed and improving the income status of people who are too often trapped below the poverty line. Because the economy can grow as a result of economic inclusion, everyone can benefit." According to Mr. Johnson's survey, many Black people believe we should remain the "included" rather than the "includers."

Let's look inward as well as outward for solutions to our problems. Let's create our own economic inclusion policy by dusting off "Twenty by Ten" and renaming it "Twenty by Twenty." Do you think that is achievable?

Blacks in Politics – Blacks in Economics

"It seems to me," said Booker T.
"I don't agree," said W.E.B.

A poem by Dudley Randall

It has always been intriguing to me that we have elected thousands of Black politicians since 1970, while the number of Black economic advocates pales in comparison. Understanding that Black economic advocates are not elected per se, it makes sense to me that if economics is at the bottom of everything in this country then Black people should have at least as many Black economists, economic advocates, and economic literacy instructors as we have politicians.

Marcus Garvey said, "The most important area for the exercise of independent effort is economic. After a people have established successfully a firm industrial foundation they naturally turn to politics and society, but not first to society and politics, because the two latter cannot exist without the former." Obviously we should have listened to and followed Garvey's advice; he was one of our most powerful and committed economic advocates.

There were many others who attempted to school us on the importance of economic empowerment, folks like Maria Stewart, William Wells-Brown, T. Thomas Fortune, Booker T. Washington, W.E.B. DuBois, and Mary McLeod Bethune. Today we have a relative few who are striving to do the same. But are we listening to them and following their advice?

We would much rather listen to the empty rhetoric of political hacks and rely on our emotions rather than our intellect to make decisions about the direction we will take vis-à-vis our votes. We also fail to properly align our priorities, as Garvey suggested, in an effort to achieve true economic freedom.

Our present condition, both economic and political, is dire. Unfortunately, we are being led to believe that politics is the answer and that some politician will solve our issues for us. Even worse is the fact that some of us truly believe that nonsense.

My local newspaper, The Cincinnati Enquirer, featured a story that questioned why no Blacks were running for Mayor this year. The piece cited the fact that Black people comprise nearly 50% of this city's population, and although we have had a Black Mayor for nearly eight years now, the paper posed the question and slanted the story as though it was truly disheartened at the lack of a Black candidate this time. Let that marinate a little while.

Since when has anyone other than Black folks been concerned about the absence of Black political candidates in any race? We don't see many stories in dominant media dealing with the dearth of Black ownership of major corporations, the overwhelming number of Black owned businesses that have only one employee, or the disparities of the prison industrial complex. So why this concern in politics? Is it that Black politics is viewed as nonthreatening, while Black economics is viewed just the opposite? Could it be that Black politics is full of emotion and symbolism, while Black economics is pragmatic and substantive in nature?

Is economic empowerment threatening? The following quote from George Meany, ALF-CIO President, in 1969, might answer that question for us. "At its worst, 'black capitalism' is a dangerous, divisive delusion – offered as a panacea by extremists, both black and white... Attempts to build economic enclaves with substantial federal tax subsidies within specific geographically limited ghetto areas is apartheid, anti-democratic nonsense."

Had enough yet? It's easy to see that Black people in 2013 are used and misused by the political system. All of you emotionally engaged political devotees please sit down for this next statement. It matters not what "color" a politician is, even the color of the person who resides in the White House. Black folks had better get that through our thick heads and start pursuing an economic agenda, first, as Garvey said, and then a political one. Believe me, when a group's economics is in order, their politics will fall in line accordingly.

For the life of me I cannot fathom why Black folks in this country, after all that we have seen and experienced, are still waiting on politics to save us. And it's hard to understand why we think Black politicians will do right by Black people, simply because of their skin color. To make matters worse, we are still trying to figure out "Who is Black in America?" despite the so-called "one drop" rule, which was made up by White people. He who defines you controls you. (By the way, wouldn't the "one drop" rule make everyone in the world Black, since mankind started in Africa? Just a thought.) Being Black is not as much about skin color as it is about consciousness.

Economics is about empowerment, and our dollars should be used more wisely to that end. Politics is about self-interest, and our votes should reflect that truth. White politicians can help Black people just like Black politicians can. The same applies for White and Black capitalists. The question is, "Will they?"

The best help is self-help, however. We must organize and rally around basic economic principles. And until we are really serious about playing the politics game, we must wean ourselves off the milk and Pabulum of political dependence, and get on a steady diet of cooperative economics and mutual support.

Blacks moved to the end of the line – Again.

"When the ax enters the forest, the trees view the handle as one of their own."

Many of us have heard the saying, "If you're white you're all right; if you're yellow you're fine and mellow; if you're brown, stick around; but if you're black get the h--- on back."

Once again, we have been moved to the end of the line, even behind those illegal immigrants who are told they must go to the end of the line in order to become legal. When the Obama administration touted its number one agenda item shortly after his 2013 inauguration, it became immediately clear that Black people, along with whatever "agenda" we might have, would be pushed further down on the Presidential "need to do" list. Hispanics are the minority group *du jour* pushed ahead of Black folks that have been waiting in line for 400 years.

The number one political priority is now immigration reform, not Black unemployment, Black incarceration, Black economic inclusion, or Black anything. The gay people have had their turn at the front; the Jewish people have had their turn; the "mainstream" Hispanic folks are now getting their second turn; and now illegal immigrants have their turn at the head of the line. In street vernacular, "Where da Black folks at?" Oh, I see them; they're waaaay back there at the end of the line – again. Here, use my binoculars; you'll be able to see them back there.

Individuals and organizations are lining up and complaining about the lack of attention being given to Black people by the Obama administration, especially since Black voters overwhelmingly supported the President's reelection. Hispanics gave 71% of their support, while Blacks gave around 95% of theirs. So why is illegal immigration, which is an issue of great concern to Hispanic people, the number one priority?

Ben Jealous, President of the NAACP, on Meet the Press, said, Black Americans "...are doing far worse" than when President Obama first took office. The country's back to pretty much where it was when this President started. White people in this country are doing a bit better. Black people are doing far worse."

U.S. Representative, Alcee Hastings, reflecting on the President's nearly all-white inner circle and his second term appointees, says President Obama has disrespected Black folks by failing to choose not even 1 of the 61 names recommended for administration positions by the Congressional Black Caucus. I don't know; maybe the President just doesn't know a lot of Black folks. Hastings also cited the meager and insulting amount of Obama campaign funds spent with Black newspapers. So what else is new? But why market to a constituency that automatically gives nearly 100% of its vote and asks for nothing in return?

The same principle applies Supreme Court appointments Maybe the next time around folks like Deval Patrick and Charles Ogletree will be considered – no, nominated.

Anyway, here's the deal. We are at the back of the line when it comes to issues that directly impact Black people in this country. Somehow we cannot get it through our heads that we are still relegated to a subordinate position, politically and economically, and will remain that way until we change our behavior, as Amos Wilson advised in his book, <u>Blueprint for Black Power.</u> There is no reason or need for anyone to change the way they treat us if we continue to accept mistreatment from them. And this goes well beyond mere skin color, folks. After all, who is more "colored" than Clarence Thomas?

This is about consciousness, commitment, and a willingness to stand up and accept no less than what is right, equitable, and just. It is also about refusing to fall for the political games that are being played on us every day. Our votes are only good for one thing: counting – if they are even counted at all. But after the counting is done, it's back to the end of the line for Black people, despite the so-called agenda that Ben Jealous, Marc Morial, and Al Sharpton carry to the POTUS. Question: If they are so important (or should it be impotent?), have so much influence, and are so close to the President, why are Black people still at the end of the line?

Malcolm said it best: "Any time you throw your weight behind a political party that controls two thirds of the government, and that party can't keep the promise that it made to you during election time, and you are dumb enough to walk around continuing to identify yourself with that party, you're not only a chump, you're a traitor to your race."

Hire Yourself!

"Let's be judged not by the color of our skin but by the content of our business plan."
Fred Terrell, Owner, Provender Capital

In consideration of the latest shenanigans from Congress as it pertains to the economic conditions facing most Americans these days, unemployment and underemployment being the most serious, the case for entrepreneurship is more important than ever. For Black people especially, whose unemployment rate is double that of the national average and even as high as 50% in certain cities, the need for entrepreneurship cannot be denied.

Education and training, business startups, and firms that have the ability to grow and increase their number of employees are all essential factors for any group of people interested in economic empowerment. Black folks have an urgent imperative to revert back to the days when we owned and operated not only individual businesses but also entire economic enclaves in various cities across this country.

The nostalgia we feel when we remember Black Bottom in Detroit, Hayti in Durham, Harlem in New York, Greenwood in Tulsa, and Sweet Auburn in Atlanta should provide us with the incentive, well beyond the emotional side of it, to move in that direction.

In my entrepreneurship classes, after teaching the glowing history of business ownership in this country by Black people, as well as our entrepreneurial skills and acumen even before we were brought here, I offered the following suggestion: "Make something or do something and sell it to someone." That's simply what entrepreneurship is all about. Of course, we need to heighten our presence and participation in manufacturing, distribution, and starting businesses that lend themselves to growth or "scale," as some would say, in order to move to a point of being able to control projects, industries, and systems rather than always be at the mercy of those who do.

How do we accomplish that? We can start by simply hiring ourselves, individually at first and then expanding to hire others. We cannot afford to wait for the folks in Washington to provide jobs for us, nor can we sit back and think the private sector will help decrease our collective rate of unemployment. Even if they do finally get it together in Washington and on Wall Street, hire yourself by starting some kind of business, and when things get better you will be ahead of the game.

Hire yourself by turning a hobby into a revenue stream. Hire yourself by offering your skills to someone who needs your services. Hire yourself by selling what you know; after all, we are in what Peter Drucker called a "Knowledge-based Society." Hire yourself and make your own job, and stop allowing the sweet sounding political rhetoric to lull you to sleep.

In his book, <u>Job Shift – How to prosper in a workplace without jobs,</u> William Bridges writes, "The first thing we must do is to demand that our politicians have the courage to abandon the fantasy that jobs can be recovered or recreated as they once could have been. We need to understand that there is no way we can pump out more jobs as though they were industrial products, and every time our leaders play into our old fantasy that that is possible, they do us an enormous disservice… promising more jobs is an effective electoral tactic. Furthermore, it sounds public-spirited and humane."

Bridges also says, "The disappearance of jobs, with every passing month, is … a change that has already happened. It is also a change that can be exploited by individuals and organizations that know how to do so." You can find more information on this subject in William Julius Wilson's seminal work, <u>When Work Disappears</u>, which should be a staple in your personal libraries.

Another writer named James Brown, also known as the Godfather of Soul, put the following words of advice to music when he said, "Let's get together and get some land; raise our food like the man; save our money like the mob; put up a factory and own the jobs." How are we ever going to be economically empowered if we do not own our jobs?

"Less than half of the workforce in the industrialized world will be in 'proper' full-time jobs in organizations by the beginning of the twenty-first

century" – Charles Handy. We are already 15 years late, folks. Whether you like it or not, jobs as we have known them are gone for good. So even though you may not be convinced of that reality, encourage your children to hire themselves by pursuing some form of entrepreneurship; even as they look for and secure jobs from someone else's company, they can still own a business.

2014

"Mo' Money, Mo' Money"

Well, I've learned my lesson and now I know
The sun may shine and the winds may blow.
The women may come and the women may go,
But before I say I love you so,
I want
Money, honey.
Money, honey.
Money, honey,
If you want to get along with me.
Elvis Presley

Remember that movie with the Wayans Brothers? After stealing some credit cards, Damon's character, Johnny Stewart, had everything he ever thought he wanted. He spent a lot of money on "things" and still found himself with more than enough cash to do whatever he wanted. I am also reminded of another movie back in the 1980's, Wall Street, that featured the infamous Gordon Gekko whose mantra was "Greed is good." When King Solomon wrote, "Money answereth all things," I don't think he had Stewart and Gekko in mind.

To expand on that point, the Pope and President Obama will be kickin' it in March (2014) to discuss the issue of economic inequality, which is graphically described by the following three points cited in an Oxfam Briefing Paper:

"The wealth of the richest one percent in the world amounts to $110 trillion. That's 65 times the total wealth of the bottom half of the world's population;"

"The bottom half of the world's population [3.5 billion people] owns the same as the richest 85 people in the world;"

"In the US, the wealthiest one percent captured 95 percent of post-financial crisis growth since 2009, while the bottom 90 percent became poorer."

Do I have your attention? It is definitely too large a number for me to wrap my brain around, but I do know that $110 trillion dispersed among just 85 families is a whole lot of jack! That makes Gordon Gekko and all of his friends look like paupers, and Johnny Stewart isn't even in the game. What does this mean to Black folks in the United States? And let's not even talk about the other countries.

A previous piece, "The revolution must be financed," pointed out that everything we say we want and need to do begins and/or ends with someone writing a check. Juxtapose that fact against the Oxfam report and marinate for a while on our relative economic position in this country.

During the housing collapse Black people lost hundreds of billions of dollars in wealth, more than any other group. We were already way behind before the recession; where do you think we are now? What is our children's economic position? What does the future hold for Black Americans, collectively, especially since we are a microcosm of the world's wealth concentration model?

That's right; we have the same relative situation going on with Black money. A small percentage of Blacks holds a large percentage of all Black wealth. You know the most popular ones, from Oprah and Bob Johnson on down to the entertainers and athletes, but there are other business owners whom many of us have never heard of who hold billions as well. This is not an effort to make them out to be culprits; this is merely about facts, and then what if anything you are willing to do to help change our situation.

Now let's get one thing straight, those 85 families are not going to come to our neighborhoods and drop bags of money from helicopters, and the richest Black folks are not going to do that either. As a matter of fact, some of them are too busy being Johnny Stewart (Gotta have that bling). So once again the call goes out to our people to look at the facts and get with the program. Economic inequality will always be with us; therefore, we must not waste our time and resources trying to reach "equality;" we simply need to spend as much time raising our individual and collective wealth as we spend trying to have an impact on politics.

It is now estimated that Black people in the U.S. have exceeded $1 trillion in annual income, which only means something positive to those on the receiving end of that money. Income vs. wealth? No brainer, right? Yes, it takes some sort of income to create wealth, but it will also take good stewardship and "common cents" among our people to reach the lofty heights of economic stability.

Look at economic indicators across the board and you will find Black folks at the bottom of every category. Unemployment, business growth (not start-ups), Black owned firms with employees, average annual sales revenue, poverty, health, education, and a lack of structured economic empowerment initiatives are challenges to our wellbeing and future prosperity and, if not changed, will prove to be our demise. And they say our economy is doing much better, that it's growing. For whom?

Our President subscribes to the Reagan model of economics that says, "A rising tide lifts all boats." I say, if you have no boat a rising tide can also drown you. Blacks need to save and pool mo' money, buy some boats, and get in on this rising tide of economic prosperity.

Accelerating Affluence and Perpetuating Poverty

"It turns out that advancing equal opportunity and economic empowerment is both morally right and good economics, because discrimination, poverty and ignorance restrict growth, while investments in education, infrastructure and scientific and technological research increase it, creating more good jobs and new wealth for all of us."
William J. Clinton

The role we play in our own economic demise is mind-boggling. First of all, our priorities are screwed up. We place more emphasis on some of the most meaningless issues and aspects of life. We use much of our time talking about the preachers, the husbands, the housewives, the Grammys, the Oscars, the fashions, and yes, politics, and fail to do what it takes to empower ourselves. This is a case of the poorest in our society doing everything they can to further enrich the affluent.

Of course, it is by design and there has to be a willing and, as Amos Wilson said, "stupid" consumer class to maintain our capitalistic system. But this is not a diatribe against rich people; as a matter of fact, I wish we had more rich people rising from the ranks of the poor. The intent of this article is to illustrate our participation in keeping ourselves in the very place we complain about being.

The affluent are piling up more cash than they could spend in three lifetimes, and they never get distracted from that mission. They do not succumb to being dumbed down by silly, time-wasting, no-redeeming-value, TV shows. They are not swooning over politics; they know it's nothing but a game and a means for them to get even richer. Yes, some of them are even willing to break the law, sacrifice their morality, and do unethical things to get what they want; but I am certainly not suggesting we go that far.

I am suggesting that we stop being the fodder for this economic system, at least not to the extent we are now. I am suggesting that we take ourselves more seriously and start playing to win. Aside from the obvious problems for our children, this is also a problem for the country. The rich save and the poor spend, which heightens the importance of income inequality. If the vast majority of the money in the system always finds its way to the top 1%, thereby, not very likely to be spent, as it relates to Black and poor people, how does that affect consumption, which comprises two-thirds of our GDP?

It's one thing to talk about income and wealth disparities, but it's an entirely different thing to get down to the business of doing something about it. We can, as Red said in the movie, Shawshank Redemption, "Get busy livin' or get busy dyin'" and that begins by studying and learning how business is done in this country. Find out what your individual role is and what our collective role is, and then change the paradigm.

Stop buying so much stuff that others make; start buying more of what we make. Stop complaining about others starting businesses in our neighborhoods; start our own. Slow down spending; increase saving. Use Black financial planners, tax preparers, accountants, lawyers, and yes, sports agents, start building a relationship with a bank, a Black bank if possible, and stop falling for those celebrity prepaid debit card rip-offs.

I understand that some folks cannot get checking accounts, which causes some of them to fall prey to high profile celebrities who endorse cards that charge usury fees. But regardless of your situation, you should try to build a relationship with a bank or credit union, and stop paying outrageous fees to spend your own money?

Those cards, backed by the likes of Russell Simmons, Magic Johnson, Lil' Wayne, just to name a few, only increase their affluence and perpetuate your poverty. They charge loading fees, monthly fees, ATM fees, and even "inactivity" fees, of which the so-called "Rush Card" has the highest. Check them out for yourself, and stop being clowned by these guys and their backers. If you must use a prepaid card, find the cheapest one; you don't need a celebrity's face on it or an endorsement by a celebrity for it to work for you.

Finally, in his SOTUS the President said no one should to have to raise a family in poverty, and therefore we need to raise the minimum wage to $10.10. Poverty level for a four-person household is $23,850; at $10.10 per hour and with one person working, that household would earn $21,008. Duh! Don't get emotionally hyped by mere words; do some research and know the facts. Accounting for inflation and productivity, some reports indicate the minimum wage should be even higher, and unless it is tied to inflation, with raises every year, "10-10" will go down in history as just another cute political phrase.

Sure, we should raise wages for the lower tier of workers, but that in and of itself will not make a dent in the "inequality gap" now being discussed. As stated earlier, poor people spend; rich people save. Thus, the cycle continues. Unless we change our economic habits there will always be an acceleration of affluence among the affluent and a perpetuation of poverty among the impoverished.

Employed by the unemployed

"Because the Negro does not own and control retail establishments in his own community, he is unable to stabilize his community... The Negro must pool his capital in order to help himself.... This will enable him to solve his own problems." S.B. Fuller

Has the thought ever occurred to you that despite having the highest unemployment rate in this country, our job creation rate is perched at the other end of that spectrum? That's right; Blacks are some of the best job creators in this nation. We have created jobs in the clothing industry, the entertainment industry, the communications industry, the food industry, the liquor industry, the music industry and, oh yes, the prison industry. There are many other areas I could name, but I am sure you get what I'm driving at by now.

Amos Wilson, in his book, Afrikan-Centered Consciousness Versus the New World Order, posits, "How different our education would be if we sent our children to school to create jobs for themselves, to create their own economic and political systems, to see themselves as the major source of their own employment." He continued, "…I heard about some people protesting for jobs and pushing other people for jobs. I asked the question: Do we know how many jobs we really create for other people?"

No, Brother Wilson, I don't think we do. Paradoxically, and much to my chagrin, Black folks, the very ones who need jobs the most are too busy *maachin'* and begging someone else for jobs, rather than using the same money we spend to create jobs for others to create jobs for ourselves. In other words, we, the unemployed, are virtually employing others via our silly response tactics and our ridiculous spending habits.

We live our lives vicariously by buying a $500.00 bottle of vodka because we want to run in Diddy's circle of friends. We hoist a bottle of outrageously expensive cognac up in "da club" trying to be Jay-Z, a guy who could buy and sell most of us in a heartbeat. These celebrities and others hawk the wares of folks who make a very good living from the $1.1 trillion Black people earn each year. We provide the profit margins for several industries, thereby, keeping many people employed.

The other point is that high profile Blacks, mainly entertainers and athletes, earn a large portion of their money by being entrepreneurs. They sell stuff, some of which creates jobs for others, but all of which allows them to fly on private jets and drink high-priced liquor. We cannot do that, and all the fake, pretentious, wannabe spending in the world will not make that possible; what it does is continue the cycle of the unemployed: create jobs and keep others employed.

Economic freedom, not "economic equality" must be our goal. Equality requires measurement against someone else's standard; it requires the party seeking equality, by default, to elevate someone else and seek his standard, his approval, and his acceptance. It makes little sense to get into that game because every time we reach that standard, it can—and will be changed to an even higher standard.

Economic freedom was the clarion call in years past, just as it is now. Many have propagated that message and we have yet to heed it in a collective manner ever since we lost our minds over politics in 1965. Economic freedom means setting our own standards, and not having to meet those set by others. Economic freedom means the ability and willingness, and dare I say eagerness, to create jobs for our children.

Economic freedom means that we have multiple streams of income that can, of course, empower us individually and then empower us collectively. Economic freedom means producing, manufacturing, and distributing; it means owning natural resources to whatever extent possible and vertically integrating our businesses.

Economic freedom, as Dr. Claud Anderson advocates, means aggregating our dollars and utilizing them to our own advantage rather than some else's. Economic freedom means what Pastor Jonathan Weaver and the Collective Empowerment Group are doing: leveraging the large number of church members and their spending capacity, and obtaining reciprocity from the marketplace. Economic freedom means, as S.B. Fuller and Malcolm X said, "Control."

Currently Black folks for the most part are out of control and/or under control. We cannot be economically free under those circumstances. *"No people can be free who themselves do not constitute an essential part of the ruling element of the country in which they live. The liberty of no man is secure who controls not his own destiny. For people to be free they must necessarily be their own rulers."* Martin Delaney – The Political Destiny of the Colored Race on the American Continent"

How strange it would be to our elders if they knew we, the unemployed, were creating jobs and wealth for everyone else except ourselves.

Black Business—Start-ups vs. Growth

I'm a fundamental believer in strong partnerships. My success is written through partnership relationships. My first partner at BET, John Malone, gave me the capital, gave me the support, and gave me the mentorship. All of these things were vital to my success and I believe that in every business I go in, I look to see if I can find a partner who shares my values, shares the vision,

and believe that working together, we can achieve more in partnership than we can achieve separately.
      Robert Johnson

While the 2012 Economic Census data have not yet been released, I am certain we will see another increase in the number of Black owned businesses in the past five years, since the last census was taken. As a matter of fact Black business start-ups increased at the highest rate during the previous census period. It's great that we are going into business, but shortsighted for us to stop there and celebrate just the number of businesses and overlook the growth of those businesses. Understanding that most small businesses go out of business in a few years, it is vital that we concentrate on growing the businesses we have in addition to merely counting them.

The 2007 census data indicate that of the nearly two-million Black owned businesses, only 106,566 had employees; the total number of employees is 909,552, not all of whom are Black, of course, with an annual payroll of just over $23 million. Please take a moment and juxtapose those stats against the $1 trillion annual income of Black people in this country, and then analyze the information relative to our population size and the percentage of Black businesses that are sole proprietorships.

One-person businesses are not inherently bad; don't get me wrong. However, the problem with approximately 5% of Black owned businesses having employees indicates a dearth in business growth within our ranks. With that same scenario being repeated from census to census Black economic empowerment via the very engine that moves this nation and the world—business—will never be achieved. That is a prescription for falling even further behind, especially when you consider the realignment of geopolitical power and influence; Black businesses must not only be started, they must be grown to a scale that hires more people and increases their value proposition.

We have heard and continue to hear the litany of excuses and reasons for why our businesses are in the shape they are in and, believe me, I have heard just about all of them. I understand the history connected to our businesses and how they were excluded from the general marketplace and how they have been discriminated against by lenders and equity funds. I know we had to take nontraditional steps to establish our businesses, and we did pretty well at it, in spite of the treatment we received and the government actions that inhibited us.

The main question now is, "How can we make the appropriate changes necessary to attain business growth in today's economy, which is the measurement of business success?" Several come to mind. Equity Funds specifically earmarked for Black businesses and lending programs are the two most cited answers to the problem. Equal access to capital by traditional credit organizations and consumer support are also mentioned quite frequently.

There are other creative ways to provide an influx of capital to Black owned businesses, but there are also a few caveats that include the responsibility of the business owner to take care of his or her business by providing great customer service, operating an ethical business, properly managing their finances, staying informed and educated about their particular business field, providing good products and services, adding value to their customer base, and simply doing what they say they will do, i.e. showing up on time, and charging a fair price for their goods and services. Notice I said "fair" not "cheap."

In the vein of being informed, educated, and honest business owners, and since capital is nearly always the issue that prohibits business growth, let's look at what Leonard Greenhalgh and James Lowery say in their book, <u>Minority Business Success</u>, about access to capital. "… *increasing access to capital without making sure the money will generate long-term revenue streams amounts to 'throwing money at the problem,' and we have squandered billions of dollars demonstrating how ineffective that tactic is. The emphasis needs to be on development of minority businesses, of which capitalization is just one element. Successful development involves a comprehensive integrated set of interventions. Piecemeal solutions have never worked and will never work. That is why our efforts need to be refocused.*"

They were absolutely correct in their assessment and recommendations, and I invite you to get a copy of their book to see the entirety of their presentation on business growth. Yes, we definitely need to refocus from how many businesses we have to how much they have grown. Take the lessons of successful Black owned businesses operating today; learn from them and mimic them as much as possible. That way Black people can live out the entrepreneurial legacy left by our forebears

So let's spend a little less time complaining and more time building our businesses with tried and true strategies and positive traits of great entrepreneurs—Black and any other color; because the main color in business is green.

Voting - A Means, Not an End

"The vote is precious, it is almost sacred...It is the 'most powerful nonviolent tool' we have in a Democratic society. And we got to use it!"
John Lewis

I believe the dollar is the most "powerful nonviolent tool" in a Democratic society. Why? Because this society is more capitalistic than it is "Democratic." This "precious vote" thing has really gotten to me. It's precious but we loyally and eagerly give it away to a party that gives us nothing in return. If it is so powerful, why isn't that power working on our behalf? Abraham Maslow said, "If a hammer is the only tool you have, you will see every problem as a nail." If the vote is our only tool, we will see voting as the solution to every problem we have. We have one trillion more tools in our toolkit; they are called dollars.

So let's stop believing that all we have to do is vote to make it all better. Further, it's so silly for Black people to fight over the Dems and Repubs, and it is counterproductive for us to be enslaved by either party. Between the late 1800's and the mid-1900's we voted nearly 100% Republican. Now we vote nearly 100% Democrat. What has that gotten us besides being ignored and taken for granted? Do we have any real political power? If we do, why are we so far behind?

We have been instructed and admonished to be independent and only give our votes to individuals who act in our best interests, but we have failed miserably in response to that advice by doing the exact opposite. It makes no sense to give virtually all of our support to one political party and receive patronizing crumbs in return.

To a large extent, our problem is centered on our romance with the vote itself. We hold our ability to cast a ballot in such high esteem, sadly, as though that alone will solve our problems. Not so. Voting is simply the first step, not the final step. Without power behind our precious votes, we are a paper tiger, helpless to effect positive change for ourselves in the political arena. The key word in the last sentence is, "ourselves," because we have certainly helped make things better for other groups.

So, with our political predicament in mind, here are my thoughts: If we are unwilling to vote as independent critical thinkers, we should stay out of the voting booth. If we are not inclined, on a local and national level, to collectively leverage our voting power, then all we will ever have is the power to vote. If all we are going to do is vote, there is no need to vote at all.

Now before some of you get your jaws tight, just think about all the energy Black folks have put into voting. Think of all the sacrifices we have made, all the mistreatment we have suffered and even this month (March 2014), as we remember "Bloody Sunday," how we are still fighting to keep our precious vote. Compare all of that to what we have gained by merely casting our votes and then going back to sleep. We have treated elections like popularity contests and euphoric exercises that only give someone a "job" for as long as they want it, whether they produce or not. We have misused and abused our votes by being uninformed on issues and candidates alike, and by being unwilling to do anything except vote for whatever or whomever the party tells us to. That's sheer nonsense. If our vote is so sacrosanct, why do we mistreat it?

As much as we say we need "power," both political and economic, our actions belie our words. Dr. Claud Anderson, in his book, <u>Black Labor White Wealth</u>, wrote, "...groups aspiring to gain political power can only obtain and use it if they have economic power as well...Voting rights have pacified Blacks by allowing them to make choices but never decisions."

If voting alone gave us power, we would not have heard "You lie!" during the State of the Union Address; if it gave us power, Darrell Issa would not have dissed one of our most respected and respectable congressmen, Elijah Cummings; and Paul Ryan would not have uttered his ridiculous comments about "inner city" men. Voting is part of the process that, if supported by economic power, leads to real political power.

Amos Wilson wrote, *"The idea that [Blacks] can exercise effective power, political or otherwise, without simultaneously exercising economic power is a fantasy...In the absence of access to and influence on relevant government centers of power, the absence of an 'independent' political party, and the absence of an influential, wealthy, nationalistic upper or leading class [Blacks] are unable to effectively secure [our] special interests."*

For example, Wilson also said, *"We have a leadership that talks about income equality. A man can have $1,000,000 worth of land and get an income of $10,000, and another get an income $10,000 working for someone else. Even though they have equal incomes, they are not equally wealthy."* Politics leads to incomes; economics leads to wealth. That's why back in 1998 I coined the term, "Blackonomics" rather than "Blackolitics."

Brother Tarikh Bandele wrote in 2006, "Indeed, Black people should register to vote, but not to become lackeys for [any] Party...voting, by itself, should never be looked upon as the ultimate solution. Voting is but a tactic, a strategy, or a means to an end...far too many are promoting the idea that all Black people need to do is vote, and heaven is just around the corner."

We want "voting power" but we settle for the "power to vote." We fight for the "right to vote" but we fail to "vote right." Voting is a means to gain political power, not an end that simply allows one to participate in the act. If we fail to follow that truism, we may as well not vote.

When Elephants and Donkeys Fight

Politicians fight all the time, but they never really lose. We lose.

The Kenyan Proverb, "When elephants fight the grass suffers," is very apropos to us, the grassroots. Only in our case, we are fighting over elephants and donkeys, but we are still the ones suffering. We watch the two parties fight every day, and then we take sides and jump in. Who is hurt by that? Certainly not them; it's always us who are hurt, us who are left behind, and us who are ignored and taken for granted. They get rich while we suffer.

Is the term "political hypocrisy" redundant? Don't worry, that's a rhetorical question; I know the answer, and I am sure you do as well. In follow up to the previous essay on "Voting," I could not help but stay on the political subject a little while longer. After all, the mid-terms are coming up and, as usual, Black pundits are telling us this will be the "most important election of our time,"—again. How many times have you heard that?

I must reemphasize, don't mistreat your precious vote by giving it away to someone or some issue that is not in your best interests. Don't be swayed by the talking heads that would have you walk lock-step with one political party or the other and vote a "straight" Democrat or Republican ticket. Strengthen your vote by being informed and casting it wisely.

The road to political power is paved with hypocrisy—on both sides of the aisle. We can look back and recall many things that have been said relative to a position taken and later that position was switched to the complete opposite side of the argument. One egregious example is the continued insistence by the warmongers to "get to the bottom" of the Benghazi situation. They use the "four" lives that were lost to justify their ire and outrage against Hillary Clinton; but the same crowd, led by Chaney, Rumsfeld, and Condoleezza Rice, was responsible for some 5000 lives lost in that unnecessary war in Iraq. What hypocrites! All life is sacred, but politicians only value the lives of our soldiers when it's convenient for them and fits their agenda for reelection.

A similar example of hypocrisy is the President's use of drones that have killed innocent people. Railing against the killing of innocents in Iraq and then killing more innocents in Afghanistan and Pakistan is hypocrisy. How about raising the debt ceiling? Many politicians are for it when their guy is President, but against it when the other guy gets in.

Hypocrisy reigns among the elephants and the donkeys as they fight each other. The rancor and hate-filled speeches and remarks by party sycophants on so-called television "news" shows are disgusting and hypocritical as well. We have dueling networks, Fox and MSNBC, who make no bones about showing us how much they hate and love President Obama, respectively. Fox vilifies Obama and MSNBC holds him up like he is a god. Both are wrong, of course, but we take sides and suffer even more from their fight.

I am sickened by the shameful acts of various politicians and the parties they blindly support. But even worse is the grassroots crowd and how we relate to so-called leaders who are supposed to be concerned about our wellbeing and this nation's future. We eat up anything they and their lap-dog mouthpieces say, and then we regurgitate it to our own people like it's the Gospel itself—suffering all the more for our lack of inquisitiveness, critical thought, and knowledge.

Here's the bottom-line: We must stop falling for the hype and being used and abused in the process. While the elephants and donkeys fight, and as we take sides, our children's futures are going down the drain; our hope of economic empowerment is waning; our status and position in this country are diminishing; our gravitation toward politics and aversion for economic empowerment continue to push us further down the ladder; and as we continue to follow self-aggrandizing mis-leaders we will slowly but surely die, and our children will end up being permanently dependent and at the mercy of those in control of this country.

Let the elephants and donkeys fight, just get out of range and off the field of battle so you will not be trampled under their feet. Notice that while they fight all the time, neither one dies. That's because one does not want to kill off the other. They just want you to keep watching the fight and keep your mind diverted from the important things—like your own wellbeing and your own future.

If you are not convinced to stop enabling the elephants and donkeys by cheering for one or the other, grab your popcorn, keep our ringside seat, and enjoy the fight; but know that only you will be hurt in the end.

The cost of getting older

"If I knew I would live this long I would have taken better care of myself."

We are at a critical stage in the economy when "more than one-third of workers (36%) have a measly $1,000 saved for their later years," according to a study by the Employee Benefit Research Institute. "Compare that to the 28% of workers who said they had $1,000 saved in last year's survey, and the picture gets a little more grim," the article continued. The report refers to all workers; that 36% likely skyrockets when applied to Black people. You know what happens when America gets a cold—we get pneumonia.

With baby boomers at the head of the mortality line, all we can do now is reflect on the financial "what ifs" in our lives and try to figure out how to live with $1,000.00 or less in the bank. The millennial generation had better pay close attention to their finances and start saving as early as possible to keep from making the same money mistakes their parents and grandparents made.

First and foremost, be very careful with those student loans. Leaving school with a debt of tens of thousands of dollars, even before you get a job, is a prescription for financial disaster. I know the money is great to have, especially what some of you call your "monthly check," which is in excess of what your tuition requires. But you will have to pay it back no matter what, with interest of course. Imagine trying to find and keep a job, a car, a place to live, and food to eat, while having to pay a monthly note of $400-$600 for a student loan for the next twenty or thirty years! When you get old you may also end up in the group with less than $1000.00 saved for retirement.

Keep in mind that a college education, while it is very important and necessary in this economy, is not worth what it used to be. Thus, it would be prudent to forego that high-priced school you want to attend and consider a smaller community college, a tech school, or an HBCU. Unless you get a scholarship that covers most or all of your costs, a smaller less expensive school is the way to go.

I know most young people refuse to acknowledge it, but if you keep living you will get old. Question is: "What will getting older cost you?" In today's economy it is very expensive. And who knows what will happen to Social Security and Medicare? The way things are going now, young people will be pretty much on their own when they get old, so it's best to get a Roth IRA started now, or at least some kind of saving plan that will multiply and be there at retirement. (A few dollars saved each month now will multiply into hundreds of thousands or even a million dollars by the time you reach retirement age.) Don't put all your eggs in one basket by simply depending on your employer's contribution to your 401-K and insurance plan. Unless you "own" the job you have, it can be taken away from you at any time, along with your retirement plan and your insurance policy.

Understand, young people, that if a young athlete or entertainer can go broke after making unwise decisions with his or her millions of dollars, your $80,000 per year will evaporate at a much faster pace, especially if you try to live like they live. Be smart, learn from the mistakes of others, and understand that you do not have to end up like the current 36% in this country.

The other caveat for young people as they prepare for their retirement is the dreaded conspicuous consumption syndrome. In an article I wrote some years ago, titled, "Supply and Demand," I noted that Black folks demand and others supply us with their goods and services. Anything someone makes we will buy it, no matter how much it costs. Just look at Nick Young of the L. A. Lakers who recently had his home burglarized of a pair of $6,000.00 shoes called "Nike Air Yeezy 2." That reminded me of basketball star, Antoine Walker, getting robbed of a $55,000.00 watch.

A great article on this subject is featured on The Root website, written by Demetria L. Lucas, titled, "Fronting: We Need to Stop Living the 'Fabulous and Broke' Lifestyle. It's time to put the 'fake it till you make it' philosophy out to pasture." She wrote, "My wake-up call came… when my friend called me in a panic, not knowing what to do. He was around $30,000 in credit card debt and had student loans. That friend ended up moving back in with his parents for a year-plus so he could save money to pay off his credit cards. (More than 10 years later, he's still paying off student loans.)"

The cost of getting old is high—be prepared.

Black Capitalism – Fulfillment or Failure?

"We must produce more than we consume and earn more than we spend. Otherwise, growth and wealth-building are impossible…if we remain weak economically, it will make little difference how educated we are or how many politicians we have. In Capitalist America, you cannot build wealth and financial security with just a job. You must own…businesses to generate profit income and invest to generate interest income."
Robert Taylor, Better Life Club

In light of what most of us know about the economy and where Black people fit, mostly as consumers rather than producers, a discussion of Black Capitalism is in order. The term was promoted by Stokley Carmichael in 1966 as part of the "Black Power" movement, but came into vogue in 1968 when the Nixon administration adopted it from a proposal by Robert Kennedy. Black Capitalism originally called for loan assistance, credit guarantees, and technical assistance for Black owned businesses in an effort to stimulate economic development in the ghettos.

Black Entrepreneurship in America, by Shelly Green and Paul Pryde, cites, "[Black capitalism] constituted a movement by Blacks to gain control over the business development of their own communities... Directing business growth in the Black community was considered the first step toward achieving a powerful Black economic presence in the larger American economy. [It] called for a new kind of social contract among racial groups in America—one based on mutual self-interest rather than integration."

Andrew Brimmer, noted economist and Lyndon Johnson appointee to the Federal Reserve Board, had a different perspective on Black Capitalism. In the book, A Different Vision: African American Economic Thought, edited by Economist, Thomas Boston, Brimmer wrote, "...the strategy of Black capitalism offers a very limited potential for economic advancement for the majority of the Black population."

In support of his contention, Brimmer posited, "The ghetto economy...does not appear to provide profitable opportunities for large scale business investment." He noted a large part of the problem was due to "a tendency for affluent Blacks to shop in the more diverse national economy."

Brimmer says Black Capitalism fails because it is founded on the premise of self-employment, as opposed to employment in salaried positions where the rewards are greater and the risks are much lower. (That reality gives credence to Thomas Boston's "20 by 10" strategy of Black businesses hiring Black employees.)

Brimmer suggested that Black Capitalism "may retard Blacks' economic advancement by discouraging many from the full participation in the national economy..." His position assumed that corporations would hire Blacks; but his concern about the greatest risk being placed on those who can least afford to take risks is quite valid. We have several examples of that reality in Black businesses today.

Has Black Capitalism worked? Is it working? One thing is certain: Korean Capitalism is working. They control the Black hair care market via their stores in the ghettos, where Black folks are their only customers; and Koreans hire their own people as well. This is a great example of how "segmented" capitalism can and does work.

Economist, Milton Friedman wrote, "History suggests only that capitalism is a necessary condition for political freedom [since many nations can be identified that have] economic arrangements that are fundamentally capitalist and political arrangements that are not free."

History Professor, Dr. Juliet E.K. Walker, wrote, "The existence of Black entrepreneurship... provides an example of an economic arrangement in this nation's antebellum free enterprise system that was fundamentally capitalistic, but within which some of the capitalists, the African Americans, were not fundamentally free."

The problem with Black Capitalism is structural inequity due to a paucity of government support. Just as the government has subsidized large corporations, it should do the same for Black businesses. The International Journal of Humanities and Social Science (November 2012) carried a paper written by Ryan Very, titled, Black Capitalism: An Economic Program for the Black American Ghetto, in which Mr. Very made a good case for government support of Black Capitalism.

Here is the Abstract from that paper: *The American federal government supported the creation and expansion of economically depressed urban residential areas where blacks live in segregation from whites. These ghettos face barriers to economic development including high unemployment, a low wage labor market, capital drain, and market dualism. Three popular ghetto economic development strategies are ghetto dispersal, corporate branch planting, and black capitalism. Black capitalism breaks the ghetto's economic barriers better than ghetto dispersal and corporate branch planting, but it will only be possible with significant support from whites and the federal government.* In other words, the government caused the problem, and the government should fix it.

Mr. Very continued, "Black access to capital coupled with subsidized entrepreneurial training services would...allow more residents to start their own potentially successful businesses in the ghetto. With a sizeable government subsidy, ghetto residents could even build manufacturing plants. If ghetto residents would export enough manufactured goods, both the drain of capital and the (neighborhood) trade deficit would decrease."

Until Blacks understand our economic and political positions in this country, we will continue to languish in what Dr. Ron Daniels calls, the "Dark Ghettos" of *either or*, and we will never move to the land of *both and*.

Where do we stand?

"Tell me somethin' good."
Chaka Khan

The 2014 National Urban League (NUL) report, <u>State of Black America, "One Nation Underemployed</u>; Jobs Rebuild America," contains a lot of great information, but it will only prove to be "good" if we use it to build a solid and long lasting economic base. The 236-page report has statistics and insights Black people need to know—and act upon, but knowledge is only power if we use it.

For the most part, Black people in this country are at the bottom of every good category and at the top of every bad one. Of course most of us don't need the NUL or anyone else to tell us that; we see it every day all around us, but supporting statistics are a great way to drive the point home. Sad to say, our overall "state" is not good. (Sorry, Chaka)

I would love to see a report on the "Fate" of Black America. Maybe that would wake us up and get us involved in changing our "state." Reports on our "state" are nice but they usually tell us what we already know. Acknowledging and discussing our fate might scare us into implementing long term, solution-based, and work related approaches to our challenges.

I was intrigued by some of the responses to our "state" by Black folks. For instance, an article titled, <u>NUL State Of Black America 2014 Report Says Minorities Losing Economic Ground</u>, by Jesse Holland, states, "Despite the 'dismal' numbers an analysis by The Associated Press-NORC Center for Public Affairs Research found African-Americans significantly more 'optimistic' about their future standard of living than whites…" Holland went on, "The survey found high optimism even among Blacks who say racism is a cause for economic inequality." My reaction was, "Say what?"

Another irony in the NUL report referred to the new "Chocolate City," Memphis, TN., which is 63% Black, according the 2010 U.S Census (The NUL report says 46%), yet ranks the "most equal for 'Hispanics' in unemployment equality" (3.8%), compared with a 6.5% unemployment rate for whites." The unemployment rate for Blacks in Memphis is 16.6%. What's wrong with that picture?

Optimism is commendable, but apathetic responses to old problems, and using the same failed measures of the past, is irrational. We should know by now what relying on hope and optimism brings. MLK's words, "Why we can't wait," and the "Fierce urgency of now" ring true. Do we just recite his words, or do we act upon them? As I have asked before, "Just how long is 'now'?"

It's been 46 years since King died in Memphis, fighting for economic rights. An article on nashvillescene.com stated, Memphis is "Among worst of the U.S. cities to be Black, male, and unemployed." The city just spent $28 million to revamp the civil rights museum; I wonder how many jobs were created for Black men on that project, and how much of the $28 million went to Black contractors. Did Blacks in Memphis settle for symbolism over substance, or did they get both?

Information on the State of Black America is great, but if we don't change our inappropriate behavior we will continue to be distracted from the real solutions to our problems. Heck, Tavis Smiley televised the revolution for several years. What did we do with that? I am worn out by our tepid and sometimes total lack of response to the problems we face in this nation.

It's frustrating to see Black people settling for a nebulous request for "jobs" and an increase in the minimum wage to $10.10. We do need more jobs, but we must create some of those jobs ourselves, and be able to hire a higher percentage of our own workforce.

We must have entrepreneurship included in our schools' curricula, and grow our businesses via support and strategic alliances. The NUL report states, "We must recognize…entrepreneurship as the most important vehicle of economic development in the Black community." To that, I say, "Amen!"

Our "high optimism" alone will not take us to the promise land of "economic equality"? Complacent optimism makes us feel good in our misery; pragmatism makes us work to "do good" and do well at the same time. It also motivates us to do the work necessary to get out of our miserable position.

Curtis Mayfield wrote it, and EnVogue sang, "Giving him something he can feel." Great song, but it's better when coupled with the Isley Brothers' classic, "I got work to do." Let's move, as the Temptations sang, from "Standing on shaky ground" to "Standing on the top."

Crisis in Education

"What does 3.8% interest translate to for students? If we go back to that average figure of $26,600, compounding for interest year over year using the 10-year-payback plan that is the standard, the total cost of your $26,600 loan is about $38,600. Break that down by monthly payments and you are looking at about $320 per month going toward student loan payments. 'Debt costs you time in savings, pushes back when and whether you can buy a home, start a family, open a small business or access capital,' says Lauren Asher, president of TICAS. Not to mention the opportunity cost of the education itself at almost $40,000."

Forbes

We may as well call it "Edu-pay-tion," as far as many prospective students are concerned. The cost of a college degree has risen 1120% since 1978, but wages have increased a mere 6% during that same period. The national collective college debt is more than $1 trillion! We have college grads mired in $29,000 of debt, on average, while they are looking for jobs that do not exist. Parents and grandparents of those grads are also saddled with much of that debt, which is immune to bankruptcy, and they will have to make the payments until they die.

What have we gotten ourselves into? The greed that accompanied those easy-to-obtain, just-sign-here college tuition loans, borders on immoral. Financial institutions were like Black Friday crowds, trampling one another to get in on the act. New lending operations cropped up every day, and new proprietary colleges and universities opened their doors throughout the nation, advertising their degrees and easy to get loans for tuition. What would happen if students and parents just stop paying on that $1 trillion debt? Who would pay then? Bingo! I can see another bailout coming, and this time it will be for student loans.

Ethical implications exist on both sides—the lenders and the borrowers, but no matter what side you take the problem is still here and is looming as yet another bubble about to burst in the near future. As many schools are raising their tuition costs, despite the ominous specter of a meltdown, many prospective students are opting out of their plans to attend college. But where does that leave them in today's "jobless market"? Sounds like a catch-22.

This nation trails many other countries in various fields of education, and we will find ourselves even further behind if this tuition bubble is not deflated very soon. Our young people will not be able to compete on a national level, much less on an international level, without access to adequate, relevant, and higher educational experiences. In other words, the famous mantra, "Leave no child behind" will soon become, "Help every child catch up."

We have smart bombs and dumb children. We have the ability to kill people with drones without even seeing them, but we cannot—or will not—provide adequate education for our children whom we see every day. We have spent trillions destroying and rebuilding Iraq and Afghanistan, but a relative meager amount to secure the future of our own youth. Now we are sending money to Ukraine, along with all the other places to which our dollars flow, while our young people slip further down the education scale. Our priorities are all screwed up.

This is not to say that money alone will solve all of our education problems, but more of it, pointed in the right direction, sure would make a positive difference in our current educational crisis—and that's exactly what it is. Simply throwing money at a problem usually results in that money being caught by folks for whom it is not meant. The students are at the bottom of the food chain and see little or no benefit from money meant to help them.

Meanwhile, as we teach our children how to take tests rather than how to use their critical and analytical thinking skills, we are doing them a gross disservice. And similar to what we saw with the sub-prime housing debacle, if we continue to make financial institutions even wealthier by allowing them to make outlandish loans to college students who cannot afford to repay them, we will soon have another piper to pay.

So what do we do? Prospective students should start looking at less expensive alternatives to attain their college degrees. For instance, go to a local school and live at home (I know that's a tough one, but it beats having to go back to live with your parents when you graduate); stop treating your student loan like it's a free monthly check that you can use to buy everything but educational necessities; and, here's a novel idea: work while you are in college. It may not be the most glamorous job, but if it helps pay your tuition and keep you out of thousands in debt, that's a good thing.

Government and financial institutions worked so well when it came to the bailouts. Banks were too big to fail and had to be helped with $780 billion or so. Aren't our children too important to fail? Maybe they are not; at least not in this country, huh? Anyway, if they care to listen, banks, proprietary schools, and government officials should get together and stop the madness that has led to $1 trillion in student loan debt while graduates cannot get commensurate employment and cannot compete in a global society.

We cannot allow education to turn into "educ-pay-tion."

Obama courting billionaire kids

Unlike oil and water, politics and money mix very well.

The New York Times carried an article titled, "White House Hosts 'Next Generation' Young and Rich," in its Fashion and Style section, of all places, on April 18, 2014. The piece revealed several issues we need to be aware of as we move toward 2050; the year demographers say White people will be the minority in this nation. Unless you are among the most naïve people in the world, you know why the rich kids were summoned to the White House in the first place. So let's look at the bigger picture and its implications for Black people.

The piece notes, "Policy experts and donors recognize that there's no better time than now to 'empower' young philanthropists. Professionals in the field, citing an Accenture report from 2012, estimate that more than $30 trillion in wealth will pass from baby boomers to younger generations by around 2050." What an interesting convergence of events. Whites become the minority and $30 trillion is transferred to their children. Another interesting point is the apparent need to "empower" the young philanthropists. Since when have billionaires needed to be empowered?

The headline also discussed, "Including the Young and the Rich;" since when have billionaires needed to be included? They have always included themselves. Money controls politics; it's not the other way around. Thus, bringing rich kids to the White House for a tête-à-tête is nothing more than pandering, but the larger issue for Black folks is that we are not and will not be included in economic discussions as they pertain to control and empowerment. It ensures, as if that needs to be done, that while the political majority may be "minorities," the overwhelming economic majority will remain in the hands of the rich kids. But as the saying goes, "I ain't mad at 'em." They are taking care of their interests and their own people, while we continue to rely on charlatans and hucksters to show us the way to the next "maach."

There are two groups of people: those who are seeking power and those who already have power. It is pretty obvious what group the rich kids are in. By the way, I wonder if Bob and Sheila Johnson's kids were invited to the billionaire soiree. There were no Black kids in the photos I saw. But maybe the Johnson's don't have enough billions to qualify.

It is disheartening to watch Black people settle for so little from our abundance. No, we do not have the same resources as the rich kids, but we do have enough to command respect and to leverage economic and political benefits. But we have this "messiah complex" when it comes to leadership; we continually vie for the "HNIC" position in politics, religion, community activism, education, sports, and every other category, instead of establishing a cadre of proven, intelligent, unafraid, and un-beholden men and women to lead the way forward to economic empowerment.

Our attempts to gain economic freedom, since Martin Luther King, Jr. was murdered, have not worked, which is another reason Black rich kids were not summoned to the White House. To politicians the

Black elite are folks who have no independence. Heads of nonprofit organizations dependent on the largess of corporations owned by the rich kids, preachers who capitulate to the political whims of groups with whom they disagree on basic Biblical tenets, and talking heads who have been chosen by the rich kids to speak for Black people, are the ones called to the White House. They have no power; they only have influence.

In 2050 only the demographics will have changed. The real power—economic power—will still be in the hands of the rich kids featured in the New York Times article, and the so-called minorities will still be "maachin" and decrying voting rights infringements. The rich kids are planning for 2050 right now, and so are the top political players, while Black folks are celebrating the fact that we will be in the majority by then. What benefit will that bring us if we have no collective economic foundation from which to support ourselves and obtain reciprocity in the marketplace?

Land, labor, and capital, the basic assets necessary for economic empowerment, are what Black folks need to prepare for 2050. We don't need a bunch of bought-and-paid-for puppets bloviating about issues that hardly affect us at all. We don't need more photo opportunities, superficial press conferences with little or no follow through, and certainly not a continuation of endless rhetoric that rings hollow when it comes to our economic advancement. We are still economically enslaved in 2014, after all we have been led to believe by the HNIC's, and if we don't change now, we will still be economically enslaved in 2050.

In 2050 the rich kids will be in charge, and as the article cited, "Justin McAuliffe, a 24-year-old heir to the Hilton hotel fortune, was similarly impressed by the crowd. 'Hilton, Marriott, and Carlson,' he said. 'That is cool.'" Cool indeed!

City for Sale—Cheap

"The home of Motown, Cadillac, and Joe Louis
Through all this, we cannot be defeated, because we have never been
defeated.
You've built us, you've moved us, you've shaped us
Sometimes down, but never out
Take strength in us, your people
Stay up Detroit."
Eminem – "Letter to Detroit"

I remember when Vice President, Dan Quayle said we should be glad that foreigners are buying properties and land in our country; "America is for sale," he said. I guess he was correct, considering what we have seen over the past 25 years, especially what we see going on in Detroit now, where the most powerful person is the bankruptcy judge. It looks like the Chinese people want to get in on the Detroit property bonanza, along with many other Detroiters and Michiganders, of course. One person bought 428 homes for $379,100, and some are buying individual homes for as little as $500.00 each. According to the Detroit Radio website, "In Wayne County's 2013 auction, nearly 20,000 properties hit the auction block – about 90% of them in Detroit. Some could be had for as little as $500."

Since Detroit filed bankruptcy, and even before then, property in that town has been selling at an unprecedented pace. No one can blame folks for speculating and buying the land; we know Detroit will come back and once again be a great city. For Black folks, however, who comprise as high as 90% of the population, it will mean even less control of the economics of that town, despite occupying much of the political strata. Is this a microcosm of Black folks in general?

Surely Black people are buying some of the property too, but at the rate and volume others are buying it, including Chinese buyers, the Motor City is definitely in for a major transition as it emerges from bankruptcy. But as the sayings go, "Money talks" and "He who has the gold makes the rules."

Much has been written about Detroit's bankruptcy, but the bottom line is that it is being sold. Articles abound about China buying Detroit;

some say it's true others say not true. Forbes wrote a piece in December 2013, titled, "China's newest city: We call it Detroit," in which was stated, "Detroit, broke with almost no prospects for recovery, is the fourth most popular U.S. destination for Chinese real estate investors." If the buying spree keeps up, there is no way Detroit won't recover; folks aren't investing their money to take losses.

My Quayle memories notwithstanding, a little common sense tells me that America is for sale—to anyone who has the money to buy it, but my memory of the proposed "Maroon City" by former Detroit resident Dr. Claud Anderson, still haunts me. In 2005, during the comedic reign of Kwame Kilpatrick, Claud was quite prepared to develop a Black economic enclave in the heart of Detroit, but the Mayor and a few of his cronies decided that would be "racist," "divisive," "a suicidal form of 'reverse racism,' and a bad deal for Detroit," despite the existence of other ethnic economic enclaves in that Chocolate City. Black folks said those things, not Whites.

Fast forward to today, and we see a continued movement by everyone other than a major contingent of Black people buying Detroit properties. I wonder how Detroiters feel about Dr. Anderson's plan now as they watch the economic takeover of their city. Anderson, along with the support of Joann Watson, Kwame Kenyatta, and hundreds of citizens, were desperately trying to do what others before them had attempted.

In 1968, Detroit icon, Albert Cleage, said, "...This marks a new day for black people... The black community... must control its own destiny... this means political control of all areas in which black people are a majority... Politics is only one aspect, however. It is also necessary for blacks to have economic control of their community. In Detroit we are trying to invent strategies for this, such as the development of co-op retail stores, co-op buying clubs, co-op light manufacturing, co-op education...These ventures will give black people a sense of their economic possibilities and a realization of their need for economic training." The "Black Madonna" must be weeping right now.

While we have a tendency to revere folks like Cleage and Anderson and drop their names from time to time, we seldom follow their lead, as Carter G. Woodson said about Black folks in his book, <u>The Mis-Education of the Negro</u>. We love symbolism more than substance.

So as the sale of Detroit continues, I pray Black folks will carve out a significant piece for themselves in the city they have supported and built up for decades. If they don't capture this latest opportunity, Detroit will come back and Blacks will continue to be the fodder from which the wealth of other groups will be generated. Black people may indeed hold on to the politics, but the more important ingredients, economic control and ownership, will remain in the possession of others, thus, maintaining a system of dependence by Blacks upon those who own the assets.

The cost of doing business

"Let me issue and control a nation's money and I care not who writes the laws."
Mayer Amschel Rothschild.

I often wonder if most Black people in America really understand the across-the-board impact economics has on our daily lives. Or have we just been beaten down so badly that we have fallen into a state of apathy when it comes to our collective pursuit of economic empowerment? The above quote by Rothschild always reminds me of the kind of nation and world in which we reside. It also makes me even more aware of Black folks' economic position in this country, and our lack of emphasis on what's really important vis-à-vis real power.

What are the messages being given to Black people by many of our leaders? Well, they run the gamut from "civil rights" to "voting rights" to "gay rights" to "immigration reform" to someone calling one of us or all of us a name we don't like. Many unsuspecting Blacks are riled up about issues that do not and will not affect us one iota when it comes to being able to obtain power for ourselves. We spend an inordinate amount of time caught up in nonsensical discussions that only keep us from devoting energy to self-empowerment.

Maybe we are simply unwilling to "pay the cost to be the boss," as we like to say. Or, maybe the "cost of doing business" is just too high for us. Maybe we just want to continue to buy everything and anything other folks make and distribute rather than do those things for ourselves. Maybe we are just content to be the primary consumers in this nation.

The engine of the U.S. economy is fueled by consumption, which is 70% of our Gross Domestic Product (GDP), and that does not include purchases of new housing. Our current GDP is more than $15 trillion; do the math and see how much is being spent on goods and services. Question: Doesn't it make sense for Black people to be producing and selling much more than we do presently? With an aggregate annual income of more than $1 trillion, we could carve out a few niches in the business world and make a veritable killing.

When we look at per capita GDP by country, interestingly, we see that Liberia ranks among the lowest in the world. Why? Well, I have writings from Booker T. Washington to the officials in Liberia and Haiti warning them to be independent and to take full advantage of their land and natural resources by maintaining ownership and control over them. He admonished them not to allow foreigners to buy their land and use it for their own economic advantage. Unfortunately, they did not follow Washington's advice, and Liberia ended up signing 100 year leases on its rubber tree plantations to Goodyear, and Haiti, now the poorest nation in the western hemisphere, failed to control its beautiful island and turn it into a primary tourist attraction.

We are so hung-up on meaningless and powerless political discussions, and instead of mimicking even the smallest measure of what Rothschild said, we obviously keep thinking the politicians are going to take care of us. But they keep telling us things that will not move us forward economically. When it comes to economic advocacy, where is our voice in Washington?

Let's be honest. Over the last 50 years, Black people have cast millions of votes. We have helped elect thousands of Black public officials—and White ones too. In 2012, Black people voted at a higher rate than other minority groups and by most measures surpassed the white turnout for the first time. What has that gotten us, as it pertains to what Rothschild said? Suppose for the past 50 years we had cast our "little green ballots," as Booker T. directed us, to build our own economic infrastructure and support system. Had we done that, we too could say it does not matter who "writes the laws;" we would be true political powerbrokers.

Take reparations, in whatever form you support. What politicians in DC are seriously advocating for what Louis Farrakhan called, "Reparatory Justice?" John Conyers' bill has been languishing for decades now. The President says he does not support reparations for Black people, so where does that leave us? How about the political talking heads on TV? Are they devoting a serious amount of time talking about economic empowerment for Black people, or are they just trying to get us to vote a certain way?

Wake up, Black folks! The cost of doing business requires commitment and sacrifice. The Rothschild's were ruthless and unethical, but they knew that economics runs politics. We can build an ethical and moral economic foundation, but we have to jettison our current way of thinking and take on an economic mindset.

Economic Collapse

"On Oct. 29, 1929, the U.S. stock market crashed. America's economy collapsed, pulling many international markets down with it. It was the beginning of the Great Depression: an era of long bread lines, bankruptcies and hungry Dust Bowl sharecroppers that would last through most of the 1930s."
NPR

Imagine the U.S. dollar being worthless. Picture all of our millionaires and billionaires becoming "thousand-aires" overnight. Think about the possibility of two hundred million U.S. citizens being unable to eat unless the government provides food for them. Fathom a day when you check out your 401-k or your bank account and find nothing there. What would happen to social security and Medicare if the dollar was devalued to the point of being virtually worthless? The short answer to these scenarios: We would be in a world of hurt and misery.

As the recent Urban League Report stated, despite our current fiscal situation, Blacks are "optimistic" about our economic future. So it naturally follows that we seldom, if ever, give a thought to the possibility of an economic collapse in this country; after all, we are the world's "top economy" the "biggest, strongest, and the 'baddest' nation on earth." Our dollar is the reserve standard for the world; oil is traded in what we call "petrodollars," which assures that our economy will always rule because everybody needs energy, right? We are the "breadbasket" of the world, and everybody needs to eat, right? We are indeed "all that," aren't we?

In case you have been spending most of your time watching all of the award shows on BET, or the many other mindless, non-thought provoking distractions being tossed at us 24/7, you have no idea about the true state of our union. You are hung-up on what Donald Sterling said, what Stephen A. Smith and Michael Eric Dyson said, what that police commissioner in New Hampshire said, and what Mark Cuban said. You are ensconced in what Michelle Obama is wearing, what brand of Vodka Diddy drinks, Solange's elevator beat-down, and buying a $200.00 ticket for the Beyonce/Jay-Z concert.

While I understand the need for us to get away from the real world and reside in fantasy land for a while, the amount of attention we give to the 140 character banter of some celebrity or athlete, no matter how mindless or ridiculous it may be, is very dangerous. We have no sustainability, no patience, and no staying power when it comes to the things that really affect our lives and our very survival. In other words, we have been swept away from reality by reality shows through which we live vicariously; and to make matters even worse, we have fallen for the absolute delusion of economic progress in spite of all the indicators that point to the complete opposite.

We are not teaching our children and grandchildren about economics, wealth building, finance, entrepreneurship, inflation, hyperinflation, deflation, quantitative easing, cashless society, bartering, self-reliance, gold, silver, bitcoin, fiat, and the role of money in general. In many cases we adults have very little knowledge of these things. We are too busy working 70 hours a week to earn dollars that could be worthless in the next decade or two. We are not making efforts to prepare for the worst; we are not "hedging" our bets against economic collapse, and we are definitely not working to become more independent, which includes, at a minimum, being able to grow food and feed our children.

In general, we have very little understanding of what our government is doing and the plans it has for us just in case things get really bad financially. Yes, we talk about conspiracy theories all the time and we think we know about the Bilderbergers, the Council on Foreign Affairs, the Illuminati, Skull and Bones, the Boule, and all the other so-called secret societies that run the world. While they may make for great conversation, we cannot affect them one bit. They are doing their thing, and all we do is "talk" about them. Do you really think they care? When it's all said and done, if a collapse does come, they will be the ones we will have to depend upon because they have the vast majority of the wealth.

This is not meant just to instill fear in us, albeit, we are at the very bottom of every economic category; it is to stimulate us to use that fear to change our minds, to be more informed and active, and to direct our attention to economic empowerment in a world where that's all that counts. It is an effort to bring us back to where we once were when we took care of ourselves and built for future generations. It is a cry for a stronger and collective foundation of Spirit-led people who know that while we are on this earth we have an obligation to share our talents and to multiply them rather than squander or "bury" them in the ground of conspicuous consumption.

As for our position in this country right now, as a citizen of 1st century Rome said, "I smell smoke!"

How much are you worth?

During the enslavement of Black people, we were placed on the auction block and examined by prospective buyers to determine our worth. We were prodded, probed, poked, inspected, and sometimes rejected. "Open your mouth, boy; turn around, wench." Some would demand our mothers and fathers spread their legs to have their genitals inspected. "This one is well endowed, and he will be a good stud." Another would say, "This gal has strong legs and broad hips, and she will be able to bear many children."

In a 2010 report titled, <u>Lifting as we climb: Women of Color, Wealth, and America's Future</u>, posted by Insight - Center for community and Economic Development, a startling and unbelievable statistic was cited. Written by Mariko Chang, Ph.D., with the help of Meizhu Lui, Director of the Closing the Racial Wealth Gap Initiative, the report stated the median wealth for Black females from "36-49 years of age is $5.00!"

If you took statistics you may remember that the "median" is the number in the middle of a given set of numbers arranged in order of increasing magnitude. That being true, this statistic also means that some Black women in that age group have even less wealth, while the others cannot be too much higher, considering that $5.00 is right in the middle. Just for disclosure sake, the report used the term "women of color," which includes Hispanic women.

So what are we to make of yet another indicator of Black economic disparity—or should I say economic despair? Do we just shake our heads and continue down the path of apathy, giving into the notion that there's nothing we can do about it? Do we view it as a microcosm of our overall economic condition? Or, do we address this issue head-on with our "leaders" and demand economic, political, educational, and social change?

For perspective, the report also cites the following: "White women in the prime working years of ages 36-49 have a median wealth of $42,600. Prior to age 50, women of color have virtually no wealth. Moreover, in comparison to their same-sex white counterparts, women of color in the two youngest age groups, have less than 1% of the wealth of white women..." The report also noted the same relative statistics for Black men.

Compared to White people, Blacks are so far behind that it's almost meaningless to even discuss the "gaps" in income and wealth. In addition, compared to Asians and so-called "East Indians," who even exceed Whites in some categories, we have moved to fourth place on the economic scale, only barely ahead of Hispanics.

Notwithstanding what John Sibley Butler called the "Economic Detour" that Black people had to take to create wealth in this country, the discrimination against us in credit and land ownership, the lack of government assistance as opposed to the subsidies White companies received, we have come quite a distance in spite of having to run from behind with weights tied to our feet. But how much consolation can and should we take from that?

We are still in very poor economic shape as a whole, which the $5.00

wealth of Black women 36-49 years of age graphically indicates. Our families are still at the bottom in median net worth; our businesses are at the bottom in receipts and number of employees; and our children are still at the bottom in education and employment, but at the top in incarceration.

Doesn't this suggest to you that we have to change our economic behavior? Doesn't it indicate a dire need to develop multiple streams of income for our people? Doesn't our position in this country, much of its wealth having been built on the backs of our enslaved ancestors, point out that business as usual is a prescription for failure? How many more reports do we need? The one I cited was written four years ago in 2010, but there are so many others that were written over 100 years ago. What are we waiting for, the next crisis?

Some of our women are worth less now than they were on the auction block, and we are sitting around waiting for Barack Obama to make things right. We are ensconced in discussions about politics and politicians who are doing absolutely nothing to help us. We are spending our time on voting rights instead of economic rights, not understanding that our voting rights only lead to economic rights for the politicians and their hacks. We are not asleep; we are in a coma!

For twenty-one years I have been sounding the alarm via my column, first locally in Cincinnati, Ohio, and then nationally via the National Newspapers Publishers Association (NNPA), and others have done much the same thing for even longer. It is beyond frustration, beyond disappointment, beyond discouragement, and beyond disillusion that I submit another wake-up call to my people in hope and prayer that we will work together to change our economic situation in this country. Even though a segment of our women only have a net worth of $5.00, which is shameful and insulting, we have the collective wherewithal to raise that value exponentially. We have the economic capability to determine our own worth. Do we have the will do so?

The Black Power Conundrum

"Black power can be clearly defined for those who do not attach the fears of white America to their questions about it."
Stokely Carmichael

Frederick Douglass said, "Power concedes nothing without a demand, it never did and never will." I often wonder what Black people do not understand about that statement. We love to quote it, but when it comes to putting it into practice we fall far short of the spirit of Douglass' words. Maybe Douglass should have added this caveat: A demand is nothing without power to back it up.

In response to incidents of injustice we are quick to resort to the same old tactics directed by leaders who sell us out. They tell us, as our President told the Congressional Black Caucus a few years ago: "Take off your bedroom slippers. Put on your marching shoes," and hit the streets chanting and singing in an effort to show our discontent.

We gather in churches and listen to fiery speeches; we hold press conferences and show our disdain for the system and its oppressive behavior toward Black people. We offer milquetoast solutions to the worst of crimes against us. For instance, in Ferguson, Missouri, Al Sharpton advised us to stop having "ghetto pity parties." John Lewis called for martial law in Ferguson. (I am still trying to figure how he thinks implementing martial law, which has the power to suspend civil rights, is the answer to a problem he and others consider to be a suppression of civil rights.) Other iconic leaders say the problems in Ferguson can be solved simply by "voting."

Tepid solutions offered by our "leaders" do absolutely nothing to change our situation, because there is no power behind them. Demands sound great and make for good photo opportunities and press conferences, but they fall on deaf ears because they have no power backing them up. Thus, the conundrum of so-called "Black power." We know that power concedes nothing without a demand, but a demand not backed by real power gets no concessions.

In their quest to be important, many of our leaders are, as a comedian once said, "Impotent," which only exacerbates our collective situation and keeps us running like a hamster inside a wheel—going nowhere.

What we hear and see from some of our leaders is really embarrassing. Instead of, or even in addition to, putting forth their weak responses to killings on all levels, they should also offer strategies based on economic power. That's where the issue will be solved, but we are woefully inadequate when it comes to implementing economic sanctions that will bring real change.

Some of the local leaders in Ferguson understand the power of economics and have been promoting solutions thereof, but they had to take a backseat to the fly-in crowd, toward whom the media gravitated. Now that things have calmed down and the opportunists have left Ferguson, the folks who live there, along with continued collaboration with young advocates for economic solutions, can work together.

It is sad to see Black "powerbrokers" strut to the microphones and threaten folks, only to walk away with their proverbial tails between their legs, having received absolutely no concessions from the establishment. Rather than contenders, these folks are pretenders; and rather than powerbrokers, they are really "power-broke." The conundrum of today's notion of Black power resides in false bravado and impotence.

Anheuser Busch (A-B), Radisson, and Nike withdrew their economic support from the NFL. They know exactly where power resides: in dollar bills, y'all. They wielded their power immediately to show their "outrage" about domestic and child abuse.

A-B, domiciled in St. Louis, said, "We are not yet satisfied with the league's handling of behaviors that so clearly go against our own company culture and moral code." A-B took serious action against child abuse in Adrian Peterson's case, but did nothing in response to Michael Brown's abuse that occurred in their back yard. Did that go against their "moral code"?

Apparently Nike was not outraged by Eric Garner, Ezell Ford, and John Crawford, being "abused." Pardon me, but isn't abuse—no matter the form—still abuse? Pepsi Cola CEO, Indra Nooyi, spoke against the NFL but voiced no indignation about Marlene Pinnock's abuse on a California highway. Hypocrisy abounds in reactions to Ray Rice and Adrian Peterson, as with Michael Vick and his abuse of dogs, for heaven's sake. Dogs! But those company execs and others fail to speak out and use their economic clout to put a stop to the abuse of their

Black consumers by police officers because we have no power behind our demands.

Folks with power are not reluctant to use it to punish those who do not operate in their best interests. Black power has been reduced to calling for and falling for voting rallies and worn out speeches laced with demands not backed up by any real power at all. If we want others to change, we must change.

Frederick Douglass shed light on what freedom is when he said the turning point in his life as a slave was deciding to fight back and not allow himself to be whipped by Edward Covey. After defeating Covey by fighting back, Douglass said, *"I was nothing before ... I was a man now." The experience of fighting back made Douglass even more determined to be a free man. He described a feeling he never had before, a feeling of being released from the "tomb of slavery, to the heaven of freedom."*

He went on to say, *"My long crushed spirit rose, cowardice departed, bold defiance took its place; and I now resolved that, however long I remained a slave in form, the day had passed forever when I could be a slave in fact. I did not hesitate to let it be known of me, that the white man who expected to succeed in whipping [me], must also succeed in killing me."*

Praying and Fasting in Ferguson

"Paper Tiger" - *a person or thing that appears threatening but is ineffectual.*

Remember the Jena Six? Some 15,000 to 20,000 protesters went to Jena, Louisiana in 2006 to demonstrate against injustice. After all the speeches, threats, marches, and church rallies, the people went home and nothing really changed. The prosecutors did their thing and the system rolled right over Mychal Bell and the other five defendants. It was business as usual. Did we learn anything from Jena that we can apply in Ferguson?

What will take place in Ferguson when the protesters leave? What happened in Sanford, Florida when they left? What has happened in Staten Island since Eric Garner was choked to death and the marches have ended? The latest report says the prosecutor is still trying to "collect the dots," much less connect the dots, and most have forgotten about Garner and his family and moved on to Ferguson, as it now becomes the crisis *du jour* for Black people.

Eleven years ago Kenneth Walker was shot and killed by a police officer on I-185 in Columbus, Georgia. He was in a car that was pulled over by mistake. He was on the ground, unarmed, when a police officer shot him twice in the head. After protesters and marchers went home, the officer was acquitted.

Many Black men have been killed by police with impunity. So what's my point? As I listened to the speeches in Ferguson, I eagerly awaited solutions. I could have missed it, but I never heard a solution that centered on economics. I heard the obligatory voting solution, in light of an embarrassing 12% turnout among Black voters, but an "I Voted!" sticker will not stop a policeman's bullet, and voting alone will not change our condition in this nation.

I also heard the praying solution, and I do believe that prayer changes things. However, I am suggesting that the folks in Ferguson and all across this country not only pray but fast as well. That combination will definitely create change.

I am not talking about giving up food for a period of time. The kind of fasting I am suggesting is a "product fast," which does require doing without and less buying; but isn't the cause worth it? Maybe the "leaders" who came to Ferguson were afraid to call for a product fast because they could lose a check or a contract or an endorsement or their status among corporate giants. Capitalism can tolerate marches that call for voting and prayer, but it has a great deal of angst when a decline in consumption and sales occurs.

"Black-Out" Days and other shotgun approaches are nice gestures but have no overall affect; they are simply more symbolism without substance. They make you feel good but won't cause anyone to change, because we go out the next day and buy what we want.

A product fast is quite different. For instance, Black folks consume a lot of soft drinks, gym shoes, liquor, fast foods, and other items we don't think we can do without. Just stop buying some of these products until corporate CEO's tell the President who would tell the governors who would tell the mayors and prosecutors who would tell the police chiefs who would tell their officers to stop violating our rights. You better believe their voices will be heard.

Money runs politics, and when campaign donors are against something they will get results from the politicians they support, especially when their bottom-line is adversely affected. For example, can you imagine Starbucks CEO, Howard Schultz, Coca Cola CEO, Muhtar Kent, Pepsi Cola CEO, Indra Nooyi, NBA Commissioner, Adam Silver, Nike CEO, Mark Parker, McDonald's CEO, Steve Easterbrook, Diageo Liquor's CEO, Ivan Menezes, and even Anheuser Busch's CEO, Thomas Santel, standing before national media and calling for an end to injustices against Black people? Nothing personal against these companies; it's just as they say in war, "collateral damage." But the damage would stop when the folks who run this country speak out.

We have been marching for decades; still we have Michael Brown, Eric Garner, Trayvon Martin, Sean Bell, Oscar Grant, Timothy Thomas, Nathaniel Jones, Kenneth Walker, Patrick Dorismond, Amadou Diallo, John Crawford, Ezell Ford, and nameless others.

Stop the insanity of doing the same thing and hoping for different results. We need leaders who call for economic solutions, not leaders who will hurt you if you get between them and a news camera or microphone. Get the folks who are really in charge of this country to speak out, and we will see a positive change. Start your local Prayer and Fasting campaign now; and use the money you save to build businesses, create jobs, and recreate real Black communities.

Selling Black Businesses

"The reason why black businesses have to sell to major corporations is because we do not have businesses with the type of capital it takes to acquire another business. Also, those who do have the means to purchase a business don't see the importance of keeping Black-owned businesses in the Black community."

Lanee Javet, CEO and Founder, CulSire

The news about Black owned beauty/hair care company, Carol's Daughter, being sold to L'Oreal USA is rife with opinions, both positive and negative, especially from Black people. Some say Lisa Price grew her business to a point where she could no longer support it and did the right thing by selling it. Others say she "sold out" as in being a "sell out." When I see stories like this I always think about our recent history as it pertains to Black firms being bought by non-Black businesses, one of which was Johnson Products, in 1992.

Lisa Price owned and ran Carol's Daughter for more than two decades. Like other businesses, operating capital became an issue. Price filed bankruptcy, as many businesses do in order to reorganize. Subsequently the deal was struck with L'Oreal USA. Price is staying with her former company in some capacity, which will help with brand continuity and consistency.

Small businesses are like newborn babies. Their owners take care of them, nurture them, mature them, and then, in many cases, have to let them go. I imagine this is what Price had to face in making her decision to sell her business. Like parents, you don't hold on for 20 plus years and not have some reluctance to let go.

History shows that even the largest Black hair care company had to make the same decision in 1998. Soft Sheen Products, founded and operated by Ed Gardner and his family, was also sold to L'Oreal. Prior to that time, in 1987, a Revlon V.P., named Irving Bottner, predicted Black hair care companies would be taken over by White companies in about 15 years. We got mad, but he was right, as other Black hair care giants fell to corporate raiders in the ensuing years,

Now, Carol's Daughter is another in a long line of Black businesses sold to White and other companies. Motown was sold in 1987 to MCA and Boston Ventures. Essence Magazine was sold to Time Warner; and BET was sold to Viacom. So what's the problem with the sale of Carol's Daughter? Is it because it's a Black hair care business?

In 1949, at a Black Beauticians' convention in Washington, D.C., attendees voiced their concern about Whites pushing their way into the lucrative beauty shop business, "The old line beauticians were losing a long-waged battle to keep the $450,000,000 beauty business in 'tan hands'...Big laboratories and constant experiment cost money...

Whatever the blame, the fact remains that a highly profitable field is surely and not so slowly being taken out of our hands." Their concerns then are still ours today, 65 years later.

If a 21 year-old firm has to file bankruptcy it is a pretty good indication of a serious cash flow problem. Where will the owner get the money necessary to keep the business open? If the bank is unwilling to lend it, and there is no angel investor at hand, selling is a logical option. The Black haircare industry is now worth several billion dollars; large companies can't wait to buy smaller successful competitors, especially those that have already established brand loyalty among Black consumers.

L'Oreal's purchase of Soft Sheen and Carol's Daughter, while under completely different circumstances, points to a larger issue for Black people. What is our role in the sale of businesses that we support? Many Black folks get upset at these deals, but we never get upset enough to invest in Black companies or provide cash infusions before they are on the ropes. Black investment groups could have a huge impact on small Black businesses—with due diligence, of course—and make a profit at the same time.

Wealthy Black folks could do the same for the larger Black businesses. Motown sold for $61 million and, shortly thereafter, was resold for $325 million. Imagine earning that kind of profit. Soft Sheen sold for $120 million; would you have turned that down? Essence Magazine was sold without even inviting Black Enterprise Magazine to make an offer, according to Earl Graves.

If we want to hold on to Black businesses, we must work together to save them. In 1998, I wrote: "The sale of Soft Sheen and other Black owned firms is merely a sign of the times. In the merger-charged atmosphere that abounds in this country, everyone seems to be forming partnerships and alliances except Black people. Thus, our companies are being devoured by the highest bidders. There is a literal feeding frenzy for the Black dollar. Black people are throwing our dollars to the sharks, and they are getting fat and happy at our expense. The sad part is we continue to do so, even after being insulted by those who benefit from our dollars."

Let's stop crying and start buying—other businesses.

Black vote in vogue—again

If our votes are so precious, so sacred, and so powerful, why do we give them away without reciprocity?

The Black vote is said to be the determining factor in whether the Democrats hold the U.S. Senate in 2014. President Obama is on Black radio shows, and of course "Little" Al's TV show, giving us the rundown on how important our turnout is in this mid-term. The Dems and Repubs are outwardly admitting that the Black vote is the X-factor. Isn't it great to be wanted and needed, even if it is just for one day? All across the nation, Black is popular once again, because it's voting time.

How should we react to this latest patronization of the Black vote? Well, let's look at our situation. Black folks are being beaten, shot, and killed, and we are told to vote. We have the highest unemployment, the lowest net worth, the highest incarceration rate, and many of our leaders tell us simply to vote. We are treated unfairly and excluded from economic opportunities, and we are told to vote.

Young Black males are 21 times more likely to be fatally shot by police than their white counterparts. The 1,217 deadly police shootings from 2010 to 2012 captured in the federal data, show that Blacks, age 15 to 19, were killed at a rate of 31.17 per million, while 1.47 per million white males in that age range died at the hands of police. All of this, and we are told to vote.

It's no wonder young Blacks are turned off by many of their elders. They are the ones taking the tear gas, the batons upside their heads, the abuse, and the lethal methods used by police officers; it is only after that or between the real battles that the usual suspects show up to march, hold a press conference, make a speech, and high-tail it out of town on the next thing smokin'.

Political hacks are telling Black voters to cast our votes to make sure Democrats maintain control of the Senate during the last two years of the Obama Presidency. My question is: What happened during the past six years of a Democrat controlled Senate? Other than Obamacare, which was passed strictly along party lines in the Senate, what has that body done for Black folks?

One of our Black Senators, Republican Tim Scott, is busy "discovering" what it's like to work at low level jobs in South Carolina; and since Democrat, Corey Booker, accepted a "challenge" to live on a $35.00 food stamp budget for one week, albeit, while earning $13,000 per month as Mayor of Newark, New Jersey, you haven't heard a peep out of him. As Malcolm said, Black voters are political "chumps."

To add insult to injury, the DNC is busy buying ads in Black newspapers, now that they need us again. The ads, titled, "Get his back," come after the 2012 Obama Presidential campaign raised $1 billion but only spent $985,000 with the Black press.

Since the Senate Democrat Class of 2008 took control, Black folks have done worse. The Wall Street Journal (August 2014) reported, "The real median income of African-American households has fallen by 9.5%, more than any other major census classification." Since MLK spoke in 1963 we went to sleep and co-opted his dream; and we have not awakened yet. No one can work while asleep.

Now we are being told we must keep the Democratic Senate in order to allow Barack Obama to build his legacy during his final two years. Well, I ask: What about our legacy? What will be the legacy of Black voters, without whom there would not be a Black President? Will our legacy simply be that of a bunch of emotional automatons who just felt good about having a Black President? A naïve voting bloc that gave its entire "quid" but received no "quo"?

Politicians work for us; we don't work for them. At least that's the concept. Politics is, to borrow a phrase from Dr. Freddie Haynes, a "Cauldron of contradiction," and we are lost in that morass of political never-never land, thinking that voting is the answer to all our ills.

Black people should not become lackeys for any political party, but in total contradiction to that, we allow ourselves to be taken for granted and used during every election. The current message to Blacks is simply, VOTE! They don't even have to say for whom because they know we will vote Democrat. That's insulting to Black people, but it's quite obvious that we don't care.

But, in yet another effort to admonish and beseech the Black people to be critical and analytical thinkers, especially when it comes to voting, I leave you with two questions for this upcoming election: What will Blacks gain if we vote? What will we lose if we don't?

The cost of not doing business

If there is no cost to pay for mistreatment, no price to pay for indifference, and no reciprocity between Black consumers and the businesses they support, we may as well call this whole protest thing off. It will take much more than marching and symbolic gestures; it's going to take serious economic responses from Black consumers if we want things to change.

Over the past few decades Black people have been led to believe that we have "power" because we earn and spend so much money in the marketplace, now having eclipsed the $1 trillion mark. As the most studied consumer segment in the world, Black Americans are touted by dozens of studies as the most brand loyal and the biggest spenders, especially on specific goods and services such as fast foods, movies, cellphones, hair and skin care, and sweetened drinks, just to name a few. Is that power? Well, it is for those on the receiving end of those dollars, but not so for Black consumers. It's more akin to a weakness.

You have heard the term, "The cost of doing business," which means that folks in business have certain costs that come with the territory. Some characterize it by saying, "It takes money to make money." Agreed, of course; but how much money does it take for businesses that Black consumers support to make more money? What is their cost of doing business within the Black consumer segment? The answer: little or nothing. They get our money with little effort or reciprocity.

So why do studies always point out that we have power in the marketplace? Black spending power, Black purchasing power, and the power of the Black consumer are all phrases that are utilized by researchers who point to our billions in consumption spending. The question is "power." Are we powerful simply because we spend a lot of money?

Power has many definitions, the most comprehensive list of which is noted by Dr. Amos Wilson, in his seminal work, <u>Blueprint for Black Power</u>. In a general sense, according to Rollo May, as quoted by Wilson, power is, "...the ability to cause or prevent change." The application of that definition of power to Black consumers falls short, however, because of the word "ability." How do you know if you have the ability to do anything until you actually put that ability into action? It's much like another word we like to apply to Black folks: "potential." The only way we really know we have potential is to utilize it—or do away with it, as I like to say.

Batteries hanging on a rack in a store are believed to have power, but the purchaser will never know if that's true until those batteries are put to use. Likewise, all the power that researchers say Black consumers have will never be seen or felt until we exercise it. Until we change our consumption habits we will never have true power; instead we will only have the illusion of power. Influence, yes, but never power.

So we must change the phrase, "The cost of doing business" to a new phrase, "The cost of not doing business." As consumers, and voters I might add, we are largely taken for granted. Our dollars continue to flow outward and continue to empower everyone except ourselves. Our votes are always on parade, as is the case now with the upcoming elections, but with no reciprocity. How can we even think we have power?

A paradigm shift to the cost of not doing business would cause an enormous change in how things are done in his nation and their effect on the lives of Black people. Moving from business as usual to "business unusual" would send a strong signal that Black consumers are tired of being the profit margins for companies that fail to respond appropriately to our brand loyalty. It would cause the CEO's and board members of those firms to step up and speak up on our behalf.

When the cost of doing business rises, the producer simply raises prices or hands out pink slips. When the cost of Black consumers not doing business hits those company balance sheets and cash flow statements, the 2% or so they currently spend on Black advertising will rise. The meager sums of ad dollars currently being spent with Black newspapers will explode. And the amount spent with conscious and conscientious Black media will also increase.

Understand that reciprocity works in a variety of ways. Those Black media firms that reap the benefits of Blacks not doing business must reciprocate by circulating some of their newfound wealth to other Black businesses, and they must make drastic improvements in their programming to Black audiences.

Media is certainly not the only category to leverage reciprocity. Issues of injustice, discrimination, and disparities can all be addressed within the context of not doing business with a targeted group of corporations until they appropriately respond to Eric Garner, Michael Brown, et al.

If we want real power, pursuing a "cost of not doing business" strategy is one way to obtain it.

No Justice, No Profit!

"This new generation has an intersectional analysis, grassroots legitimacy, intergenerational connections, social media savvy and, above all, prophetic rage. They are willing to risk life and limb for the project of freedom. Indeed old things have passed away."
Ebony Magazine, October 2014

Through the years I have wondered when we would "get it." It took a group of young people who went to Ferguson, Missouri over the Labor Day weekend to encourage me in that regard. They get it.

The Howard University Student Association (HUSA), led by its incoming President, Mr. Leighton Watson, organized a 13-hour bus trip from Washington, D.C. to protest alongside other students from Washington University and other colleges. They went to stand with the residents of Ferguson to seek real solutions to the issues that plague that city.

An interesting thing happened on their way to the march. Those young people marched to a Black company to charter their bus. When they got there they marched to a Black restaurant to eat. They made every effort to find a Black owned hotel, but the hotel owned by the Roberts brothers was closed. They did, however, manage to get accommodations at a black owned franchised hotel. They let their money speak as they protested; I even saw a sign that said, "No Justice, No Profit."

I was blessed to speak at a teleconference of HBCU's at which they sought appropriate responses to what took place in Ferguson—and what is taking place around the country between police officers and Black folks. The more I listened to the students, the more I knew that our future was in good hands with them. They are not only intelligent but they are conscious and they have the courage of their convictions. They showed their willingness to sacrifice for a just cause, to stand up against wrongdoing, and to speak truth to the powerful.

I could hardly hold back my emotions as I watched and listened. Leadership, discipline, and respect for one another permeated the teleconference. I thought about how long our elders, who now include me, have tried to make us understand the priority of economic empowerment and economic leverage, how they have screamed at us to use our collective income to obtain reciprocity and equity in all areas of our lives.

I thought about Joshua and Caleb, two young men who were not afraid to stand up against what the older men thought was an unconquerable obstacle, which led to 40 years of meandering in the desert until all of that older generation died, leaving only Joshua and Caleb. Instead of cowering in the face of evil, the students were willing to "go into the land" and fight for a righteous cause, and they were willing to do it in a way that makes economic sense.

Howard students attended Ron Daniels' recent symposium in Washington, D.C. and Leighton Watson spoke from the perspective of young people, whom Daniels encouraged to be there and step forward to carry on the battle for justice. They heeded his call to show up and speak up, and now they are putting up, not shutting up.

Plans are in the works to confront the real powers in this country, those who are in charge and in control the vast majority of the money, primarily by leveraging our economic resources, Black "buying power" as it's called, to elicit appropriate responses to Ferguson and elsewhere. Money runs politics and everything else in the U.S. and the world, and college students understand that withdrawing their consumer dollars from various product categories is the only way to get the attention of those who can put an end to the blatant injustice that festers in our land.

Finally, HUSA members connect with other HBCU students across the country, and they are building a coalition in the mold of Joshua and Caleb. I can only dream of a day when students, their organizations, their families, and many of the rest of us collectively work for justice and economic empowerment. All we need to do is heed the words God spoke to Joshua: "Be courageous."

I am so proud of the students at our various HBCU's as well as those in other colleges and universities, who have taken up the gauntlet by

228

bringing not only their intelligence but their energy and seriousness to the frontlines of this fight. Like Moses and Dr. King, I may not see it or get there with them, but I am confident in their ability to take us to the next level of economic empowerment, from "No Justice, No Peace!" to "No Justice, No Profit!"

Note: *Mr Leighton Watson has since been invited to the White House to give his perspective and advice relative to strategies that could be implemented to alleviate the injustices against Black men and women. He has also appeared on the major cable news channels, and was invited to speak before the U.S. Congress on the topic, "Racial Profiling–What next after Ferguson and New York City?"*

Maybe our wait for the next Black President will not be that long after all.

All Quid and no Quo

"You give me something, I give you something"
Chicago Mayor, Harold Washington

The term "Maát" is familiar to many of us. I give credit to the youth at the SBA ("Saba") Academy in Ft. Wayne, Indiana, under the superb leadership of Brother Kweku Akan and his staff, for enlightening me on the exact meaning of the term and the principles it embodies: Truth; Justice; Righteousness; Balance; Harmony; Order; and Reciprocity. I want to speak about reciprocity in politics for Black folks.

It simply means something for something, for mutual benefit, between two parties or entities. In politics they use the Latin term "*quid pro quo*" probably because the majority of the electorate does not know what the term means. It sounds nice and sophisticated but it simply means reciprocity. You give me something and I will give you something. In political circles, of course, it could be boiled down to dollars for votes, or votes for dollars.

Blacks are the most loyal voters in this country but not the most generous when it comes to campaign donations. So our quid pro quo should be "votes for dollars." Although we call them programs and benefits, nonetheless, our "quo," in return for our "quid" should be flowing back to us like a rushing stream. We should not have to beg, march, demonstrate, or fight for our quo; if reciprocity is the name of the game Black voters should be sitting pretty right now. But for all of our quid, election after election, we have little quo to show for it.

Politically speaking, Black people are being played. The sad part about it is that we don't seem to care. The lower we sink, politically and economically, the more we are available "to get off the couch and put on our marching shoes" to demonstrate our dissatisfaction about the political system, as though our anger alone will change it.

The mis-leaders keep telling us how powerful our vote is, but in spite of turning out in greater proportionate numbers that Whites in 2012, we still suffer from a lack of reciprocity. Despite our undying loyalty we are still an all quid and no quo voting bloc. Frederick Douglass warned, "When we are noted for enterprise, industry, and success, we shall no longer have any trouble in the matter of civil and political rights." Makes me almost wish he had said, "When we give all of our votes to one political party, we will achieve full political reciprocity."

To many Black folks, Maát has real meaning. We recite the principles, chant, sing, and teach them, but a relative few of us actually practice them. As for reciprocity, Black people have far to go in the marketplace and in the political arena. We give but we do not receive. All quid with no quo.

Why do we accept such a one-sided deal, especially from those to whom our loyalty is pledged and given? Politically we are taken for granted, obviously because of our staunch loyalty; and economically we suffer the same result because we do not command and demand a reasonable return on our dollars.

One example that captures both the economics and politics of this issue is the $1 billion in President Obama's 2012 campaign war chest contrasted by the measly $985,000 spent with the Black press. In exchange for our 93%-95% quid, our quo was one-tenth of one percent, or 0.1% in media buys, and that was up from the planned spend of $650,000, which was raised due to "pressure" on the campaign managers. Taken for granted is putting it mildly.

Rep. Alcee L. Hastings (D-FL), accused President Obama of "consistently disrespecting the Congressional Black Caucus (CBC), the Black Press, and graduates of historically Black colleges, key groups that were critical to his re-election in November."

Considering the number of years that Blacks such as Douglass, Booker T., Garvey, and Malcolm have been telling us how to play the political game to win, we continue to play it just to play. Considering our penchant for ancient African principles and tenets, such as reciprocity, we insult the memory of our ancestors by giving our quid without demanding and receiving a quo.

Our response to the political landslide

"The difference between a democracy and a dictatorship is that in a democracy you vote first and take orders later; in a dictatorship you don't have to waste your time voting."
Charles Bukowski

Relative to the "Tuesday Evening Massacre" by the Elephants over the Donkeys, in January 2009 I wrote an article that warned about our being complacent and resting on the mere fact that we had elected a Black President. I suggested that we should get busy right away doing the commensurate work it would surely take for us to get something more for our votes than just a good feeling about "making history." Obviously, we failed in that regard, and now we are crying about the massacre that took place on November 4, 2014.

As far back as 2006 this column and my television show warned against our complacency and settling for an emotional victory rather than a substantive victory. Now we have very little, if anything, to show for our record turnouts of 2008 and 2012, because we failed to act appropriately on the morning after those elections.

For the next two years the elephants and donkeys will continue to fight and we will continue to suffer. Why? Because we have no clout with either party; we have no say-so about what happens to us.

Black voters have been lulled to sleep by patronizing gestures and platitudes from politicians who only want and know they will always receive our votes. They also know that we will not leverage our votes against them nor make demands on them in exchange for our votes. They know all we want to do is vote, and then we will go home and await the next election.

When the donkeys won they did not move us to the front of the reciprocity line. They did not acknowledge us by putting forth specific legislation to benefit Black voters. They did not show their appreciation by spending more with our media during their 2012 campaign. No, they needed our votes, which we gave so generously in prior years, but they refused to reciprocate in any meaningful way. Now the donkeys are blaming us for their defeat, saying "too few" of us voted.

Is it really our fault? Are we the reason many of us are crying about the results of the last election? Are we, the Black electorate and the political talking-heads whom we follow, the reasons we will likely spend the next two years in political purgatory? Maybe so, but the real question is: If we got nothing during the first two years of the Obama administration, when the donkeys controlled both houses, what would make any of us believe we will get anything during the next two years? Maybe this is the slap upside our heads that will make us change the way we play politics.

Here is a solution. Mr. Theodore Johnson III wrote an article in Atlantic Magazine titled, Black America Needs its own President (September 5, 2014) in which he stated, *"The call for a President of Black America may, at first blush, sound odd...But Black America is about 45 million people strong and has buying power of just over a trillion dollars... an economy roughly equivalent to Portugal's and a population that is about the same as Spain's. That should translate to a significant amount of economic and political power. But without a leader to marshal this capital, we're treated like a subcultural afterthought..."*

Johnson continued, *"Of course, the President of Black America is just a symbolic label, not an elected position. But it needn't be. After all, who elected Frederick Douglass, Booker T. Washington, and King to be the personification of Black America in their respective eras? He or she would carry a big stick, and that big stick would be the marshaling of the Black electorate and Black purchasing power...the Black American economy sustains numerous businesses and products across the nation; no dollar leaves a community faster than the Black dollar. This is unfortunate, but it is also leverage."*

Interestingly enough, a group formed in 2007 devised a plan for a President of Black America, which we called the "POBA." Unfortunately, Black folks decided to take another nap when it looked like Barack Obama would be elected as the POTUS, and our plan was shelved. In light of Mr. Johnson's article and our previous attempt, now is the time to find the POBA.

This is a call for one million conscious Black voters to join the POBA movement. These voters/consumers will use our leverage to positively impact political outcomes and the Black economy, locally and nationally.

Still hoping for change?

"Simply hoping will not change anything for Black people. We must create the change ourselves, collectively and individually; and, rather than hoping it is sustained, we must build upon it, maintain it, and sacrifice for it along the way to victory."

As the end of another tumultuous year approaches, Black people again find ourselves in the relative same economic and political position as we were the year before, and the years preceding. In 2007, leading up to 2008, when the ultimate level of political history had finally come to fruition, Black folks and others were citing the mantra, "Hope and Change!" Quite frankly we got more hope than real positive change—for Blacks, that is.

Just as our emotional bubble was inflated to its maximum capacity, now the air is coming out and we are heading back down from our lofty height, about to burst in a very short while. Instead of saying, "We are the change we've been looking for," in light of all the unrest and injustice, I and others say as we have said for decades, "The change you are looking for is in your pockets."

Slowly but surely, albeit very late in the game, Black folks are learning that economic empowerment is the key to our progress and prosperity in this nation. Years of instructions from elders, scholars, and activists are taking hold in the minds of young people, despite the tired messages coming from some of our current leaders.

Black people must first acknowledge our situation, admit our mistakes, and work cooperatively to improve our economic status, from which we can then build true political power. It's not the other way around, and fortunately the younger generations see and understand that reality. I am encouraged by our youth.

Although we still get our "marching" orders from political icons and media talking heads, many are determined to blaze a new trail that leads us to real power. The sad part is that all we have to do is look back at the past 60 years and we can see how wrong and misguided we have been in our quest for parity and fairness. Now, there is an enlightened, determined, and unwavering group of young people who are neither intimidated by the powerful nor swayed by the mis-leadership of the old guard and political gatekeepers. It looks to me that they are in it for the long haul.

While Ferguson brought about an awakening of sorts, the solution-based messages we still hear are, "March" and "Vote." The NAACP, as big and bad as it purports to be, issued a call for a 130-mile walk from Ferguson to the Missouri governor's office, the same guy who insulted them with his decisions after Michael Brown's death. Walk 130 miles? The only thing we got out of that was sore feet and worn shoe leather.

Oh yes, the businesses along the route benefitted economically; as long as the marchers were not staying, I'm sure they said, "Y'all come." We counted the miles, and they counted the dollars. It's no wonder the younger generation is marching to its own drummer. They look back and see all the marching we did and ask, "Why are we still being subjected to the same things they marched against back in the day?" Can you blame them?

While many in my generation and older are still hoping for change, young folks have come to the understanding that the change they can and should control is in their pockets. They are committed to implementing economic solutions to address the problems they face, not only in Ferguson, but across the nation. They know that politics alone will not solve their problems; they know that the hue and cry from folks like Congressman John Lewis, who is now saying, "Republican voter suppression efforts played a crucial role in driving voter turnout to historic lows in 2014," is ridiculous.

Mr. Lewis is calling for more involvement in the voting process rather than more involvement in the economic process of leveraging Black spending throughout the year. He suggests that Republicans went into the homes of Black folks and forced them to stay away from the polls during the past election. While there certainly are efforts afoot to curtail and suppress the vote, Black folks still have the right to do so. Many chose not to vote because of nonsensical remedies put forth as relief for the inequities against Blacks in this country; they didn't vote because they are frustrated by the past.

Young people are not following the political practices of the past. Where we used politics to solve our problems, they are using economics. This "new guard," is saying: "No more symbolism; we want substance; no more speeches, we want specifics; no more rhetoric, we want results; no more dallying, we'll use our dollars; and you know what, rather than rely on hope, we'll use our change."

2015

Between Barack and a Hard Place

What are Black folks going to do in 2016? We landed our best political shot in 2008; we threw a haymaker and the establishment took it on the chin, shook it off, and kept on fighting. We didn't even get a knockdown. Well, it's the 12th and final round; and "the loser is…"

The "experiment" that featured a Black man in the White house is on the downside now. Folks in the Obama administration are busy looking for their next job and jumping ship faster than rats. But you can't blame them; that's the way it is in politics. You ride your horse as long as you can and then you find a new horse. That's just what folks in Presidential administrations do. The question is: What horse will Black folks ride now?

With Barack, came new line-dances at the clubs, new phrases, and new "hope" that would finally move Black people to the front of the line for a "change." We were large and in charge, big-ballers and shot-callers, cool and stylish, but we soon found that we were not really running anything. Having bet the farm on our horse, we now look on in agony as he comes down the home stretch. We want to move the finish line a bit farther down the track because we don't yet have the victory, and it looks like we're not going to get it. All we can hope for now is just a little more euphoria before November 2016.

Right now many Black folks are between Barack and a hard place. We don't know if we are pitching or catching. As that Richard Pryor movie asked, "Which way is up?" We invested nearly 100% of our political capital in our current President, thinking we would get a decent ROI (Return on Investment). Unless there is a drastic uptick in the next few months, our investment will be lost forever, because we know it will be years before this experiment is done again.

Between Barack and a hard place means that Black people, collectively, are now without a comfortable place to turn, without someone we can look to for hope and change, and without what we considered to be a foothold in politics. Being between Barack and a hard place is causing anxiety, doubt, and even fear among some of our people.

Being between Barack and a hard place will make many of us revert back to our docile political ways by staying on the Democratic wagon because the Republicans ignore us and don't like us anyway. We will rationalize our loyalty and allegiance to the same party that takes us for granted, however. And some of us will even opt out of the system altogether, because we are so frustrated and angry at how the previous two terms went down.

It's very uncomfortable being between Barack and a hard place. To whom will we now turn? Will Hillary help us? Will one of the Republican candidates help us? Maybe Doctor Ben will win and come to our rescue. What are Black folks to do in 2016 as we now find ourselves wedged between Barack and a hard place with no wiggle room? Maybe we could "apologize" to Hillary for abandoning her in 2008; maybe we could do a public mea culpa to the Republicans. After all, we need someone to turn to now, right?

Well here are a few thoughts: Maybe we can now turn to ourselves; maybe now we will fully understand the error of our ways and make appropriate change; maybe we will finally work together as a solid bloc to leverage our precious votes against the 2016 candidates; maybe we will understand that no matter who resides at 1600 Pennsylvania Avenue, Black folks still have to be vigilant about our political and economic position in this country; and maybe, as we struggle to remove ourselves from between Barack and a hard place, at least a small percentage of us will organize around economic and political empowerment.

The Barack experiment was cool. He could sing like Al Green, dance like the steppers in Chicago, shoot three-pointers on the basketball court, play a little golf with Alonzo Mourning, have a beer with the guys, and even get his preach on when speaking to Black audiences. In other words, Barack could make us feel real good, so much so that we kicked back, relaxed, and waited for him to fix our problems, to speak on our behalf, and to give us the same deference he gave to other groups. Now, we find ourselves between Barack and a hard place—no turning room, very little breathing room, and much uncertainty about our future in the political arena.

There will be a new sheriff in town in January 2017, and our guy will stand there with him or her to give congrats and well wishes right before he rides off into the sunset, back to Chicago, Hawaii, or wherever, to enjoy the fruit of his labor, and I do mean fruit. He and his family will be well taken care of, but most of our families will be in the same or worse condition, having been stuck between Barack and a hard place for eight years.

What now?

What now my love, now that you've left me?
How can I live, live through another day?
Watching my dreams turning to ashes
And my hopes turning to bits of clay.
Carl Sigman (English version)

What a raucous, topsy-turvy, heart-wrenching, angry year we experienced in 2014. We had everything from the sadness of lives lost on airplanes and ferry boats, to the anger of Black men being killed and Black women being beaten by police officers, to the elation of a record-breaking stock market and the lowest gasoline prices since 2008. Certainly our emotions were mixed as we witnessed a potpourri of ups and downs while we pondered the question: "What's next?"

Of course none of us knows what will happen the next minute, much less the next year, but there are things we can do from day to day to solve some of our problems and improve our lot in life. I invite you to think about your personal and our collective situations, and make a commitment to do what you can to make the much needed changes we must have for self-empowerment and self-determination. After you seriously and honestly think about those things, I implore you to take appropriate action.

What happened during the past year is now a lesson for all of us, whether positive or negative. We must move forward. We cannot live in the past; we can only learn from it. In light of that reality, here are a few suggestions to help get you moving in a positive direction in 2015.

First and foremost, build, strengthen, and nurture your spiritual foundation. Be thankful for each day, and use it wisely. Stay informed with real news, not with mere views from talking heads. Remember that followers pick their leaders; it's not the other way around, so pick leaders who work in your best interests rather than self-serving charlatans who are only concerned about themselves.

Make an even stronger effort to support Black businesses and, Black business owners, take care of your business by doing what you say you will do with honesty and professionalism. At tax time, if you need a tax preparer, use a Black firm; Compro Tax Service is an excellent and wise choice. Look online to find the office nearest you. Talk to your church leadership about joining or forming a local chapter of the Collective Empowerment Group (CEG), also found online.

Don't waste your vote. Give it to someone who is not afraid to state their position regarding Black voters during the campaign and afterwards—and then fulfill their promises. If they fail to do so, don't vote for them. Also, on the political side of things, stop putting the same old folks into office, especially if they have not delivered anything to Black folks and/or if they have been in their particular office for decades. Put some new "young-bloods" with fresh ideas into office. We will never be politically empowered until we start playing to win instead of playing just to play.

Find a Black certified financial planner and get involved in some level of investment in the stock market. As we are standing in line to buy Nike shoes, we should also be teaching our children how to buy Nike stock. Also, teach entrepreneurship to our youth. Let them know they can own a business even if they end up working for someone. Teach them early by using examples of young Black business owners like Jasmine Lawrence, Moziah Bridges, Cory Nieves, Omar Bailey, and many others you can find on the Internet.

Make it a habit to listen to the Carl Nelson Radio Show (1450AM WOL in Washington, DC or www.woldcnews.com), Brother Daren "State of the City" Muhammad in Baltimore, Michael Imhotep, in Detroit, Dr. Rosie Milligan in L.A., Keidi Awadu on LIB Radio.com, Elliott Booker (Time for an Awakening) in Philadelphia, and other conscious and informative radio shows.

Finally, in response to the outrageous treatment some of us have received from the police and the criminal justice system, first, let's boycott prisons, that is, stop committing crimes and putting yourself at the mercy of a system that cares absolutely nothing about you.

Second, in addition to the protests the young folks are doing now, add a strategy, an end game that uses economic sanctions (No Justice, No Profit!) as leverage to get the CEO's of various corporations to come out publicly and denounce the abuse being inflicted upon our people.

Remember, it's not simply about withdrawing our money just to hurt someone else; it's about using that same money to help ourselves by building our own economic infrastructure.

Last but certainly not least, sign up as one the Million Conscious Black Voters and Contributors by simply going to <u>www.iamoneofthemillion.com</u>. One million Black folks willing to leverage our votes and our dollars can change our situation. Get involved in 2015; let your actions outweigh your words, and let's move forward.

We Must Change

"There comes a time in the course of human events for persons who have been mistreated to dissolve the political bands which have connected them with those who mistreat them. In the interest of self-respect and to claim the respect of others, after a long train of abuses, such persons have the right and the duty to throw off those who mistreat them and provide new guards for their future security."
<u>The Declaration of Independence</u>

This country was established on the simple facts that people were being mistreated, they were tired of it, and they were not going to take it anymore. One cannot help but admire people who come to the end of their rope, defiantly proclaim the truth about their condition, and then do something about it.

I long for the day when Black people finally get so tired of the abuse we suffer all over this country that we will decide to spend much more of our time, not trying to hurt someone else, but to use our resources to help ourselves. Our plight is similar to that of the founders of this country. The big difference: They were fed up and determined to make a change; we are just fed up. They had to go to war, as we must do if we want change. Our war must be revolutionary as well, but it must be fought with dollars rather than musket balls.

Our resolve must be the same as the Patriots. We must "admit" our problem and then "commit" to doing what we have to do to get what say we want. Why would we continue to hope and wish for change from people who have demonstrated no indication of their willingness to do so?

Check out how Patrick Henry put it: *"I have but one lamp by which my feet are guided, and that is the lamp of experience. I know of no way of judging the future but by the past. And judging by the past, I wish to know what there has been in the conduct of the British ministry for the last ten years to justify those hopes with which gentlemen have been pleased to solace themselves..."*

Henry knew he had to fight rather than hope and wish for change. He asked his compatriots what would make them believe their captors would change. "Is it that insidious smile with which our petition has been lately received? Trust it not, sir; it will prove a snare to your feet."

Patrick Henry continued, *"They tell us, sir, that we are weak; unable to cope with so formidable an adversary. But when shall we be stronger? Will it be the next week, or the next year? Will it be when we are totally disarmed... Shall we gather strength by irresolution and inaction? Shall we acquire the means of effectual resistance by lying supinely on our backs and hugging the delusive phantom of hope, until our enemies shall have bound us hand and foot?"*

Henry reminded the people of their futile petitions, their arguments against oppression, their entreaties and supplications to the King. He reminded them of their demonstrations, their protestations, and their humility, all rejected by the power structure. He told them it was time to take things into their own hands and stop begging their oppressors to come to their rescue. He said, "There is no longer any room for hope. If we wish to be free... we must fight! I repeat it, sir, we must fight!" Until Black people decide to fight against negative external forces and our own internal economic recalcitrance, things will not change.

If we do not act upon the historical juxtaposition of David Walker's Appeal to Black people, and Patrick Henry's words to Whites, we are doomed to permanent underclass status. We must leverage our economic capacity against corporations that treat us like afterthoughts. And, we must combine our intellectual and financial resources to build our own political, economic, educational, and social independence.

Having written my newspaper column for 22 years, I figured I'd let a white man do the talking this time. That way more of our people will listen and act; because if a white man called for a revolt, it must be all right for a Black man to call for one.

So I leave you with Patrick Henry's most famous words: *"Why stand we here idle? What is it that gentlemen wish? What would they have? Is life so dear, or peace so sweet, as to be purchased at the price of chains and slavery? Forbid it, Almighty God! I know not what course others may take; but as for me, give me liberty or give me death!"*

Fifty Years of Economic Futility

Dr. Martin Luther King, Jr. was killed while fighting for an economic cause. Five decades later our lack of economic progress in this nation is an insult to him and the sacrifice he made for us to be empowered.

During the fifty year period from 1963 ("I have a dream!") to 2013, Black people have been on a virtual economic treadmill. Our relative economic position has not changed; our unemployment rate has consistently been twice as high as the White unemployment rate, which was 5% for Whites and 10.9% for Blacks in 1963, and today it's 6.6% for Whites and 12.6% for Blacks. Our aggregate annual income is $1.1 trillion, but it's not what you earn; it's what you're worth: The typical White family had $134,200 in wealth in 2013, while Black families had $11,000, lower too than Hispanic families, at $13,700.

The U.S. has a $17.7 trillion Gross Domestic Product (GDP), the world's largest economy. The total Gross Domestic Income (GDI), which some economists say is a better measure of an economy, was $9.3 trillion as of the 4th quarter of 2014. A recent Pew Research study indicates that the financial gap between Blacks and Whites is the highest it's been since 1989. In 2010, the median wealth of white households was eight times higher than blacks; now it's seventeen times higher. The African-American economy, by either measure, GDP or GDI, despite reports of robust economic growth, remains mired in a recession. Or is it a depression?

You awake yet? So what can we do about it? Please, don't take that fatal leap of faith in thinking the "guvment" will take care of it. They are too busy counting our income as a huge part of GDP, because we spend nearly all of our $1.1 trillion on goods and services, which comprise 70% of GDP.

We must extrapolate a logical and appropriate response from the above information. All the reports in the world will do us no good if we fail to learn from them and then act upon what we know. After that, we must do our part as individuals to contribute to the collective economic/political uplift of our people and future generations.

What do we have, as individuals, to contribute to our economic and political success? We have votes and we have dollars; and if we cast our votes with leverage and spend our dollars strategically we can achieve parity. Let's face it, to chase the illusion of economic "equality," via income and wealth, will only keep us diverted from setting practical and achievable goals.

MLK was partially correct when he posited that by obtaining employment in White corporations and using either strategic consumption or boycotts as leverage, Blacks could secure economic equality, just as we had secured civil rights. He was right about the leverage of our dollars, but wrong about the result of us getting jobs in corporate America. The above statistics prove that. Chasing equality instead of parity is futile, in that we are always chasing someone else's standard, a standard that can be elevated at any time, thus never to be attained by the pursuer.

We must use our own intellectual and financial capacity to change our shameful and static economic position in this nation. Fifty years of chasing an illusion are enough? We squandered our economic base and abdicated our personal economic responsibility when we abandoned our businesses to buy from others. We gave in to the notion that we could be equal if we elected Black folks to political office. So it's up to us to admit those near fatal mistakes and work together to rectify them by pooling our resources, locally and nationally, and growing our businesses to the point where they can hire our own people. You know, just as other groups do.

We must gather enough conscious independent-thinking voters who will cast their votes as a bloc for the candidate that supports our best interests. Enough with the pre-election condescending rhetoric, kissing our babies, and coming to our churches at election time; they must explicitly state their support of our issues and follow through on that support. If we cannot win at politics, why play?

We must save more money, irrespective of how much or how little we have. We must own property, or at least rent from one another. Blacks collectively lost between $164 billion and $213 billion in housing wealth as a result of the sub-prime debacle. (And we are seeking "wealth equality"?) Therefore, we must also invest in stocks, and not tie all of our assets to real estate. We must find ways to decrease or eliminate our reliance on college loans, which will be a generational albatross around the necks of our youth, their parents, and even grandparents. And while we are at it, we should be petitioning the "guvment" for a massive student loan bailout similar to the way the banks got bailed out of their debt.

Finally, Black people must be more circumspect and get more involved in things going on around us; in many cases we are oblivious to the channels and programs through which public money flows. The billions of dollars spent on local, state, and national construction projects is one example. Black businesses rarely get their "fair share" of the contracts that emanate from these projects. Yes, there are Small Business (SBE), Women Business (WBE), Minority Business (MBE), and Disadvantaged Business (DBE) programs that are supposed to oversee an equitable process of inclusion for Black people, but many of them are dysfunctional, and that's putting it mildly.

If you examine the information contained in many of the inclusion reports put out by these programs, you will find great disparities among the groups supposedly being served, i.e. "minorities" and women. The number of contracts secured by MBE's pale in comparison to those given to WBE's, which are exclusively White female owned companies started and operated by White men. In other words, they are "front" companies. Black firms, male and female owned, on the other hand, must compete within a category that includes several other ethnic groups in order to obtain a small share of those public construction dollars. This is especially true and embarrassingly blatant within DBE programs.

Check it out for yourself; learn about it, and act on it.

Selma, 2015

"Fifty years from Bloody Sunday, our march is not yet finished, but we're getting closer. Two hundred and thirty-nine years after this nation's founding our union is not yet perfect, but we are getting closer. Our job's easier because somebody already got us through that first mile. Somebody already got us over that bridge. When it feels the road is too hard, when the torch we've been passed feels too heavy, we will remember these early travelers, and draw strength from their example, and hold firmly the words of the prophet Isaiah: "Those who hope in the Lord will renew their strength. They will soar on [the] wings like eagles. They will run and not grow weary. They will walk and not be faint."

President Barack Obama, Selma 50th Anniversary

I remember back in 1999 when my daughter came to me crying about something she had seen on TV. It was the movie, "Selma, Lord, Selma!" She was distraught, even at six years old, at the mistreatment of Black folks in Selma in 1965. My daughter related to Jurnee Smollett and Stephanie Peyton in their portrayals of Sheyann and Rachel, two young girls growing up in Selma during that time. That being a teaching moment, she and I had a talk about Selma and other issues pertaining to injustice toward and mistreatment of Black people in this country.

Adding to the title of that movie, by making it "Selma, Lord have mercy, Selma!" captures my effort to highlight and reemphasize not only the historical tragedy of Selma but also its current political and economic condition in light of the 50th Anniversary of Bloody Sunday.

March 3-7, 2015, tens of thousands of people converged on Selma, including politicians, of course, celebrities and corporate executives.

Selma enjoyed the national and world spotlight for a brief time, but I wondered if those folks would leave Selma without addressing current critical issues that exist there. Daily life in Selma includes a 40% poverty rate, high unemployment, low median family income, crumbling infrastructure and building facades, and closed businesses.

I could only pray that some of the folks who visited and made speeches also left some money there, maybe to start a micro lending fund, an equity fund, or even invested in a business in Selma. I hope the politicians who say they hold Selma in such high esteem went back to their respective offices committed to allocate funds to help the city that some refer to as, "The Third World of Alabama."

As Representative Terri A. Sewell (D-Ala) said, "We have to move beyond the bridge." Along with all the crying, preaching, inspiring speeches, and marching back across the bridge, I trust that on this 50th anniversary of Bloody Sunday the folks living in Selma received more than just well wishes.

During our family visit there in 2001, former head of the National Voting Rights Museum and Institute, Joann Bland, gave us a tour (Even though it was past closing time); she told her personal story of being in the march at 10 years of age and shared her wealth of knowledge with my then 8-year old daughter. My eyes were opened to the history and the present state of Selma, a city still waiting for change, especially economic change.

Fifty years since 1965 that famous bridge, named for Edmund Pettus, a former U.S. Democratic Senator, chairman of the state delegation to the Democratic National Convention for twenty years, and Grand Dragon of the Alabama Ku Klux Klan, has even greater meaning. Back then it symbolized the struggle for voting rights; today it is a guidepost for a new struggle, the struggle for economic justice and empowerment. Those who walked that bridge in 1965 won their battle; we must be as strong and as determined as they were then to win the battle we face today.

Obviously the political environment has changed in the city that elected as its Mayor the sheriff who supported the beat-down in 1965, and kept him in office until 2000. Selma leaders like Terri Sewell know, however, that political change is not enough; they know change must also come in the form of economic empowerment and federal support.

Is it enough to have gone to Selma simply because it was the 50th anniversary? Albeit a treasured occasion, for some it has become more symbolism than substantive, a photo-op, just as the 50th anniversary of the famous March on Washington was in 2013. Today our words and activities in Selma must result in progressive and appropriate action, so that next year we can celebrate the victorious culmination of that revered freedom march, rather than lamenting our continued frustration over the fact that 50 years later, as some of the dignitaries and the President said, "Our march for justice continues."

Selma needs much more than an annual celebration. It needs economic development, businesses, employment, and revitalization. It should be valued well beyond the platitudes, pretentiousness, and pontification proffered by politicians and their pundits. That city, so important to our history, should be held in the highest esteem by Washington D.C., the State of Alabama, and the rest of us. In addition to an annual spotlight, we must keep it on the political radar screen throughout the year, until it is given the assistance it certainly commands and truly deserves.

The culmination of true freedom is economic freedom. Selma citizens and those who endured the batons, horses, dogs, and those who were murdered leading up to and during the march, are certainly deserving of more than 50 more years of "The struggle continues," and "We 'shall' overcome."

What's in a million?

That's a nice round number, a tidy little sum if you're talking about dollars; but it's much more valuable when you're talking about people.

Exactly what is there in one million Black folks united in their will and purpose? What is in a million brothers and sisters who are tired of the same old rhetoric, the same old leaders, and the same old ways of dealing with political and economic empowerment? What's in a group of one million Blacks who are unapologetic about their identity? What's in such a group that, collectively and cooperatively, is willing to sacrifice some of its members' time, talent, and treasure for the uplift of Black people in this country?

Considering our relative position within the political system, is it rational to believe that one million like-minded Black voters could affect positive change by leveraging their votes to obtain concessions from candidates prior to and after an election? What would be the result of one million Black independent-thinking voters deciding to register as "No Party Affiliation" rather than as Democrats, Republicans, or any other formal political party? What if we followed through on Theodore Johnson's article on The Root.com, "Black America Needs Its Own President"?

Is it reasonable to think that one million conscious Black consumers would have the power to affect the bottom line of corporations to the point of getting those companies to take public positions in support of justice for Black people? Could those one million consumers ultimately obtain reciprocity in the marketplace by leveraging and redirecting a greater portion of their dollars to their own businesses?

Just imagine one million consumers purchasing just one product made by a Black person. In an instant a Black multi-millionaire would be created. Think about one million people sending five or ten dollars to a Black school or a Black museum. Instantly that entity would be the recipient of our own largess and not have to depend on donations that come in every now and then. Creating more conscious millionaires and taking care of the things we say are valuable, are just a couple of victories we could have via one million committed and determined Black folks.

All of these questions and commitments point to choices; they will suggest to some of us, first, that Black people would never declare themselves independent of the Democrat Party and that Black people will never cooperate in support of one another economically. But to others of us those questions raise attractive alternatives to what we are doing now; they suggest very strongly that we can be more self-determined via simple but powerful tactics that impact the two systems that run this nation and the world.

Recognizing that everyone will not want to walk the road toward economic and political transition (After all, everyone did not want to go with Harriet Tubman), there are no "marching orders" being trumpeted by the group that is shouldering the responsibility of bringing together one million conscious Black folks. This is a "Whosoever will, let him come" movement.

The movement is simply called, "One Million Conscious Black Voters and Contributors." To the skeptics out there who think Black folks are too individualistic to come together in such a large number, that one million Black folks will not cooperate, that we have too many schisms among us, and we will not trust one another, we say, "Not so." The key word in the name of the group is "Conscious." Even further, there is no need to pressure anyone to join. I know there are one million conscious Blacks in America (about 2%) who will join this movement without being prodded, which eliminates our need to cajole, persuade, or spend a lot of time trying to convince them of why they should. If we can't find two in every hundred among us, the result would be analogous to Abraham failing to find a few righteous men in Sodom and Gomorrah.

The Million Man March proved that Blacks will come together across religious, ideological, and economic lines for a righteous and necessary cause. Those who attended nearly 20 years ago will remember the cooperative and accommodating spirit among the men, the supportive attitudes of the women who stayed home and encouraged their men to participate, and the subsequent follow through by many of the men upon returning home. Much good work was done by individuals who were committed and determined to keep the promise they made that day.

As Amefika Geuka always quotes Marcus Garvey, "There is nothing common to man that man cannot do." We have already shown through many collective efforts that all we need are a relative few conscious, committed, dedicated, and intentional men and women to accomplish the tasks at hand.

With that in mind, rather than ask "what's" in a million, we must see "who's" in a million? If you have not added your name to the list, one thing is for sure: You are not in the million. Names are being added every day; just go to www.iamoneofthemillion.com to sign up.

We can do more to help our organizations, our businesses, and our schools by leveraging our votes and by "contributing" our resources to this movement, thereby, getting more political quo in return for our political quid. We will also obtain reciprocity in the marketplace and a cadre of new multi-millionaires that can, and will, use their wealth to help create more.

Be "One of the Million" and let's finally let our people and everyone else know that we are very serious about being economically and politically empowered. Whosoever will...

Arrest the Black dollar

"Here's how I think of my money – as soldiers – I send them out to war every day. I want them to take prisoners and come home, so there are more of them."
Kevin O'Leary

Here's an intriguing concept: Arrest the Black dollar. Say what, Jim? You read it correctly. We should arrest our dollars and charge them with neglect. Put them on trial, call the witnesses to testify against them, and convict them of crimes against Black people. Sentence them to a minimum of five years hard labor with no possibility of parole. That's right, lock them up and make them work for their keep by producing distribution companies, supermarkets, financial institutions, and entrepreneurs.

Since our dollars are not making sense, we should discipline and punish them by keeping them locked up and making them work until they do start making more sense. Right now our dollars are "wilding out" in the marketplace, making everyone happy and secure except us. They are "raining down" at strip clubs; they are beating a path to jewelry stores and exchanging themselves for gaudy trinkets and ornaments; they are hangin' out at "da club" to pay for expensive vodka, champagne, and other top-shelf liquors. They definitely need to be disciplined.

Our dollars are filling the coffers of profiteers who know that all they have to do is make the most ridiculous item in return for them. Black dollars are strewn at the feet of shyster preachers who "anoint" them by running back and forth on top of them, as they shout, "Money cometh to me!" At least they are telling the truth about that part.

Black dollars are running wild, out of control, in our neighborhoods. They run as fast as they can to the businesses of everyone other than Black people. They are jealous as well and are always trying to outspend one another by purchasing a bigger car, a bigger house, the latest gym shoes, clothing, and all the accoutrements of what they believe to be the "good life."

More than one trillion Black dollars are acting inappropriately, committing economic crimes against Black people. They really need to be controlled and contained before they destroy us. Our dollars are weak, and are vulnerable to the constant lure of trivial things and dishonest people who are waiting to trap them with their platitudes and false doctrines. If we put our dollars in labor camps where they could work for us all day long, imagine how quickly we could revive our economic power.

Keep in mind though, when we charge our dollars and put them on trial for neglect, we will be charged as willing accomplices and co-conspirators in their criminal acts. Yes, we are guilty too; even more guilty than they are. Slothfulness is a crime; poor stewardship is a crime; waste is a crime; and failure on our part to multiply the dollars we have is indeed a crime that carries the penalty of being "cast into outer darkness where there will be weeping and gnashing of teeth" because, "To whom much ($1 trillion) is given, much is required."

The rich man in Luke 12 who had so much "stuff" that, when he asked himself what to do about it, said, "I will build bigger barns" in which to store my stuff, well, he was called a fool and his life was "required" of him because his dollars made no sense.

This graphic illustration of the crimes we commit with and through our undisciplined dollars is played out every day in our homes and neighborhoods, and we deserve the punishment we have received for decades now. We must now punish our dollars by first arresting them and then making them work for us.

Why don't you start an Arrest the Black Dollar campaign? Look around; they are everywhere. Arrest your own first, and get others to arrest and charge theirs. Let's give our dollars the charge to be responsible for taking better care of our children. Give them the charge to be more accountable to us and our families. Give them the charge to work harder for us. Give them the charge to act appropriately. Give them the charge to make some sense for a change.

Instead of allowing our dollars to run wild, let's circulate and recycle them among ourselves as much as possible before they leave us. Instead of handing them over willy-nilly to others for their fried chicken and fish, let's just grow and cook our own, and sell it to one another and to everyone else. Instead of whining every time a supermarket closes, let's buy our own, bring in the best managers and support it with our consumer dollars. Rather than decrying what others are doing to us, let's start doing more for ourselves. As we charge our dollars with being more responsible, let's make sure we are taking responsibility in this matter as well.

Arrest the Black dollar; it is committing economic crimes and wreaking havoc on Black folks. Arrest the Black dollar and teach it how to make more sense.

The Bottom-line--Black Dollars Matter!

"Money can't buy love, but it sure does improve your bargaining position."
Christopher Marlowe

The protest slogans relative to our latest struggle for justice and equity compel me to come up with a new phrase. The signs and T-Shirts emblazoned with "I Can't Breathe!" "No Justice, No Peace!" and the latest, "Black Lives Matter," carry connotations related to action. I often wonder what the folks who wear the t-shirts and hold the signs are doing to back up the slogans thereon. More importantly, I wonder who makes the shirts and who sells them. With that in mind, my slogan for action—economic action is, "Black Dollars Matter!"

The "I Can't Breathe" shirts worn by the Brooklyn Nets and Cleveland Cavaliers, for instance, were sold by NYC Customs, a shop in Long Island, owned by Helen Mihalatos, a friend of Rameen Aminzadeh, member of Justice League of NYC. The initial gesture and resulting "hook-up" came from Nets team member, Jarrett Jack, followed by help from LeBron James and Russell Simmons' political director, Michael

Skolnick. The shirts were ordered by Jay-Z, who bought 1000 more shirts after the basketball game.

I truly hope those "Big Ballers" and "Shot Callers" had enough consciousness to give the profits to Eric Garner's family. The Washington Post reported that "Skolnick obtained shirts from a store in Long Island City, whose owner confirmed in an interview that the shirts were manufactured by Gildan, a large Canada-based apparel company... According to pro-labor activists, Gildan has a poor record when it comes to respecting workers in its manufacturing plants in Haiti." The story discloses that Gildan's workers are paid $6 per day for their work. Skolnick's response was, "I think we want to assume sometimes when we're ordering shirts that they're not being made in a sweatshop; we've got to do better." You think?

Now you would think that someone in this chain of events involving t-shirts that carry the last words of a Black man who was killed on the streets of New York by police officers would be conscious enough to say, "Hold up! Let's not just settle for the symbolism of wearing shirts on the basketball court; let's make a substantive statement as well, via a Black business transaction and a financial benefit for the Garner family." Sound reasonable?

Instead we now have "I Can't Breathe" shirts sold on Amazon and elsewhere as if they are some kind of novelty rather than a sincere, compassionate, and meaningful response to the homicidal death of Eric Garner, the originator of the "I can't breathe" phrase. We saw him take HIS last breath; he was the one who couldn't breathe for real. The above travesty reminds me of an article I wrote after Trayvon Martin was killed; it's titled, "The Profit of Protest."

In light of the hype of "I Can't Breathe" and now the phrase, "Black Lives Matter," the slogan we should emblazon on shirts, and instill in our brains, the one by which we should live and the one that, if inculcated into our daily lives, will move us from the rhetoric of freedom to the action of freedom is, "Black Dollars Matter!"

Despite the wasteful and nonsensical spending by Black folks, from the poorest to the super-rich flamboyant celebrities, we must all realize that "Black Dollars Matter" and they should matter to us first. Right now, they matter most to everyone else; and other folks are doing everything they can to get more of our dollars with no reciprocity other than symbolic gestures that make us feel good.

It's great for athletes to wear shirts with slogans, but they should move to the next step of starting initiatives that not only sustain their gestures but build economic empowerment for Black people. Our athletes and celebrities, as they protest inequities and injustice, should keep in mind that "Black Dollars Matter," and they should consider that as they come up with their solutions to effect real change within the systems against which they protest—and so should we.

After the chanting, the marching, the protests and demonstrations, the outrage, the threats, and the unjustified killings of our people with impunity, if all we do is sit back and wait on the next crisis, why should we even bother with the above actions in the first place? We must be smarter and we must be conscious when it comes to our strategy and subsequent behavior in response to these kinds of issues. We must always be aware that money runs this country and it has its place in everything, yes, even in the deaths of our people.

I am so sick and tired of seeing Facebook videos of police violence—and any violence for that matter—with comments like "This must stop!" and "Enough is enough!" and "When will it end?" If we are not going to do anything to stop these acts of violence except call for a march or have a press conference, then we should stop sharing the videos and making empty, symbolic, and tepid comments about them. If we are not willing to stand up, then we should just shut up.

It will take an initial economic threat to get the attention and appropriate response from CEO's of companies we support, which will surely be followed by a political response because economics drives politics. CEO's threatened to move their companies out of Indianapolis if the State of Indiana did not change its "freedom of religion" law. That law, according to the protesters, would also allow for businesses to discriminate against the LGBT community. Those CEO's got immediate political action because of their threat to impose an economic penalty against the city. It's all about economics, folks.

Indeed, Black lives matter above all; but to those who kill us, those who economically exploit us, and those who are indifferent toward us,

Black lives don't matter as much as Black dollars do. Start a "Black Dollars Matter" campaign, and act upon it.

"Black Dollars Matter," but only if we teach them how to make more sense.

Class dismissed.

In keeping with my personal philosophy of sharing and giving back, this book is available for fundraising. A bulk rate discount, with a purchase of a minimum of 50 books to be sold at events or other venues, is available to anyone interested in participating. (This does not include book sellers)

The discount rate is contingent upon the number of books purchased. In turn, books can be sold at the retail price to raise funds for various activities and causes.

My hope is that groups involved in economic literacy, entrepreneurship training, political and public policy development, especially among our youth, will take full advantage of this offer.

Our children comprise a virtual salesforce for many products; they sell everything from candles, to cookies, to candy, to coupon books, thus, creating wealth for others but not themselves. This is an effort to make a small change in that scenario.

To purchase books for your fundraiser send an e-mail to jclingman@ blackonomics.com or call 323 750 3592. Thanks so much to all who have purchased my other books, invited me to speak, and read my newspaper column. I pray that my work has not only inspired you but has also moved you to take the appropriate action necessary to achieve economic and, thereby, political empowerment.

Peace, Love, and Blessings.

Made in the USA
Charleston, SC
09 June 2015